NEW HUMANITARIANISM AND THE CRISIS OF CHARITY

NEW HUMANITARIANISM
AND THE CRISIS OF CHARITY
Good Intentions on the Road to Help

Michael Mascarenhas

Indiana University Press

This book is a publication of

Indiana University Press
Office of Scholarly Publishing
Herman B Wells Library 350
1320 East 10th Street
Bloomington, Indiana 47405 USA

iupress.indiana.edu

Manufactured in the United States of America

Cataloging information is available from the Library of Congress.
ISBN 978-0-253-02612-5 (cloth)
ISBN 978-0-253-02642-2 (paperback)
ISBN 978-0-253-02658-3 (ebook)

1 2 3 4 5 22 21 20 19 18 17

*To those whom we continue to
harm with our good intentions*

and

*to James, Sam, and Ashwin,
May you, too, in time, recognize that
poverty is the price for wealth*

Contents

Acknowledgments

No book project is an individual effort. My fortunate dilemma is to be able to reflect on who has contributed to this scholarship and in what way. And, like so many similar projects, there are always more people to thank than there is room on the page or time in the day. First, this book would not have been possible had I not been selected to be a fellow of Framing the Global Research and Publication Project. This amazing project was supported by a seven-year initiative of Indiana University Press (IUP) and the Indiana University Center for the Study of Global Change and funded by a grant from the Andrew W. Mellon Foundation. The project aimed to develop and disseminate new interdisciplinary knowledge, approaches, and methods in the field of global research and apply them to the study of global processes. I was truly the lucky recipient of a few gifted individuals' ability to recognize the scholarly and methodological need for a more grounded and critical approach to global studies. At IUP I was fortunate to work with Janet Rabinowitch, Becky Tolen, Dee Mortensen, and others. At the Center for the Study of Global Change, I had the opportunity to learn from its director, Hilary Kahn. Her unflagging dedication to our collective and individual project was only slightly overshadowed by that of Deborah Piston-Hatlen, the program coordinator. Without Deborah, and indeed Hilary, a project of this magnitude would have never succeeded.

As fellows, we meet once a month in cyberspace and once every six months in person to discuss our ideas, write, and review our work. These meetings with fellows, IUP staff, and collaborators at the Center were what I might best describe as unforgettable moments of teaching and learning—real collegiality. In many ways, our time together, for me at least, represented the pinnacle of scholarly cooperation. Tim Bartley, Manuela Ciotti, Deborah Cohen, Deirdre McKay, Stephanie Deboer, Zsuzsa Gille, Anne Griffiths, Rachel Harvey, Prakash Kumar, Lessie Jo Frazier, Sean Metzger, Faranak Miraftab, Alex Perullo, and Katherina Teaiwa all contributed to the initial framing and scholarly process of *Good Intentions*. We often jokingly referred to ourselves as the Bloomington School of Global Studies to capture the unique collaborative effort that this scholarship represented.

Others who contributed to this book project included Framing the Global's visiting scholars Matthew Connelly, Michael Curtin, Carolyn Nordstrom, and Saskia Sassen. Gillian Hart, one of the keynote speakers at the Framing the Global conference, also helped me with the conceptual framing of this project. I owe much to her close reading of my chapters. Sandra Harding also provided a careful and constructive review of the manuscript. The project has benefited greatly from her scholarly participation. The entire Framing the Global project would not have been possible if it were not for a generous grant from the Andrew W. Mellon Foundation, through its Universities and Their Presses Program.

The financial analysis of nonprofit organizations used in the analysis of this project was conducted by Jeffery Lin, a Rensselaer Polytechnic Institute (RPI) undergraduate at the time this manuscript was written. Joelle Woodson also helped with the transcription of interviews. Lindsay Poirier, a wonderfully talented graduate student in the Science and Technologies Studies department at RPI, also helped with both data analysis and conceptual framing of this project. Students in my graduate course on postcolonialism were also gracious enough to have an earlier version of this manuscript included on the reading list. I also acknowledge Judy Tyler and Fraser Murray, my friends who also contributed to this project in meaningful ways. I also thank those who took the time and, in some cases the risk, to confide in me about "doing humanitarianism." This manuscript would not have been possible if not for their trust in me. And, to the people I visited while doing fieldwork: I hope this project reflects your understandings, resentment, and ongoing frustration with postcolonial forms of help and charity.

Lastly, to Kelly Grindstaff and the boys: Kelly's editorial footprints are all over this manuscript. She remained steadfastly positive even when I was not. My three wonderful boys—James, Ashwin, and Sam—also made this project possible by understanding that Dad was not always available to them and by providing much needed distractions to writing.

NEW HUMANITARIANISM AND THE CRISIS OF CHARITY

Introduction

On December 26, 2004, in the Northern Hemisphere we watched and witnessed the human devastation from a massive 9.0 magnitude earthquake centered off the western shores of Indonesia. The earthquake triggered a series of devastating tsunamis that inundated the coasts of fourteen countries along the rim of the Indian Ocean, killing nearly 230,000 people, injuring tens of thousands more, and displacing more than 10 million men, women, and children. The scale of the harm to life and damage to the local economy, infrastructure, and government was unprecedented. In the days that followed, the South Asian tsunami became a truly global affair. Bombarded with media reporting and seduced by YouTube videos, we watched live as millions of helpless people lost their homes, livelihoods, and, in many cases, their lives. These horrific images, combined with the seemingly arbitrariness of their fate, provoked an outpouring of empathy and generosity of global proportions. Governments, corporations, and individuals[1] from around the world scrambled to offer aid, medicine, other vital supplies, and technical support to the helpless victims of this tragedy.

Airlines provided free travel for relief workers. The Coca-Cola Company and PepsiCo donated thousands of cases of bottled water. Drug makers and medical companies sent shipments of medical supplies and cash donations. Pfizer announced plans to donate $10 million to local and international relief organizations, including Save the Children and the International Rescue Committee, as well as about $25 million of its health-care products to the relief efforts. Bristol-Myers Squibb sent antibiotics and other supplies, in addition to a $100,000 donation through the American Red Cross. Abbott Laboratories' charitable fund donated supplies, including nutritional supplements, valued at $2 million, as well as an additional $2 million in cash. Merck made a cash donation of $250,000. Johnson & Johnson contributed $2 million in cash and matched employee donations to the Red Cross. General Electric pledged $1 million to the Red Cross's International Response Fund and $100,000 to the United Nations Children's Fund (UNICEF) (*Wall Street Journal* News Roundup 2004). Similar donations poured in from other corporate sectors and governments from around the world, and, within six months, official aid and private donations raised over $13 billion for the victims of this natural[2] disaster!

The emotional imagery of debris-laden coastlines, destroyed school buildings and decimated roads, tent camps and temporary shelters, and mass graves ensured that this story would not leave the public spotlight for some time. In the weeks that followed, the media turned its attention from relief efforts to restoration and recovery. It was at this point that large international nongovernmental organizations (INGOs) began to take center stage, for their participation as first responders was deemed a vital component of relief efforts to restore normal life in the region. Humanitarian agencies seized the media opportunity and pasted their logos on every available surface and raised their flags on every restored structure. And, for a while, we all felt rewarded for our efforts and hopeful about the future.

However, over the succeeding weeks, a different story came to the fore: the transparency and accountability of these large INGOs involved in the rebuilding of tsunami-ravaged areas. "I was exhausted and I was completely disillusioned with the entire [humanitarian] system," reflects Adrian Roberts, about his four-month volunteer experience with the Thai Red Cross. "I started seeing all of these organizations like World Vision and faith-based organizations," he recalled, "rebuilding people's homes and farming operations in the name of Christianity. . . . But there was no transparency. . . . Someone would get 'a five-star hotel for [their] chickens," while other families "weren't being helped out. . . . Money was being spent," Roberts remembered, "Lots of money was being spent," but "many families who I helped weren't getting the help they desperately needed. . . . So, I did as much as I could with a thousand dollars and I returned to the States." Sure enough, Roberts's experience in Thailand was not unique, as stories began to emerge about donations not getting to where they were needed. More stories started to surface about donations being diverted by charities to other non-tsunami relief efforts. To many who had donated, as I had, and others who participated in the relief efforts, such as Roberts, this seemed rather troubling.

As the media pressed the issue of where the aid was going, we found out that diverting donations to other projects is a generally accepted practice of humanitarian organizations. In some cases, much of the aid pledged (about half, in some cases) never ends up reaching the poorest people affected by these disasters.[3] Much of the money raised is used to purchase urgently needed goods and materials, such as food and medicine; ambulances and mobile medical clinics, portable water, sanitation, and housing; clothing, blankets, and other personal belongings. "Right after the tsunami hit, I volunteered for a local humanitarian organization involved in the delivery of emergency health services," recalled Naomi Cohen. "On my first day I was able to acquire a large quantity of hospital coats. They needed that immediately. We had a whole bunch of doctors and nurses going over to Aceh, and they needed those gowns donated. I spent all day on the phone and was able to get a huge amount donated from hospital supply companies." Gowns, in addition to long list of necessary relief items, are donated from the private sector or purchased from government contractors or other suppliers—all located

lo transparency

in donor countries. In other cases, international pledges, in some cases up to millions of dollars, take the form of redevelopment contracts that are given to domestic companies. These multinational for-profit companies then offer their technical assistance and engineering capacity, as well as other forms of expertise, necessary for extensive redevelopment projects in the devastated regions or countries. For example, as part of its pledge to the Sri Lanka Tsunami Reconstruction Program, the United States Agency for International Development (USAID) awarded CH2M Hill a $33 million contract to lead infrastructure redevelopment efforts in parts of Sri Lanka damaged by the tsunami.[4] Some of the redevelopment aid, however, was used to fund large-scale construction for tourism and other economic activities, which further displaces fishing and farming villages along attractive coastlines (Klein 2007). A humanitarian response of this scale, after all, could not help attracting some controversy about how funds were spent, and it is important that these types of funding issues are raised. The real question I want to explore in this book, however, is: as the shared interests that make humanitarianism possible have grown and the networks among them have strengthened, how is this assemblage of global actors transforming the politics (decisions over who gets aid, when, and under what conditions) and power-knowledge dynamics (notions of expertise, data, and measurement) of humanitarian policy and practice? How are we to make sense of the complex formal and informal partnerships that seem to be forming among states, businesses, and civil society organizations as they join efforts—and change roles—in a concerted effort to alleviate the crisis conditions of the world's poor and dispossessed? How can this new humanitarian network be analyzed and understood? And how has the production of crises and understanding of need served to organize this particular humanitarian conjuncture?

In an effort to find empirical answers to these theoretical questions, I examine the unprecedented rise in nongovernmental organizations (NGOs) and their interconnected response with donor (Northern) governments and the business sector. What does it mean if private Northern NGOs and for-profit corporations channel large sums of government and private funds, resources, and people (employees and volunteers) to the Global South as a result of their involvement in new humanitarian efforts? A great deal of debate and scrutiny has arisen in response to the transfer or channeling of funds around the globe by government and non-government agencies interested in global security, terrorism, and migration. Governments have blocked bank accounts and confiscated assets when they determined that funds circulating around the world were tied to various forms of corruption or terrorism. One way to identify corrupt activities, criminals, and terrorists, governments argue, is to "follow the money." By comparison, the same sense of scrutiny or concern has not seemed to follow funds that circle the globe in the name of this new humanitarianism, in spite of their growth and magnitude. Total government funds transferred by and through Northern NGOs (i.e., from industrialized counties) from 1970 to 1990 alone increased at twice the rate of international aid as a whole. In addition, government funding of Northern NGOs has grown at a faster rate than support for the general public during this period (United Nations Development Programme 1991). Why would Northern governments be diverting funds to NGOs working in the Global South rather than to their general public, living within their borders? Moreover, private aid has dwarfed official government aid several times over, which would seem to suggest that this new humanitarian complex might actually be sending much larger quantities of funds to the Global South than projected. Why are Northern businesses so engaged in humanitarian efforts in the Global South? Walmart, for example, reported a $2 million donation to the Red Cross for tsunami relief, yet many of their employees rely on food stamps to subsidize their low wages in the United States. How can we understand this seemingly humanitarian contradiction? Wouldn't it make more sense to pay their employees higher wages and better benefits rather than advocate charitable measures to aid strangers around the globe? What is it about the current humanitarian complex that enables corporations to be good Samaritans, on the one hand, and callous employers, on the other? And to what extent are those charitable funds a direct result of exploitative labor practices and, in some cases, criminal behavior? For example, JPMorgan Chase donated $183.5 million in charitable cash donations in 2012 (*Chronicle of Philanthropy* 2013). In 2013 the largest bank in the United States also agreed to a $13 billion settlement[5] over mortgage-backed securities sold ahead of the financial crisis of 2007–2008 (O'Toole and Perez 2013).[6] As corporations like Walmart and JPMorgan Chase continue to funnel some of their profits to humanitarian causes, it becomes increasingly important to recognize the way in which these rising profits are generated in the name of good corporate citizenship and to question to what extent this charity is, in fact, a gift.

New Humanitarianism

The crisis conditions of the post–cold war era, epitomized by virulent conflicts, inhuman genocides, and rising rates of inequality, have led to intense debates over the role and responsibility—and if we were truly honest with ourselves, the apathy and culpability—of the international community in the prevention of human suffering and intervention in genocidal events (Power 2013). Moreover, the changing nature of violence, as exemplified in the genocides in Kosovo and Rwanda—to name only two in "the age of genocide"—have called into question the principles of classic humanitarianism and the monopoly power of sovereignty, pertaining in particular to the violence of citizens. Critics have argued that traditional humanitarian aid, based on the principles of humanity, impartiality, neutrality, and independence, is not only unable to protect the most vulnerable but, in some cases, may have been complicit in their dispossession. "What got under my skin," writes Roméo Dallaire, the force commander for the United Nations Assistance Mission for Rwanda (UNAMIR), in his memoir *Shake Hands with the Devil: The Failure of Humanity in Rwanda* (2003, 493), "was the way the aid community so unthinkingly rallied behind its first principle: no matter what, they had to protect their neutrality. It was my opinion that, in this new reality we had all inherited, they were defining their independence so narrowly it often impeded their stated aims." This neutrality that NGOs clung to, Dallaire (2003, 493) insists, "needs to be seriously rethought."

But it is not only humanitarian organizations that have clung to the principle of neutrality when marshalling their efforts to aid the dispossessed. In their countless opportunities to mitigate and prevent slaughter, Samantha Power (2013) writes, US policy makers and presidents clung to their neutrality and insisted that genocidal affairs in other sovereign states were not their business. However, Dallaire observes that when NGOs were given military escort by the Rwandan Patriotic Front (RPF), which, in effect, granted them sovereign protection, they "moved in to feed and aid these supposedly displaced," while also "providing aid and comfort to a belligerent" (2003, 299). From Dallaire's vantage point, the relief work of some NGOs and the inaction of the international community "aided and abetted genocide in Rwanda" (2003, 323). Recalling the failure of the United Nations Security Council and the international humanitarian community to act in a decisive manner in Rwanda and the former Yugoslavia, then–Secretary-General Kofi Annan asked, "if humanitarian intervention is, indeed, an unacceptable assault on sovereignty, how should we respond to a Rwanda, to a Srebrenica, to gross and systematic violation of human rights that offend every precept of our common humanity?" (United Nations 2014).

The debate at the heart of Annan's inquiry and Dallaire's concern was whether states have unconditional sovereignty over their affairs or whether the international community has a responsibility to intervene in a country for humanitarian purposes, and at what point does the right to intervene supersede state legitimacy? In 2004, the High-Level Panel on Threats, Challenges, and Change, set up by Annan, declared that the international community had a responsibility to protect people, by force if necessary, "in the event of genocide and other large-scale killing, ethnic cleansing and serious violations of humanitarian law which sovereign governments have proved powerless or unwilling to prevent" (High-Level Panel on Threats 2004, 57). In effect, this "new humanitarianism" gave the international community the right to intervene in sovereign affairs when it deemed necessary. In September 2005, at the United Nations World Summit, all member states formally accepted this R2P[7] principle ushering in a new global era in humanitarian governance.

Fiona Fox (2001, 275) argues that this "new humanitarianism" is "principled, human rights based, politically sensitive, and geared towards strengthening those

Table 0.1 Classic Humanitarianism and New Humanitarianism

Classic Humanitarianism	New Humanitarianism
Humanity	Directed
Impartiality	Limited
Neutrality	Principled
Independence	Political
Universal	**Instrumental**

forces that bring peace and stability to the developing world." Whereas actors engaged in classic humanitarianism—most notably, Médecins Sans Frontières (MSF; Doctors Without Borders) and the International Committee of the Red Cross (ICRC)—have generally defended their practice on ethical terms and resisted attempts to instrumentalize it, the new humanitarianism is directly instrumental, guiding purposive action for specific outcomes—such as overthrowing oppressive groups or regimes, maintaining peace, and introducing democracy (see Table 0.1). One striking feature of this new brand of humanitarian government is that it blurs the boundaries of "who does" and "what constitutes" humanitarian relief. For instance, new humanitarianism blurs the lines between formal and informal humanitarian actors, extending that distinction from donor governments, international agencies, and NGOs to foreign and private militaries, corporations, investment and banking, private foundations, religious groups, political parties, diasporas, and any other institutions or groups extending a helping hand to people affected by crises (Bolton 2009; Labbe 2012).

In addition to introducing new actors, new humanitarianism has also blurred the boundaries of what constitutes humanitarian intervention and relief, extending them to include the training of armed forces, the support of international human rights reform, and the strengthening of the domestic justice system through regulatory reform or regime change (Labbe 2012). In effect, this ends the distinction between development and humanitarian relief by linking aid and charity to broader political and economic decision-making structures (Fox 2001; Labbe 2012; Neuman 2012). In making this observation, I am not suggesting the classic humanitarian intervention somehow lacked political and economic motivations. However, what distinguishes new from classic humanitarianism is the way in which human rights issues and political and economic reform are now joined with humanitarian intervention. In the future, Fox (2001, 280) writes, "responding to human needs will be conditional on achieving human rights and wider political objectives."

However, although it may relegitimize the role and responsibilities of the international community in the face of extreme poverty, human conflicts, and even genocide, new humanitarianism also signals the rejection of a universal right to relief in times of crisis. In effect, this technique of humanitarian governmental-ity permits the creation of "deserving and undeserving victims" (Fox 2001). Who becomes deserving and not deserving in this new goal-oriented system of relief is unclear. However, one thing is certain: decisions about who is deserving and who is not will be made based on more than need alone, leading to decisions in which aid might be withheld or suspended because of broader political and or economic objectives, or in which racial, ethnic, gender, or religious identities might influence or even take precedence over human suffering. It begs the question as to whether the international humanitarian community should be making life and death decisions—decisions previously associated with state sovereignty—in the Global South. And, if so, on what grounds will these highly political decisions be made, given the complicated and uneven power-knowledge dynamics within the global humanitarian complex?

The "State of Exception"

If the South Asian tsunami has taught us anything, it is that one enduring feature of the postcolonial condition has, and continues to be, humanitarian emergen-cies. Consider the genocides in East Timor, Rwanda, Congo, Liberia, Sierra Leone, and the former Yugoslavia; the ongoing ethnic conflict between Israel and Palestine; the enduring conflicts in Iraq, Afghanistan, Yemen, and, now, Syria; the current humanitarian crises in Darfur and South Sudan; and the most recent earthquakes in Haiti, China, Japan, and Italy. Walter Benjamin's (1942, 392) well-known formula that "the 'state of exception . . . has become the rule" increasingly appears to be not only a technique of government but also a subjective fact of life shared among those in the North as well as the South (Agamben 2005). Nowhere is this relationship more pronounced than in the humanitarian spectacle that engulfed the tiny Caribbean country of Haiti, dubbed by some the "NGO Re-public of Haiti," after its devastating earthquake in 2010. The worst natural disas-ter in the history of the Western Hemisphere also swiftly became a lightning rod for the stark contradictions and lopsided relationships embedded in today's hu-manitarian complex. On one side of the country were thousands of well-funded aid organizations that went to Haiti "and built a powerful parallel state account-able to no one but their boards and donors" (Polman and Klarreich 2012, 1). On the other side were "the many representatives of the Haitian people—elected of-ficials, civil society leaders, businesspeople—who remain broke and undermined by the very NGOs that swooped in to help" (Polman and Klarreich 2012, 1). In between these lopsided humanitarian efforts were the "Haitian people them-selves: impoverished, unemployed, homeless and trapped in a recovery effort that has all too often failed to meet their needs" (Polman and Klarreich 2012, 1).

On a global scale, the rising rates of inequity and humanitarian need are sim-ply staggering. For example, the United Nations declared in 2014 that it would need nearly $13 billion in aid to reach at least 52 million people in 17 countries.[8]

"This is the largest amount we've ever had to request at the start of the year," said Valerie Amos, the UN Under-Secretary General for Humanitarian Affairs. "The complexity and scale of what we are doing is rising all the time" (United Nations 2013, 3). This formidable humanitarian request comes on the heels of more dire warnings from the United Nations Human Settlements Programme about the future of humanity, with the prospect that by 2020 urban poverty and slums in the world could encompass 45 percent to 50 percent of the population living in cities (UN-Habitat 2003). The rapid rise of urban poverty and slums is the harbinger of the most pathetic human consequences of the past thirty years of neoliberal reforms. Moreover, slum ecology rarely comes equipped with lifeline infrastructure, and, as a result, contaminated water remains the cause of the chronic diarrheal diseases that kill at least two million urban babies and small children every year (World Resources Institute 1996). For those who manage to survive, the United Nations assesses that two out of five African slum dwellers live in a poverty that is literally "life-threatening" (Davis 2004). "It is hard to put into words their despair, but also the dignity with which they endure the most painful and difficult circumstances," said Amos, who is also the UN Emergency Relief Coordinator. "We count on the continued support from our partners as we work to save lives and support the millions of people caught in crisis" (United Nations 2013, 3).

But while the United Nations scrambles to secure resources to contain today's emergencies, the World Bank warns of greater impending crises to come from climate change—perhaps the tragic consequence of a world system dependent on fossil fuel. In the report "Turn Down the Heat: Climate Extremes, Regional Impacts, and the Case for Resilience" (Schellnhuber et al. 2013), scientists describe how rising global temperatures will increasingly threaten the health and livelihood of the most vulnerable populations across sub-Saharan Africa, South Asia, and Southeast Asia. Climate-related extreme events due to rising greenhouse gas emissions could make the extreme flooding that affected 20 million Pakistanis in 2010 commonplace, warns Jim Yong Kim, president of the World Bank, and push millions of households below the poverty-trap threshold (Schellnhuber et al. 2013)—a substantial portion of the world's people who will never have any hope of a secure life.

These enduring, and by some measures worsening, conditions of global poverty and insecurity have prompted a humanitarian response by civil society organizations of epic proportions. Data assembled by the Union of International Associations (UIA) show that three-quarters of the estimated 27,472 INGOs active in 2005 were formed after 1975 (Union of International Associations 2008). Employment at nonprofit organizations in the United States grew every year between 2000 and 2010 despite two recessions. According to a recent Urban Institute report, the number of nonprofit organizations in the United States increased 25 percent, meaning that their growth rate exceeded that of both industry and government over that decade (Salamon, Sokolowski, and Geller 2012). The annual Giving USA report on philanthropy reported that charitable giving rose 3.5 percent in 2012, to $316.23 billion, an all-time record that surpassed the high-water mark of $311 billion before the financial crisis began in 2007 (Center on Philanthropy 2013). In 2010, public charities in the United States alone, the largest component of the nonprofit sector in the country, reported $1.51 trillion in revenue, $1.45 trillion in expenses, and $2.71 trillion in assets. The 21st Century NGO report stated that the not-for-profit sector "could now rank as the world's eighth-largest economy" (Beloe et al. 2003). This now-thriving sector employs more than 19 million people and is rapidly becoming the career of choice for many college graduates in fields from engineering and the social sciences to law and those with a master's degree in business administration. Moreover, charity workers' salaries have started to rise rapidly in recent years, with those in executive positions often earning incomes of more than six figures, making humanitarianism an attractive career choice (Canadian Broadcasting Corporation 2011). According to the 2012 Urban Institute report, in addition to rising donations and employment opportunities, more than one-quarter (27 percent) of adults in the United States volunteered with an organization (Blackwood, Roeger, and Pettijohn 2010).[9]

New humanitarian government and governmentality,[10] as expressed in the Haiti earthquake and the South Asian tsunami relief efforts, have created a way to penetrate the Global South and ignore existing laws, conventions, or constraints (Duffield 2007). Moreover, Mark Duffield (2007) suggests that this newly acquired authority to describe and define the crisis conditions among the world's poor has ensured that so-called civil society actors now wield significant international political and economic power. Some scholars have argued that their endless decision-making authority concerning how particular humanitarian conditions are defined, who will be helped, how to go about helping them, and, consequently, who can be left behind amounts to a new form of sovereignty or even empire (Barnett 2011; Foucault 1997, 2008; Hardt and Negri 2001). This type of political and economic power does not reign over citizens, per se, but, rather, populations of people that are described and organized with particular conditions, such as water insecurity, ill health, or poverty (Barnett 2011; Chatterjee 2004). The strength of this nonstate or petty sovereign power, as I illustrate, comes not only from its ability to form boundaries around particular territories, peoples, and ideas but also from its ability to transgress geographic boundaries, translate meanings, and transform value, all in the name of humanitarianism. Making these thick[11] and obscure sites of humanitarian production visible offers us a glimpse of the political and economy systems, knowledge-making practices, and institutional networks associated with a global humanitarian assemblage, which seeks to do massive social good in the face of mounting humanitarian crises.

Consider again the engineering firm CH2M Hill, which received a $33 million contract to lead infrastructure redevelopment efforts in parts of Sri Lanka after the 2004 South Asian tsunami. CH2M Hill, of course, is only one of many US corporations that have reaped a windfall from postwar reconstruction. The most infamous was Kellogg, Brown & Root, a subsidiary of Halliburton—which Dick Cheney led prior to becoming vice president—was awarded more than $2.3 billion in federal contracts for aid/development work in postwar Iraq and Afghanistan. Together with contracts to restore New Orleans from the devastation of Hurricane Katrina and to rebuild Iraq after the US invasion, CH2M Hill doubled its revenues in a five-year period, to $3 billion in 2005 (McGhee 2006). War and natural disaster have been good business for this multinational corporation. It ranked no. 11 on a list of top defense contractors working in Iraq and Afghanistan. It probably doesn't hurt that CH2M Hill has former government and military personnel in important positions. For example, Robert Card, head of the company's international group, also served as undersecretary of energy from 2001 until 2004. Similarly, John Ahearn, chairman of CH2M Hill, served in the US Air Force for thirty-four years and, as a major-general, directed the development and operations of all US air bases around the world. He once headed the Air Force Civil Engineer Support Agency, an Air Force procurement agency, which recently awarded CH2M Hill part of a $10 billion contract (McGhee 2006). But in addition to being the recipient of government funds directed at humanitarian efforts, CH2M Hill is also a major corporate donor to NGOs, many of which are involved in similar humanitarian campaigns. For example, CH2M Hill is considered a "global sponsor" of Water for People, contributing from $100,000 to $999,999 to this nonprofit. However, CH2M Hill's interest in corporate philanthropy goes beyond making large donations. One of its managers, Pawan Maini, Managing Director of CH2M Hill–India, was also a voting member of the board of directors of Water for People (his term expired in 2012) (Water for People 2014). Moreover, when Water for People conducted a baseline assessment of existing water and sanitation facilities in rural Rwanda, the project fell under the leadership of an engineer employed by, and on leave from, CH2M Hill.

As a result of their involvement in humanitarian efforts, multinational corporations, such as CH2M Hill, are not simply rebuilding productive infrastructure that had been damaged or destroyed by a tsunami, earthquake, or war. Rather, these actors are now productive agents in a humanitarian aid/development complex that seeks to reassert and extend its humanitarian mission through its interactions with multiple and interconnected sites of production from the boardroom of CH2M Hill to the shores of Sri Lanka. It therefore becomes important to assess the degree to which CH2M Hill's humanitarian effort in Sri Lanka is as much about bridge engineering as it is also about social engineering. Similarly, we need to ask to what extent Water for People's baseline assessment in Rwanda is as much about counting existing water and sanitation facilities as it is also about producing certain types of knowledge and expertise. These new thick transnational assemblages, most often associated with military and security functions and global development policy, are increasingly comingling the ethos of humanitarianism with the apparatuses of the global political economy. Indeed, it is becoming increasingly difficult to distinguish military from humanitarian intervention, as they have often become one in the same.

Although humanitarian crises in the Global South have benefited civil society actors and multinational corporations in the Global North, allowing them to ignore existing laws, conventions, and constraints and secure a foothold in otherwise prohibitive markets, such crises have also provided an economic boost to distressed countries. For example, the Asian Development Bank reported that the 2004 tsunami—paradoxically—brought a measure of stability to the Sri Lankan economy, which had been straining under growing macroeconomic imbalances (Weerakoon, Jayasuriya, Arunatilake, and Steele 2007). In Sri Lanka's case, the devastation from the tsunami provided an unanticipated source of foreign capital inflows for the relief and reconstruction effort and enabled the country to avoid a slide into a currency crisis. "Not only did the additional influx of foreign capital allow Sri Lanka to maintain a fairly healthy balance of payments (BOP) during 2005–2006," the Asian Development Bank reported, "but relief and reconstruction-related expenditures also boosted [gross domestic product] growth to a healthy annual average of 6.7 per cent over the same period" (Weerakoon et al. 2007, 1). The Central Bank of Sri Lanka predicted that tsunami-related construction activities for water supply, road, and building development, port and airport development, rural electrification, irrigated agriculture, and rehabilitation and upgrading of small-scale infrastructure would lead to an increase in investment expenditure in the second half of 2005 (*Sunday Times* 2005). In effect, the tsunami prevented Sri Lanka from descending into a currency crisis and falling into a recession.

However, although the ongoing crisis conditions among much of humanity has provided the impetus for rethinking the modern humanitarian system and its moral sentiments, very little attention has been given to the way in which this transnational complex continues to expand throughout the globe, growing new productive tentacles, overlapping with and reinforcing other sectors of society, including academia, finance capital, agriculture, and information and communication technology, to name some of the most salient, and concomitantly interweaving new threads of power, politics, and indeed cultural change, into humanitarian theory, practice, and policy. The rapid growth of institutions involved in new humanitarianism has not only aided in its expansion as an ideology, a profession, and a new social movement but also influenced the means and methods by which we attempt to do massive social good in the face of global crisis conditions. The extent to which crisis "moments are also the element of profit," as Marx (1976 [1867], 352) notably predicted, is yet, I propose, to be fully appreciated. This book examines the extent to which this new form of humanitarianism presents a legitimate strategy with which to build new concepts and politics for the crisis conditions of today's unequal world. My analysis traces the social relations of particular NGOs involved in this new humanitarian movement to scrutinize more thoroughly the exact content of what is assembled in the hidden folds of new humanitarianism. Moreover, while NGOs are mobilizing billions of dollars to improve the lot of the poor, it is unclear to what extent their involvement is also partially responsible for creating the conditions that perpetuate global poverty, inequality, and, in some cases, ethnocide and genocide. It is crucial for us to understand how diverse institutions that spread throughout the world are being pieced together as part of a global agenda that is supposed to do massive social good, in an effort to locate and understand the types of logics, functions, and subjectivities that are embedded in this new global social project. Such knowledge and understanding are vital for thinking through the paradox of modern capitalism—a system that, on the one hand, has allowed unprecedented advances in the material conditions for some, and, on the other hand, has produced its opposite for others—"massive underdevelopment and impoverishment, untold exploitation and oppression" (Escobar 1995, 4).

The Present Humanitarian Conjuncture

Many development scholars and practitioners recognize the importance of President Harry S Truman's 1949 Inaugural Address as a watershed moment in constituting a global project of poverty alleviation and development of those countries and peoples who had suffered under colonialism. Truman ([1949] 1964) proclaimed that:

> More than half the people of the world are living in conditions approaching misery. Their food is inadequate. They are victims of disease. Their economic life is primitive and stagnant. Their poverty is a handicap and a threat to them and to more prosperous areas. . . . I believe that we should make available to peace-loving peoples the benefits of our store of technical knowledge in order to help them realize their aspirations for a better life.

This postwar development period pioneered an institutional reform of global proportions—one that would create complex interdependencies between so-called developed and underdeveloped countries. Since its inception more than sixty years ago, the notion of development has formed a remarkably stable problem-space within which contemporary questions about the growing polarity of postcolonial life and its relationship to state, market, and global civil society can be understood. In fact, some have argued that this postcolonial state of exception has progressively become "the dominant paradigm of government in contemporary politics," analogous to a religion of modernity (Agamben 2005, 2; Rist 2008). However, what began as a post–World War II era of state-led development to assist countries and people in the Global South recover from the ravages of war and colonialism, what Gillian Hart calls "development with a big D," has shifted to one in which nonstate actors have introduced an overtly interventionist approach to improving the human condition, "development with a small d" (Hart 2001, 2004, 2009).

Linking this form of intervention to the notion of humanitarianism—that a deep-seeded human ethos or moral obligation exists to help improve and promote the welfare and flourishing of those in need—has made it difficult to foster a critical perspective on this form of aid/development policy and practice. How could one possibly be against this now universal principle of humankind? Moreover, the urgency associated with humanitarian crises in which governmental and NGOs are scrambling with the immediate consequences of saving lives makes it acutely inconvenient to reflect on the causes of particular crises and how they may be prevented, or best mitigated, in the future. Given the particular urgency—lack of access to housing, medical services, food, or water—there is little tolerance for second guessing. "We just have to do our best" (discussed in chapter 2) was the reprimand I received by another volunteer on a baseline assessment project in Rwanda to questions that others and I had raised about the method that continued to plague our analysis. "Facts," it seems, are a distant second in the race to do massive social good. Similarly, the steadily growing humanitarian caseload has led many practitioners dedicated to relief work and the protection of human rights to turn a blind eye to ethical matters of those who support their efforts. "Does it matter how funds are raised," some ask, "as long as it is contributing to social good?" And skillfully crafted marketing strategies—conveniently placed in your inbox and mailbox; in phone messages and TV commercials; via Twitter, Facebook, and YouTube; or in churches, malls, restaurants, and coffee shops—constantly remind us that giving alms to the poor and suffering is the right thing to do (Moyo 2010). We walk, run, bike, swim, dance, eat, pray, invest, and even steal for those in need, as countless appeals remind us that we have a moral imperative to do more for those who have less. Humanitarian aid, Dambrisa Moyo (2010) suggests, has become part of the entertainment industry. "Media figures, film stars, rock legends eagerly embrace aid, proselytize the need for it, upbraid us for not giving enough," and scold governments for not doing more (Moyo 2010, xviii). In short, humanitarian government and governmentality has become a cultural commodity, and the pressures to get involved have resulted in the fact that "everyone's doing it" (Salamon 1994, 110).

Additionally, those on the frontline of redefining the cultural boundaries of the humanitarian system have asked, "What does it matter if executives of major humanitarian organizations are making six-figure salaries, if that is the cost of expertise in this and other sectors of society?" (See chapter 3.) However, managing these and other tensions will determine the extent to which NGOs will be able to live out these expectations of justice and poverty alleviation. Moreover, the notion that free trade, self-regulating markets, good investments, and entrepreneurial ingenuity combined in the "right way" can ameliorate the crisis conditions of the world's poor is a provocative one. In many ways, this coming together of profit and welfare represents a new social contract for the twenty-first century—not a contract between citizen and state but, rather, a contract between rich and poor.[12]

NGOs continue to be a growing force in facilitating this new social contract. In addition to opening up to a number of nontraditional development actors, such as business and the military, NGOs have also cultivated partnerships with multilateral organizations such as the United Nations, the World Bank, the World Trade Organization, and the World Economic Forum in Davos. Over 1,550 INGOs have been granted consultative status by the Economic and Social Council (ECOSOC), and in 1997 an NGO Working Group was established as part of the United Nations Security Council (Opoku-Mensah 2001). At the same time, NGOs have started to take on more traditional roles of government in the name of humanitarianism, such as training of armed forces or volunteer groups on international norms and standards, advocating for the enactment of international law in domestic legislation, and strengthening of the domestic justice system regarding international human rights and refugee law (Labbe 2012). Not surprisingly, as NGOs' influence on global decision-making structures has increased, they have requested that the boundaries of humanitarianism be further expanded to include the areas of disaster risk reduction, long-term development programs, education, peacekeeping, conflict resolution, and human rights advocacy. This new humanitarianism seeks to address not only the symptoms but also the systemic causes of humanitarian crises worldwide through the use of pre-emptive humanitarian intervention toward achieving human rights and political goals (Fox 2001; Macrae 2002). The question, then, is no longer whether NGOs are too close for comfort, as development scholars Michael Edwards and David Hulme (1996) asked a decade ago, but, rather, in what ways are they assembled and whose interests are best represented in this current formulation of modern humanitarianism. If, in fact, new humanitarianism is a global empire, as Michael Barnett (2011) argues, then we need to delineate how this empire works.

Part of what makes this current humanitarian conjuncture so extraordinary is the way in which the convergence of finance capital, corporate philanthropy, social entrepreneurialism, and business management principles have converged and been reconfigured to solve the most pressing problem of modern society. Today, private aid has dwarfed official government aid several times over (see Figure 0.1). This recent transformation means that future humanitarian support

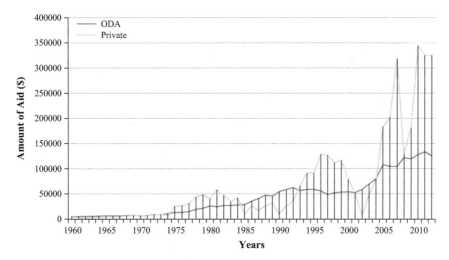

Figure 0.1 Rise in the Amount of Public (ODA) and Private Aid.

will largely hinge on the generosity of corporate philanthropy, not to mention the fluctuations of markets (see Figure 0.2). This rapidly growing network connects investment bankers in New York, engineers in London, water technicians in Montreal, celebrities in Los Angeles, and volunteers from around the globe in an uncertain and ephemeral humanitarian assemblage. This unprecedented rise and restructuring of the nonprofit sector has been described by Lester Salamon, the director of the Johns Hopkins Center for Civil Society Studies, as an "associational revolution," a revolution that might prove to be as important to matters of life and death in the second half of the twenty-first century as the rise of the nation-state was in the late nineteenth century (Salamon et al. 2012).

As I show in this book, the everyday discursive practices of new humanitarianism have proved to be powerful allies in reformulating the role of NGOs, which have increasingly become the conduit for forging all sorts of political and economic relationships, not only among countries within the North-South world system but also between rich people and poor people, or more specifically between the rich white minority in the North and the poor brown majority in the South. The persuasive power of new humanitarianism has helped NGOs receive funds from overseas governments, work as private subcontractors for local governments, and benefit from rising rates of corporate philanthropy. Therefore, the degree to which NGOs work in the service of imperialism, as James Petras (1999) has pointed out, receives little attention or is seen as a necessary evil in the larger global effort to do massive social good. The immediate consequence is that today new humanitarianism is still largely interpreted as an act of charity from Northern

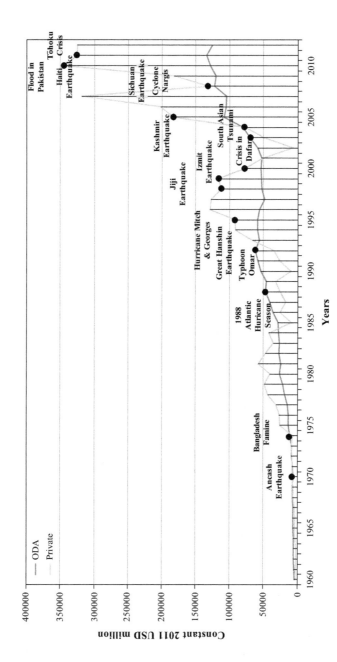

Figure 0.2 Rise in the Amount of Aid and "Natural" Disasters. Source: Organization for Economic Cooperation, 2012.

countries and business (Goldman 2005). Moreover, impediments to those acts of kindness are most often attributed to the innate corruption and irrationality of leaders or cultures of the Global South. "Corruption," World Bank president Kim warned, "is the biggest obstacle in the fight against poverty . . . it is simply stealing from the poor." In an effort to hold corrupt Bangladeshi officials accountable, Kim cancelled a $1.2 billion loan from the bank in support of the Padma Multipurpose Bridge project (World Bank 2012). However, corruption emanating from major donors in the North—Walmart, JPMorgan Chase, SAC Capital, and Johnson & Johnson, to name a few—is reduced to a few bad apples on the otherwise healthy humanitarian tree. This double standard, Michael Goldman (2005) argues, has deep colonial roots that profoundly influence our capacity to analyze the practice and outcomes of humanitarianism within its larger political and economic complex.

Changing the Way the World Tackles Poverty

The important question of how poverty can be eradicated is one that continues to disturb and agitate modern society. Poverty, according to Hegel (2005 [1821]), grows in proportion to wealth; they are the two parts of a zero-sum equation. Hegel claims that poverty is the price that society pays for wealth. Marx, building on Hegel's observation, faults the "antagonistic character of capitalist accumulation" that "makes an accumulation of misery a *necessary condition*, corresponding to the accumulation of wealth" (Marx 1976 [1867], 799; emphasis added). "Accumulation of wealth at one pole," Marx concludes, "is at the same time the accumulation of misery, the torment of labour, slavery, ignorance, brutalization and moral degradation at the opposite pole" (Marx 1976 [1867], 799). Far from being a relic of the old, undeveloped society, poverty in modern society is a phenomenon as modern as the structure of commodity-producing society itself (Hegel 2005 [1821]). However, despite years of intense Western involvement and trillions of dollars in charity and aid to so-called developing countries and humanitarian campaigns aimed at alleviating poverty and social insecurity, the welfare of the world's needy is not only still a problem but, as the United Nations (UN-Habitat 2003) and now the World Bank (Lakner and Milanovic 2013) have recently acknowledged, a problem that is actually worsening.

Debates rage over why poverty continues to increase. Within the expansive development literature, two opposing views have framed the way in which this postcolonial project has been both understood and implemented. Neither of these views does justice to the complex assemblages that constitute today's modern humanitarian practice and policy. However, both perspectives suggest that NGOS have an important role to play in the long-term fight against global poverty. One theoretical approach in the sociology of development literature has been to focus on development as a historically produced discourse or system of representation, language, and practice. This extensive body of critical scholarship extends colonial and feminist studies to reveal the many ways in which the technical discourse and strategy of development have produced its opposite—"massive underdevelopment and impoverishment, untold exploitation and oppression"—all the while obscuring the political effects (Appadurai 1990; Escobar 1995, 4; Rist 2008). Authors such as Homi Bhabha (1990), Chandra Mohanty (1991a, 1991b), Gilbert Rist (1997, 2008), and Edward Said (1979) have introduced new ways of thinking about representations of "third world" practices and peoples. Others in the development as discourse framework have chosen to examine the multitude and fragmented ways in which global domination or Empire is resisted, avoided, and negotiated (Burawoy 2001; Burawoy et al. 2000; Hardt and Negri 2004; Scott 1998). However, in spite of some progress in terms of reimagining new forms of representation, anthropology and the social sciences more generally "have yet to give satisfactory answers to the question of the production of knowledge about the 'other'" (Escobar 1995, 181). Within this perspective, NGOs are often theorized as enablers of uneven global development (Harvey 2006, 2010; O'Connor 1998; Smith 1998). Some scholars argue that they actually direct uneven development, thereby functioning as the "Trojan horses for global neoliberalism" (Wallace 2003). This perspective, however, tends to ignore the degree to which the convergence of finance capital, corporate philanthropy, social entrepreneurialism, and business management principles are shaping the way in which humanitarianism is both conceptualized and addressed by NGOs.

From an instrumentalist viewpoint, the usual concern is how to define the problem and realize the program designs in practice, usually through appropriate technology interventions and new management strategies. In the 1980s the problem was seen as a lack of technology, and the solution came in various kinds of technological innovations, of which large dams and other irrigations projects, the Green Revolution, and information technology are three examples. Today, the UN Millennium Development Goals (MDGs) (specific targets for the reduction of poverty, ill health, and illiteracy) frame development policy, and these goals are realized through various interpretations of good governance, including participatory approaches, women's emancipatory strategies, self-help groups (SHGs), and other practices aimed at enabling the world's excluded populations to become more resilient and self-sufficient.

From an instrumentalist perspective NGOs are often seen as an important and necessary actor in influencing humanitarian policy and practice. In his book *Dams and Development. Transnational Struggles for Water and Power,* Sanjeev Khagram (2004) argues that the growing struggles and campaigns over human rights, as well as indigenous peoples and the environment, can be explained, in part, by the rapid rise of transnational NGOs. The rapid rise of transnational NGOs has become a common feature of world politics, Khagram argues. As "transnational nongovernmental organizations, coalitions, and networks interact over time, " they influence "the degree to which norms and principles in issue areas, such as the environment, human rights, and indigenous peoples . . . spread globally and become institutionalized in the procedures and structures of states, multilateral agencies, and multinational corporations" (Khagram 2004, 18). However, for all the persistent optimism about the power of policy design to solve the problem of poverty, the instrumentalist perspective continues to ignore the politics of science and technology *in* humanitarianism. In so doing, critics argue, the instrumentalist perspective not only ignores long-standing traditions of domination but also contributes to permanent biopolitical restructuring—in defining the state of exception and necessity—of the world's poor (Agamben 2005; Escobar 1995; Hardt and Negri 2001).

The new visibility of NGOs as international government actors is a subject of growing interest among international relations and development scholars. Part of that attention has come from the rapid expansion of this newly (re)forming sector of civil society. In fact, NGOs have greatly proliferated in the past two decades, and some of the more established ones, such as Oxfam, Save the Children Fund, CARE, or World Vision, have expanded not only in size but also in the scope of their activities. These changes in both the magnitude and the scope of NGOs, together with growing concerns about their legitimacy, have repeatedly called for an urgent need to review and, in some cases, further transform the NGO sector (Beloe et al. 2003).

For instance, Weiss and Gordenker (1996) define NGOs as "a special set of organizations that are private in their form but public in their purpose," thus distinguishing them from either intergovernmental organizations (IGOs) or transnational corporations (TNCs). However, this characterization fails to acknowledge how both the form and practices of NGOs have become aligned with private and government interests alike. NGOs have become crucial to the United Nations' future and a salient phenomenon in international policy making and execution (Weiss and Gordenker 1996), and, at the same time, they have also been at the forefront of reforming humanitarian consultancy, education, entrepreneurialism, and financial services (Bebbington 1997). Conversely, Dorothea Hilhorst (2003, 3) has argued that there is "no single answer to what an NGO *is*, what it *wants*, and what is *does*." While an NGO might adopt a particular structure, in practice it is much more difficult to identify its boundaries (Hilhorst 2003). Some scholars argue that the NGO movement and activism against "big dams" over the past two decades has demonstrably shifted public opinion away from top-down, technocratic approaches toward people-centered, bottom-up development (Khagram 2004; Phadke 2005). This activist response has developed alongside, and often in association with, important efforts by social scientists to document the deleterious environmental and social impacts of large international water development projects. However, NGOs have been accused of "flirting with the enemy," as they have transformed their identity and objectives from empowerment to service delivery (Miraftab 1997). Moreover, Jenny Pearce (2000, 20) argues, to a certain extent NGOs have "succumbed to the pressures and incentives to pick up the social cost of neoliberal restructuring" and thus are implicated in the expansion and legitimation of market-led globalization.

The challenge to understanding the role of NGOs comes in part from conventional ways of thinking about globalization, development, and humanitarianism. Most metanarratives condense all cultural developments into a single program or trajectory: the emergence of the global era. For example, modernization theory, argues that, over time, "underdeveloped areas" of the globe will emerge from traditional societies to modern. The causes of many problems associated with underdevelopment—lack of access to drinking water, poverty, and military conflict, for example—are assumed to be mostly internal to a given country, and the solutions to these social problems to lie in more ties to the West. This conventional approach to theorizing globalization and development often pits NGOs and other civil society groups against the incapacities of sovereign state power. However, this instrumentalist perspective continues to assume a Westphalian or national frame, in which states are the only sovereign power over national territories and populations.

Moreover, even in making the observation that unregulated global markets have caused and continue to cause enormous harm to rich and poor societies alike, those at the so-called cutting edge of poverty reduction strategies continue to insist that maximizing economic integration is the best strategy in the war on poverty. For example, according to the World Bank (2002), "people rise from poverty when countries act on two pillars of development: building a good investment climate in which private entrepreneurs will invest, generate jobs and produce efficiently, and empowering poor people and investing in them so that they can participate in economic growth." Similarly, and with missionary zeal, Yasmina Zaidman, the Director of Communications and Strategic Partnerships for the Acumen Fund,[13] advised an audience of development scholars and practitioners at Indiana University that "the tools of business and partnering with corporations" *can* and *should* "change the way the world tackles poverty" (2013). In short, advocates contend not only that it is possible to get capitalism to work for the poor but also that it is *socially necessary* to do massive public good. Simply put, there is no alternative.

One goal of this book is to challenge the deeply held belief that to achieve poverty reduction "there is no alternative" to integrating the poor into the global economy. This belief is rooted in the assumption that the crisis conditions of the world's poor and dispossessed are largely a result of their social exclusion from modern life and economy, and the only way to end this condition is to include and integrate them into the world economy. What makes this particular approach noteworthy is the manner in which investment strategies, business principles, and entrepreneurialism have converged in an effort to alleviate the rising rates of inequality and conspicuous poverty that has been the hallmark of the past forty years of neoliberalism. In addition to supporting an enhanced role for free trade and economic integration, this approach has also shifted the burden of poverty reduction strategies away from national and international aid to programs supported by private donations. In the past, aid from rich countries to African and Asian governments has tended to be in the form of large concessional loans or grants (Moyo 2010). The problem for debtor countries is that these loans often come with obligations, such as selling off commonly held resources, privatizing national industries, and removing protective trade barriers, in addition to repayment of principle and interest. This form of indebtedness amounts to a new and deepening system of dependency in which debtor countries are forced to relinquish the very government assets that are needed for urgent economic recovery and long-term repayment. Moreover, critics have observed that food aid can actually undermine local agricultural production by saturating local food markets, thereby adding to the burden of farmers who were already struggling to sell their agricultural products on a heavily subsidized global commodities market. This shift from government aid to private investment, venture philanthropists argue, will reduce poverty by extending opportunities for economic integration in the developing countries and transition them away from the debt dependence that has epitomized national and international aid programs of the past forty years. In the absence of another political economic alternative, those involved in poverty reduction campaigns are encouraged to harness the power of markets in the war on poverty.

For their part, the non-profit sector have experienced unprecedented growth in recent years (see Figure 0.3). In some instances, they have replaced failing government agencies or helped to staff particular bureaucracies with paid employees or volunteers. In other instances, they have become strategic business partners or investment vehicles that are traded on global markets. In still other instances, they have advanced information and communications technology (ICT) and platforms that support and enhance their transnational networks, and, in other cases, they are actively involved in research design and data collection associated with specific humanitarian projects or emergency relief efforts. Proponents of this rapidly growing humanitarian complex argue that it merges the power of finance, the generosity of corporate charity, the spirit of entrepreneurialism, and the acumen of business to "change the way the world tackles poverty" (Zaidman 2013). Yet in spite of what amounts to sovereign decision-making authority to give life and take it away, we know very little about how humanitarian needs and efforts are determined, how money is raised, spent, or invested, how markets are "enhanced," how technology is used, how expertise is established, and how poverty reduction

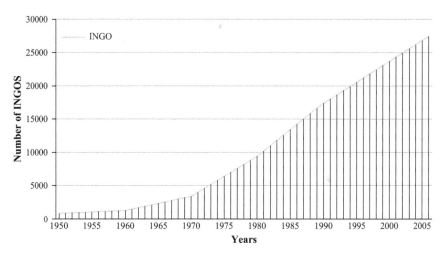

Figure 0.3 Rise in the Number of INGOs, 1950–2005. Source: Union of International Associations, 2008.

programs are supposed to work, and why they usually fail. Moreover, we know very little about the manner in which these new transnational networks of humanitarianism are assembled, expand, or are maintained. More generally, however, it remains unclear to what extent this new humanitarian complex can cope with the conflicting ambitions of human welfare and profit maximization. When people set out to change the crisis conditions in most of the world, the devil is truly in the details.

With these questions in mind, I plan in this book to place the present humanitarian conjuncture within the context of contradictory relations embedded in this new global strategy on the war on poverty. These embedded contradictions, in employment, education, finance, and technology to name four, may, in fact, represent a *release value* for the past forty years of neoliberal capitalism—what amounts to a private civil society version of the welfare state. This perspective suggests a fresh way to examine the extent to which this new form of humanitarianism offers a modern-day coping mechanism that ensures, on the one hand, that new markets are "opened up and kept open" (Polanyi 1944, 140) and, on the other hand, that demands for social protection are persistently generated. In locating the multilayered transnational networks that have produced this particular form of modern humanitarianism, we can offer a historically specific explanation for how these contradictions and tensions are first manufactured and then worked out in everyday practice.

A partial but important inspiration for this interpretation is Karl Polanyi's (1944) account of capitalism's double movement. In addition to insisting that "the road to the free market was opened and kept open by an enormous increase in continuous, centrally organized and controlled interventionism" (1944, 140), Polanyi maintained that the destructive tendencies of the so-called self-regulating market generated countertendencies and demands for social protection. However, these necessary interventions, Polanyi (1944) argued, were not external to the system but contained within capitalism itself. The empirical analysis in the pages that follow suggests that the unprecedented rise of the non-profit sector is a necessary condition of global capitalism, a condition that both constrains and enables profit and welfare.

Additionally, Polanyi argued (1944, 141), the establishment of a self-regulating market in the nineteenth and twentieth centuries was contingent on the state's developing "new powers, organs, and instruments" of governance to intervene in the market's destructive tendencies. Given this shift in humanitarian policy, it is unclear whether, and to what extent, these requisite powers and instruments of government intervention have been usurped by NGOs. Moreover, if a laissez-faire economy is, in fact, planned, rather than natural or evitable, as Polanyi (1944) reasoned, then we need to determine to what extent the current form of humanitarianism is a deliberate by-product of nongovernment management and social control.

This project also draws much inspiration from the work of geographer Gillian Hart (2002, 2013). In particular, I have been influenced by Hart's (2013) strategy of tacking back and forth between theory and practice in an effort to produce concrete concepts that are adequate to explain the concrete problems facing much of humankind. This social science method of tacking back and forth between theory and data is often referred to as the extended case method approach (Burawoy 1998; Burawoy et al. 1991, 2000). The extended case method expands the conventional limits of ethnographic analysis in order to examine how external forces shape particular social situations. It allows a researcher "to move from the 'micro' to the 'macro,' and to connect the present to the past in anticipation of the future, all by building on pre-existing theory" (Burawoy 1998, 5). I have made an effort to tell this story through the experience of humanitarian practitioners, including myself, as they/we participate in the multiple sites of humanitarian production. I try to show that these sites are filled with diverse groups of conflicted people—volunteers, employees, executives, investors, and researchers, to name a few—who are actively involved in the daily production of humanitarian policy and practice. These people do not fully agree with or consent to the particular humanitarian circumstances in which they find themselves (Goldman 2005). Moreover, many of them do not fully stand with or against universal humanitarian principles. In tracing the multilayered networks of particular people, groups, and organizations, we can better understand the key sites of contractions embedded in the modern humanitarian complex, in which ideas, concepts, and politics get deployed, negotiated, and challenged. It is only within these interstices, Michael Goldman (2005, 25) reminds us, "that we can observe concrete organic struggles over power," in an effort to rethink our political choices and claims about humanitarian policy and practice. Combining interviews and participant observation with quantitative data from baseline assessments, financial records, and corporate internet sites has resulted in multiple and diverse entry points to trace and analyze the social relations of particular NGOs involved in modern humanitarian efforts. This extended case method provides an analysis and interpretation of the experiences of humanitarian practitioners, including myself, and the practices and policies of transnational humanitarian organizations, more generally, dedicated to alleviating various forms of inequality and dispossession.

Chapter Summaries

The book provides a historical and sociological explanation for the unprecedented rise in civil society organizations dedicated to solving global poverty and insecurity. The book argues that the nature of this growth—evidenced not only in a rise in corporate charity and philanthropy but also in international schools, study-abroad programs, and "without borders" societies—embeds a contradiction in the manner in which the crisis of global poverty converges with rising global unemployment trends. For example, a recent economic data bulletin by the Center for Civil Society Studies (Salamon et al. 2012, 1) reported that "nonprofit organizations have been holding the fort for much of the rest of the economy" in the United States, "creating jobs at a time when other components of the economy have been shedding jobs at accelerating rates." Even during the recession from 2007 to 2009, the report reveals that jobs at nonprofit organizations increased by an average of 1.9 percent per year[14] at the same time that businesses averaged jobs losses of 3.7 percent per year (Salamon et al. 2012). In other words, the nonprofit sector in the United States and other core countries is the world's fastest-growing job sector. Understanding why so many institutions and people are committed to solving the "defining moral issue of our time" is a question not just of analyzing the motivations of civil society organizations but also of making sense of the larger political and economic contexts within which humanitarianism is now embedded.

In Chapter 1, I turn my attention to the fluid web of relationships within which new humanitarianism government and governmentality are embedded in an effort to draw our attention to the types of knowledge, ideas, people, and funding that move through numerous levels, sites, and associations of the global humanitarian complex. In effect, we turn to an examination of the micropolitics of humanitarianism in an attempt to reveal how welfare needs and efforts are determined and how expertise is established in this morally complicated and heavily networked biopolitical assemblage. In so doing, we draw attention to the connections between humanitarian organizations and corporate philanthropy, between institutions of higher learning and the nonprofit sector, and between voluntary associations and educational programs that have, by virtue of expanding their institutions' programs and policies, taken on new roles in the fight against poverty and dispossession. Some organizations have partnered with the business sector, others have adopted entrepreneurial strategies, and still others have looked to information and communications technology in an effort to do massive social good. Still other NGOs have turned to evidenced-based research, while others have turned to fellowship and study-abroad programs. The everyday practices of this increasingly global, diversified, interconnected, and networked complex have shaped the next wave of humanitarian ideas, devices, and practitioners. These sites of humanitarian production have become a formidable force in cultivating new kinds of organized social goods, as well as politics, and are therefore valuable applied field sites in understanding what happens in specific humanitarian spaces.

We also explore the conviction of many volunteers and employees involved in humanitarian efforts around the world when they are faced with the challenges of local conditions and everyday life in an unfamiliar place. What happens to the project or campaign when surveys do not match up, maps are not available, or data are simply missing? Do they pack their bags and return to comforts of home, or do they "soldier on" and improvise? Understanding how some of the foot soldiers in the war on poverty interpret what they see, hear, write, and feel in remote areas around the world when faced with stark contradictions raises some important questions about the "compendium of individual exchanges," necessary negotiations—with oneself and well as with others—and the politics that lie behind, and indeed support, this modern humanitarian complex (Nordstrom 2007, xvii).

Chapter 2 examines the impact and growth of a central meaning-producing institution within the global humanitarian assemblage: the education system. In particular, the rapid growth of institutions involved in humanitarian training and education has not only aided in the professionalization of the global learning experience but also been integral in shaping the means and methods by which humanitarianism is practiced and understood. The rapid rise of volunteer and study-abroad programs has allowed more students to take advantage of cross-cultural learning experiences in an effort to influence both career aspirations and personal worldviews in a global age. This practice is occurring during a period when government programs concerning global citizenship have diminished in size and importance. Today, the majority of students studying abroad are not doing so on a Commonwealth Scholarship, in the case of UK citizens, or volunteering with the Peace Corps, in the case of US citizens. Today, most Western youth and young at heart interested in a life-changing international experience are searching the Internet for innovative companies such as Frontier, Global Glimpse, and Cross-Cultural Solutions for a personalized global learning experience. The majority of international volunteer programs today are facilitated by nonprofit organizations operating in an unregulated and non-accredited industry eager to sell an "adventure of a lifetime for people of all ages and walks of life" (Cross-Cultural Solutions 2015). Moreover, this rapidly growing non-academic educational complex is increasingly merging with and influencing the curricula of more formal academic institutions. This chapter examines the effects of this educational assemblage on students who are committed to doing good but also to doing well.

Part of what makes this current humanitarian conjuncture so extraordinary is the way in which the convergence of finance capital, corporate philanthropy, social entrepreneurialism have converged and been reconfigured to solve the most pressing problem of modern society. In chapter 3, I ask, why are the nouveau riche so interested in helping the world's poor? What is notable about this new class of superrich philanthropists is that finance capital, social entrepreneurialism, and business management principles (i.e., the market) remain reliable allies in creating new possibilities for the prosperity of the rest of humanity. In effect, this mushrooming cadre of transglobal humanitarians, "partnering with corporations" and "using the tools of business . . . to finance in different ways," do not simply want to help the poor; they want to change the very nature of what it means to help those in need.

In chapter 4, I draw attention to the discourse of failure in contemporary humanitarian practice. What I find striking is the incommensurability of a humanitarian system that, on the one hand, encourages the management of failure—its predictability, its calculability, and its regulation—while, on the other hand, encouraging a culture of risk taking, entrepreneurialism, and innovation, in effect unpredictability and change. This gambling humanitarian system produces caring subjects who celebrate their failures and achievements while concurrently denouncing the conditions of its organization. This new humanitarian subjectivity pledges its faith in the magic of the market, its conviction in modern technology, and its hope in Silicon Valley–type entrepreneurialism to change the way in which the world tackles poverty. However, the deep reflections shared in this chapter, albeit comedic, at Fail Festivals seem to suggest that the making of this new subjectivity is never fully complete and always a work of malleable social construction. A *subject* that not only learns from repeated failures at saving the world's dispossessed but is also able to celebrate this achievement as a mark of leadership, innovation, and risk-taking virtue in pushing the boundaries of what is possible, yet highly improbable. An entrepreneurial *subject* who should be respected for taking the race against poverty and dispossession on, knowing that in order to win, one must be ready to lose.

The new visibility of NGOs as a possible institutional form to interrogate inequality, link local conditions with global aspirations, and cultivate new types of utopian relations is a subject of growing interest among the public, activists, and scholars. This book examines an important and enduring ethical question in development and humanitarian policy, namely: whose voice is being heard? To what extent do humanitarian campaigns champion the voices of the dispossessed? Are they championing the voices that they hear or voices that resonate with their skillset and donor interests? In other words, to what extent are new humanitarians tone deaf? Understanding how this growing force for good makes what amounts to sovereign decisions over life and death reveals some of the inherent contradictions in this new form of humanitarian government and governmentality.

Notes

1. At the time I was a graduate student at Michigan State University and, like so many others, felt compelled to donate as much as I could afford.

2. Questions continue to surface regarding the manner in which natural barriers, particularly coral reefs, mangroves, and sand dunes, have been removed to make way for shrimp farms, tourism, and other economic activities. Many countries across Asia, including Indonesia, Sri Lanka, and Bangladesh, have encouraged expansion of their aquaculture industries by destroying the coral reefs surrounding their beaches. Moreover, many reefs areas around the Indian Ocean have been exploded with dynamite because they impede shipping, an important part of the South Asian economy. This ecological damage, environmentalists argue, have left coastal communities around the world more vulnerable to natural calamities (Browne 2004).

3. Max Lawson of the charity Oxfam told CBC Radio. Lawson said when Hurricane Mitch ravaged Central America in 1998, only a third of the money promised got to the people of Nicaragua and Honduras (Canadian Broadcasting Corporation 2006).

4. AECCafe.com (http://www10.aeccafe.com/nbc/articles/view_article.php?articleid =292462&interstitial_displayed=Yes/). For more information on the redevelopment projects, see http://www.careers.ch2m.com/worldwide/en/engineering-projects/sri-lanka-tsunami.asp.

5. Of which $7 billion of the settlement was tax deductible.

6. The case is the latest in a series of legal headaches for JPMorgan, the country's largest bank by assets. In November 2013, JPMorgan announced a $4.5 billion settlement to institutional investors who suffered losses on bubble-era mortgage securities. The firm has also paid over $1 billion in connection with the 2012 "London Whale" trading debacle, and $80 million more over alleged unfair credit card billing practices. Moreover, in July 2012, the bank agreed to pay $410 million to settle charges that it manipulated electricity prices in California and the Midwest. It is also facing scrutiny over its hiring practices in China and its alleged involvement in a Libor (London Interbank Offered Rate) rate-fixing scandal (O'Toole and Perez 2013).

7. R2P states that sovereignty no longer exclusively protects states from foreign interference; it is a charge of responsibility that holds states accountable for the welfare of their people.

8. About half the aid requested will go toward delivering food, shelter, and health care in Syria and to Syrians in neighboring countries displaced by their civil war. After Syria, the next biggest requests are for $1.1 billion for South Sudan, $995 million for Sudan, $928 million for Somalia, $832 million for Congo, and $791 million for rebuilding in the typhoon-hit Philippines. Other major requests are for $591 million for Yemen, $406 million for Afghanistan, $390 million for the occupied Palestinian territories, $247 million for Central African Republic, and $169 million for Haiti (Heilprin 2013).

9. Volunteers contributed 15.2 billion hours, worth an estimated $296.2 billion.

10. Throughout this book I use the terminology of humanitarian government and governmentality. Humanitarian government entails any attempt to shape with some degree of deliberation aspects of our humanitarian behavior. This conduct is conveyed according to particular sets of norms and interests that frame and constrain ways of thinking about questions of "doing good." Governmentality refers to the way in which humanitarian actors (state, business, and non-profits), exercise this control over, or govern, the way in which we think and act upon our humanitarian aspirations, practices, and policies.

11. Here I am referring to the strategy of anthropologist Clifford Geertz towards an interpretative theory of culture where thick description ethnography is used "in the hope of rendering mere occurrences scientifically eloquent" (Geertz, C. 1973, 28).

12. For all its consequence, this social contract is rarely subjected to empirical analysis at the macro level. Of course, there is much at stake in problematizing this now-dominant approach to poverty alleviation. My fear in conducting such an analysis is that it will alienate the very audience with whom I want to have a conversation. Moreover, it strikes me that "those in the thick" of this humanitarian complex will have little tolerance or time to be self-reflective about the politics of such an approach.

13. The Acumen strategy to poverty reduction is to "raise charitable donations that allow us to make patient long-term debt or equity investments in early-stage companies providing reliable and affordable access to agricultural inputs and markets, quality education, clean energy, healthcare services, formal housing, and safe drinking water to low-income customers" (acumen.org).

14. The data revealed that nonprofit employment actually grew by 2.6 percent during the first year of the recession and 1.2 percent during the second year of the recession, for an average annual increase of 1.9 percent (Salamon et al. Wojciech Sokolowski, and Geller, 2012).

1   I Am Here to Help

"Innovation is the highway and impact is the destination."
Peter Singer, CEO of Grand Challenges Canada

I SAY ANYTHING I think. I don't hide much," admits Heather Meyer, the program advisor for the NGO Water for People, during a candid dinner conversation in Kigali. "I had for a while regular lunches with a group [of friends]. We used to call each other 'the four,' Water for People, Water for Life, Living Water International, and WaterAid. The four of us are white expatriates. We used to have lunch all the time and be able to talk openly . . . and sometimes it was absolutely hysterical. We had this conversation about sustainability, and one us, I think it was the person from Living Water International, was saying, 'oh, our website is great on sustainability,' and the other one joked, 'yeah, I thought about giving to your website.' And what happens on the ground has nothing to do with it," concludes Meyer of the daunting gap between what one reads on websites and what one does in practice. In the weeks and months that followed, I would begin to recognize the profound weight of our candid conversation, and the tensions and contradictions that surround the practices and beliefs of *new humanitarianism*, efforts repeated around the world by sincere folks such as Meyer, "trying to do something else for a while, something much more meaningful." One thing remains for certain: the governance, economics, and knowledge-making practices of "doing massive social good" have changed over the past two decades, and these changes raise important epistemological questions about the forms of knowledge, knowing, and subjectivity that are produced and sustained in the processes and circuits of the new humanitarian complex.

What is it about the current humanitarian complex that prevents many of these people—these humanitarians—from achieving their stated aims of empowering the marginalized and combating poverty? Moreover, to what extent are they becoming—knowingly or unthinkingly—carriers of the beliefs, policies, and procedures of a global agenda, which many of them openly oppose? And, having recognized their limitations, how do they reconcile them in terms of personal commitments and career aspirations. On the one hand, an army of humanitarian practitioners, employees and volunteers alike, mock the notions of sustainability, charity, and welfare that they are supposed to put into practice, while, on the other hand, these same people work assiduously to raise the profile of their organization, their donors, and their latest strategy in the war on poverty or theory on dispossession. Making sense of this striking contradiction amid the rough-and-tumble of lived humanitarian experience can help us to understand why new humanitarians offer their consent without force, how they maneuver within particular settings and organizations, and why sometimes they enthusiastically participate in agendas they actively oppose, while in other settings they dissent.

Nevertheless, amid a backdrop of personal dilemmas, doubts, and vivid contradictions, humanitarians like Meyer join an expanding empire determined to build a better world (Barnett 2011). Much attention has been paid to the growing scale and scope of this private not-for-profit humanitarian complex. For some scholars, the unprecedented growth in NGOs mirrors the scale and circumstances of contemporary humanitarian atrocities throughout the world. From this perspective, the growth of NGOs is presented as a possible nongovernmental solution to the way in which the world tackles poverty and the problems of welfare service delivery for the growing number of disenfranchised and dispossessed. As this growing network of transnational NGOs goes from one emergency to the next, they not only expand their global reach but also increasingly influence the degree to which a deepening knowledge of vulnerability and a growing ethics of care have spread globally (Barnett 2011; Khagram 2004). NGOs such as Water for People, Water for Life, Living Water International, and WaterAid are playing an increasingly dominant role in determining the parameters that we use and act on in the name of humanity. In working with donors and development agencies, corporate boards, universities and think tanks, these nongovernmental knowledge-producing institutions have been able to extend their influence and shape contemporary human rights and global aid agendas. What remains unclear, however, is how NGOs' growing influence "fits" or are being pieced together within an expanding corpus of interlocking networks and circuits through which humanitarianism is biopolitically produced, managed, and ordered. Some scholars have argued that this relationship has placed NGOs "too close for comfort," referring to the fact that nonprofit organizations are influenced more by their supporters' interests than by the interests of those they support, akin to Trojan horses, as opposed to good Samaritans (Edwards and Hulme 1996; Wallace 2003). But while these generalizations are politically and even intellectually provocative, they glaze over the everyday governing mentality of NGOs, their strategies of rule and expertise, negotiations within rapidly changing environments, and the kinds of humanitarian subjects they produce.

In other words, these sweeping generalizations about NGOs, whether optimistic, pessimistic, or supposedly neutral, fail to recognize the new relations and assemblages of power that are emerging as a result of this new humanitarian conjuncture, where the growth of financial and information flows, and the popularity of philanthropy and entrepreneurship are reshaping both the politics of inequality and the attributes of dispossession. NGOs do not work alone, nor do "they have a hammerlock on humanitarianism," as Michael Barnett (2011) has suggested. Rather, they work within a humanitarian complex of private and public actors, among them religious bodies, educational institutions, states, corporations, charities and philanthropies, and individuals. Moreover, these relations are evolving as NGOs continuously forge innovative and increasingly complex and wide-ranging formal and informal linkages with one another, with government agencies, with transnational social movements, with international development agencies, and with corporate donors (Fisher 1997).

NGOs are taking on new functions in response to the escalating problems associated with growing inequality and insecurity worldwide. They engage in empirically grounded research methods to undertake needs assessments, consult with scientists, engineers, and other practitioners to guide future work, use marketing techniques and public relations to raise funds, hire consultants to write reports and policy documents, and enlist an endless supply of students and other volunteers to help contribute much needed energy and human resources to their particular cause. These networks, alliances, and practices have opened up new sites for ethnographic research to help us understand the new relations and politics of dispossession and the humanitarian response by NGOs, in particular places and times, to manage, regulate, and order the distribution of vulnerability worldwide (Fisher 1997). Humanitarian practice is where interpretations about dispossession and victimization are produced and sustained, actors—both self and others—are enrolled, and interests and desires are translated, interpreted, and transcribed into collective stories. Examining these practices reveals how these connections are weaved with other entities, how struggles both within and between agencies are resolved, and how the everyday practices of contemporary NGOs have contributed to the expansion of humanitarianism as an ideology, a profession, and a new social movement.

In this chapter, we move away from the intense interest regarding the role of the nonprofit sector in global humanitarian efforts and turn to the hidden abode of humanitarian production.[1] We shift the emphasis from the scope and scale of humanitarian organizations to the fluid web of relationships in an effort to draw our attention to the types of knowledge, ideas, people, and funding that move through numerous levels, sites, and associations of the global humanitarian complex. In effect, we turn to an examination of the micropolitics of humanitarianism in an attempt to reveal how welfare needs and efforts are determined and how expertise is established in this morally complicated and densely networked biopolitical assemblage. In so doing, we draw attention to the connections between humanitarian organizations and corporate philanthropy, between institutions of higher learning and the nonprofit sector, and between voluntary associations and educational programs that have, by virtue of expanding their institutions' programs and policies, taken on new roles in the fight against poverty and dispossession. Some organizations have partnered with the business sector, others have adopted entrepreneurial strategies, and yet others have looked to information and communications technologies in an effort to do massive social good. Still other NGOs have turned to evidenced-based research, while others have turned to fellowship and study-abroad programs. The everyday practices of this increasingly global, diversified, interconnected, and networked complex have shaped the next wave of humanitarian ideas, devices, and practitioners. These sites of humanitarian production have become a formidable force in cultivating new kinds of organized social good, as well as politics, and are therefore valuable applied field sites in clarifying what happens in specific humanitarian spaces.

In this and the next chapter, we focus on two important knowledge-making practices that have come to dominant much of the debate about humanitarian policy and practice. The first knowledge-making practice, information gathering and data production, has become an important and contentious subject concerning assessing humanitarian needs of particular people in particular crises. The second, knowledge-making practice, discussed in chapter 2, is humanitarian training and education. Both of these practices are increasingly falling under the power (legitimate authority) and influence of nonprofit organizations, networks, and alliances.

The role of evidence and data has featured prominently in debates about measuring program transparency, efficiency, impact, and success. Proponents argue that "if we know what works and how, we could create a better humanitarian system with more efficient and effective courses of action" and institutions of care "to address needs and to reduce suffering" (Dijkzeul, Hilhorst, and Walker 2013, S1). A striking example of this widely held belief was theatrically displayed in a discussion on ending poverty in November 2013. Jim Yong Kim, the president of the World Bank, and the rock star and humanitarian Bono, of U2 fame, declared to a packed audience of World Bank and ONE staffers, civil society groups, and media correspondents that "open data and transparency" will "turbocharge the fight against extreme poverty." For Bono and other proponents of big data, "transparency is" simply "transformative" in tackling the pressing global problem of extreme poverty. In the views of many observers, the increasing use of widespread data gathering and analysis is nothing short of a revolution that is quietly transforming, or in Bono's view, "turbocharging," how we live, work, and think about enduring social problems (Mayer-Schönberger and Cukier 2013). "The benefits to society will be myriad," Viktor Mayer-Schönberger and Kenneth Cukier (2013, 17) profess, "as big data becomes part of the solution to pressing global problems like addressing climate change, eradicating disease, and fostering good governance and economic development." In effect, these protagonists argue that the rise of big data is nothing short of a historical turning point in humankind's quest to quantify and understand the postcolonial world, in order to solve its most pressing problems (Mayer-Schönberger and Cukier 2013).

This turning point is often referred to as the fourth paradigm, a new scientific methodology based on data-intensive computing, where knowledge and understanding, in effect, meaning, is gained with sophisticated algorithms and statistical techniques of extensive or megascale databases. Proponents argue that this data-exploration paradigm unifies theory, experiment, and simulation (Hey, Tansley, and Tolle 2009). Some advocates suggest that this paradigm might signal the end of theory in scientific exploration and analysis (Anderson 2008). This new paradigm, or eScience, is distinguished by four unique characteristics. First, large-scale data are captured by new instruments and sensor networks or generated by simulation. Second, software, and not individual scientists or groups of scientists or researchers, process this data. Third, information/knowledge is stored in computer databases and not with individual scientists, communities, or even disciplines. And fourth, scientists analyze the data using data management and statistics techniques, not by using qualitative or other interpretative approaches. The narrative of big data, of course, fits well with other biopolitical discourses (transparency, accountability, efficiency, corruption, and risk, to name a few) that have defined humanitarian policy and practice over the past ten years. This narrative also conveniently parallels larger conjunctural changes in governance, economics, and knowledge making that have been the hallmark of small-d development policy and practice under neoliberal orthodoxy (Hart 2009). These smaller narratives fit seamlessly within the larger *modern* narrative, or metanarrative (Lyotard 1979)—the unquestioned story—that the heroic West has the capability and the morality to save the rest (quite often from their own fate). This narrative of big data is most clearly expressed in aid agencies' preoccupation to base humanitarian assistance on solid empirical evidence—on science—and to then use this data to establish field research programs, to measure program efficiency, manage donor effectiveness, and, most importantly, predict successful campaigns. The telling and retelling of this data narrative not only serves to give purpose and meaning to the knowledge-making practices of NGOs but also is critical in establishing legitimacy in a rapidly changing humanitarian environment. It is why, in part, "data" is on the tip of every humanitarian organization's metaphoric tongue. For example, having open and transparent data is critical not only to donors, such as the World Bank, which want to been seen as funding effective campaigns, but also to recipient and donor governments that are trying to determine the costs of service delivery, as well as nonprofits that are soliciting donations from their supporters.

Yet for all its hype, data remain a scarce and elusive resource in the humanitarian world and accurate information is always difficult to establish. Necessary information is often context specific, cultivated under particular crises conditions, such as droughts, wars, and floods, over a limited duration, and involving multiple researchers with diverse interests and research training. In effect, the generation and, particularly, the application of data are never simple undertakings, and always much more than simply counting the number of people and their urgent needs. Numbers cannot speak for themselves, and data sets—no matter their scale—are still objects of human design. This is why the sociologist Steven Shapin (1998, 6) observed, "we need to understand not only how knowledge is made in specific places but also how transactions occur between places." If knowledge about humanitarian crises and needs are, indeed, a local product, how does it—or rather some version of it—travel over the uneven terrain that colonialism has reworked to spread across the world to you and I, who sit in our comfortable armchairs and tap away on our personal computers thousands of miles away?

In their evolving role as humanitarian researchers, NGOs are increasingly responsible for how actors in the global humanitarian system and the general public understand poverty and dispossession. In fact, some scholars have suggested that over the past decade NGOs have established a veritable research industry, drastically reshaping the positionality of NGOs as well as the subjectivity of humanitarians, both victims and practitioners alike (Opoku-Mensah 2007; Opoku-Mensah, Lewis, and Tvedt 2007). These knowledge-making practices include needs assessments, field research programs, programing audits, impact assessments, budgetary planning, data-driven methodologies and devices, good practice principles, agency reports, funding proposals, policy documents, the populating of website and social media sites, and the production of newsletters. This knowledge production yields a mass of humanitarian inscriptions—diagrams, prints, photographs, films, documentaries, videos, maps, equations, graphs, tables, articles, and textbooks—that together constitute a shared rhetorical space and language in which humanitarianism can be defined and debated.

A recent funding bulletin from the International Medical Corps (IMC) titled "The Numbers behind Your Support" provides a striking example of the use of inscription devices to both "make knowledge" and "establish links." The first page of the bulletin features a photograph of an African woman on a gurney. Over her stands an Asian man in a medical gown pointing to a computer beside the patient. Huddled around the doctor, patient, and computer is a group of African men. The photograph leaves the reader, and potential donor, with a pictorial representation of an IMC staff training local health-care professionals with the use of donated technology, medicines, and supplies. Flip to pages 2 and 3 of the bulletin, where the reader is informed that a $1 donation has the potential to expand to $30 in aid, "unlocking additional medicines and supplies," through the use of IMC's transnational networks in the medical services sector. On page 4, readers are informed that $1 donation will also make IMC eligible for $30 in additional grant funding from other donors. The rhetoric of leverage, displayed in text and pictures, is particularly strategic because it signals to readers, as well as others within the humanitarian system, that the practices and programs of this NGO address a generally shared concern about humanitarian aid, namely, that funds need to be leveraged more wisely and efficiently to maximize humanitarian impact (Choge, Harrison, McCornick, and Bartlett 2011).

The message on the next page shifts to an equally important rhetorical theme in humanitarian practice: the transfer of knowledge and local capacity building. "This transfer of knowledge and skills," the bulletin reports, "ensures the growth of healthy communities, exponentially multiplying the impact of your donation long after our programs have ended." Again, the message is clear: the local capacity-building programs of this NGO will improve the long-term impact of humanitarian interventions, with a lasting and sustainable influence in local communities. These types of bulletins circulate en masse, showing up in mailboxes, inboxes, on social media, and countless public places. Together, they serve as a knowledge-producing arena in which NGOs can communicate and strengthen their links with other members of the global humanitarian assemblage, including the general public.

However, it is important to recognize that these taken-for-granted knowledge-making practices serve not only to communicate and link various actors within and beyond the humanitarian system but also work to manufacture a consistent and generally shared discourse about the world's poor and their urgent needs: who or what is the cause or problem, and how their needs should be addressed, and by whom. In effect, these knowledge-making practices help shape the theories, analytical frameworks, and common sense views—cultural narratives—through which people—benefactors and beneficiaries—understand the root causes and credible solutions to global poverty and dispossession. If these numerous knowledge-making practices also provide the mechanism by which the social reality about contemporary humanitarianism comes into being (in both poor and rich countries), and if this discursive practice is also "the articulation of knowledge and power" (Escobar 1995, 39), then we need to examine how such power and authority becomes strengthened and normalized over time.

Michael Goldman (2005) has suggested that we also need to recognize how these new power relations are being constituted together within the global humanitarian assemblage, which consists of a multitude of actors with diverse goals and agendas. For instance, NGOs do not wield the massive political-economic power of the World Bank, the Asian Development Bank, or other national and regional lending institutions. Their "complementary power" lies in their knowledge-producing activities (Goldman 2005, 32). However, it is equally important to recognize that these forms of power do not work in silos but, rather, work in tandem through the myriad networks and alliances that form and structure the global

Table 1.1 US NGOs' Funding of Water and Sanitation by USAID, FY 2005–2009 (millions of US dollars)

	2005	2006	2007	2008	2009	Total
CARE	17.9	17.7	23.1	25.9	—	84.6
charity: water	—	0.1	1.1	4.5	5.9	11.9
Living Water International	4.7	4.5	7.6	11.5	11.5	39.5
Millennium Water Alliance	1.0	1.7	1.1	2.3	1.6	7.7
Water.org	0.9	1.2	2.5	2.5	4.2	11.3
WaterAid (US)	0.1	0.5	1.2	3.2	2.1	7.1
Water for People	2.4	3.3	4.4	6.5	7.6	24.2

Source: Choge, Harrison, McCornick, and Bartlett, 2011.

humanitarian system. For example, in 1970 less than 0.2 percent of overseas development assistance was channeled through transnational NGOs. However, by 1995, the US government alone was channeling 30 percent of its aid funds through NGOs (Goldman 2005). On a global scale, the contribution of all foreign aid to water and sanitation, as a percentage of official development aid (ODA) spending, peaked in 1997 at 8 percent and tapered off to approximately 5 percent in 2005 (World Health Organization 2010). Moreover, despite the global financial crisis in 2007–2008, aid commitments for water and sanitation increased from US$7.5 billion to US$7.8 billion, a 3.2 percent increase, from 2008 to 2010 (World Health Organization 2010). Private philanthropy and corporate charity are also playing a larger role in water and sanitation efforts. Some reports indicate that private contributions now dwarf ODA aid, although these contributions are generally harder to track (Organization for Economic Cooperation and Development 2012). Nevertheless this cadre of powerful international actors—banks, governments, foundations, and corporations—have actively supported NGOs, providing them with the financial resources to take on new roles and responsibilities in the war on poverty (Table 1.1).

In a recent interview, Chris Morris, head of the Asian Development Bank's (ADB's) NGO and Civil Society Department, acknowledged that financing and partnership opportunities with NGOs and civil society organizations (CSOs) can be a new and exciting opportunity for the bank to leverage its operations and resources. "What I can imagine," Morris explains in an interview with Devex[2] reporter Lean Alfred Santos, "is working with large international NGOs, and they're doing the *softer* aspect. If one just looks at the grant side of things, [some of them] have raised more money than ADB has," he explained. "We're actually contracting [with NGOs] to implement some of our work. That way, we could pool our money in one pot and let them get on with it." Looking to the future, the bank's chief expert on NGOs indicated that collaborating with large and established international aid groups, such as Plan International and World Vision, "who have the experience, credibility, and even financial muscle to partner successfully with international financial institutions" would be most beneficial to the long-term success of the bank (Alfred Santos 2014, 1). To Chris Morris and many other heads of donor organizations, NGOs offer an institutional alternative to directly dealing with so-called Third World governments, which donors believe are generally hampered by bureaucratic inefficiencies, resource constraints, and widespread corruption. NGOs, many believe, are more flexible in their approaches and are able to adapt to varying local environments, allowing them to work more closely with the poor and with intimate knowledge of local situations. In effect, partnering with NGOs to "do[ing] the *softer* aspect" allows banks and other donors to directly influence (and watch over) their humanitarian efforts, albeit from a distance, translating otherwise risky ventures into tangible humanitarian investments.

A report prepared for the United Nations Food and Agriculture Organization (FAO) echoes the virtues of partnering with NGOs (Asian NGO Coalition for Agrarian Reform and Rural Development 1994). The report claims that because NGOs have little to no bureaucracy, they are able to minimize the time between planning and implementation. Moreover, their intimate local knowledge, the report (1994) suggests, allows them to experiment with different and alternative development models. The report (1994, 11) goes on to list other strategic areas where NGOs may have comparative advantage over government organizations, including

- *Commitment.* NGOs have dedicated and committed staff able to mobilize a vast reservoir of talents and experienced volunteers rendering needed services out of their sense of dedication rather than for personal gain;
- *Ability to stimulate a sense of genuine self-reliance.* NGOs are good organizers, trainers, and facilitators. They are more capable of organizing the rural poor, provide continuous education and training (both formal and informal), and facilitate rural people's organizations (RPO) meetings and conferences for effective mass mobilizations and for issue advocacy;
- *Responsiveness.* NGOs are good at research and documentation. Their presence at the grassroots gives them an advantage in closely monitoring and documenting people's experiences. They can easily respond and develop appropriate and relevant programs/projects based on people's needs.

In effect, donors and agencies alike argue that NGOs offer a humanitarian bridge between people and government, between the West and the rest, between the helpless and the helpful, which is direct, efficient, and responsive to local needs and conditions. This comparative advantage comes from the fact that NGOs are "over there" doing humanitarian work "behind the scenes" or "in the trenches"

of humanitarian crises. In "being there," sponsors and supporters, located mostly in the West, argue that NGOs are better positioned to employ reliable methods to locate poor people, identify their needs, and validate results. This, in effect, creates a new disciplinary science of humanitarianism. Yet as these partnerships develop and stabilize over time, and the lines between NGOs, governments, and the private sector start to blur, it is becoming more difficult to differentiate whose interests, ambitions, and agendas are being served and whose are being compromised within this new disciplinary science.

So if much of the power of NGOs lies in their knowledge-making practices, then we need examine how this science of humanitarianism—in the form of baseline assessments, surveys, national databases, agency reports, funding proposals, and so on—produces permissible modes of being and thinking about contemporary humanitarianism while disqualifying and even making others impossible? Moreover, we need to ask: to what extent do these humanitarian products or artifacts reflect the diverse interests and ambitions of the institutional and individual actors involved in these knowledge-making practices, and, if so, to what extent does this self-serving process come at the expense of local humanitarian efforts, empowering the poor, improving health, and ultimately saving lives? As NGOs work ever more closely with development banks, government agencies, and venture philanthropists in poverty reduction efforts, they have amassed considerable work and authority in defining and measuring poverty. However, it remains unclear to what extent their knowledge-making practices acknowledge the complex and particular mechanisms underlying continued dispossession in the Global South. Worded slightly differently, in their efforts to intervene, to what extent do these new humanitarians recognize the destructive tendencies of previous free-market and structural adjustment policies (largely from the West) of the past decade or so?[3] How they view the past will, in effect, influence how they "make sense" of poverty conditions today and their knowledge claims about how to relieve it in the future. Another tension within the present conjuncture worth thinking through is that in their efforts to do massive social good, how do NGOs reconcile working with institutions and governments that in one way or another were behind the "free-market" policies responsible for causing global inequality? In an effort to understand this tension, we reflect on the creation of a baseline assessment, one of the most important artifacts in which people in the global humanitarian system and general public come to understand poverty and dispossession. I begin with a personal reflection.

Scaling up Our Presence in Sociological Circles

In the spring of 2010, I received an email from a member listserv of the American Sociological Association. The message outlined a volunteer opportunity for sociologists to help conduct a baseline assessment of water, sanitation, and hygiene

construct and
verify

education programs in the Rulindo District of Rwanda. Two sociologists were sought to join an eight-person interdisciplinary team from Water Research,[4] an international volunteer research partner of Water Water.[5] In conversations with the manager, it was explained to me that the main function of the Water Research was to serve as an independent body of experts that monitor and evaluate Water Water's work in an effort to ensure integrity and transparency in data collection and reporting. I would be joining other volunteers—engineers, water quality technicians, resource managers, students, and others—to conduct and evaluate a large-scale survey of water and sanitation conditions and write a report of our findings to be distributed to the district government and funding agency. The guiding principle behind this volunteer, independent, and expert peer-review process, I was told, was that it ensured "integrity and objectivity in the data collection and reporting" process. On its website, readers are informed that, through observation and interviews with people on the ground in homes, clinics, schools, and community water points, Water Research is on the front lines of determining what is happening and what is needed by the people who need it the most.

Volunteers, Water Water noted, bring in the vital data the organization needs to improve its efforts in the field; moreover, because it does not have to employ this team of researchers directly, Water Water can afford to dedicate more resources to critical programs instead of overhead. "As a secondary objective," I was told by a manager of the World Research, "sociologists' expertise is needed to adapt the baseline questionnaire to a format which can be used to survey the remaining sectors in the district."

My participation as a social scientist in this baseline assessment, I was told, would be crucial in helping Water Water and other humanitarian organizations reflect on their current approach to fieldwork in an effort to help them improve future humanitarian efforts in the field and in policy discussions with donors and other supporters. "We are trying to scale up our presence in sociological circles," Adrian Roberts, a water research manager, revealed, "as sociologists play an integral part understanding the socioeconomic relationships communities have with the technology and other stakeholders." No sooner had we worked out an agreement to work together[6] than my name appeared on the Water Water website as a sociologist and World Research volunteer currently on assignment in Rwanda. In spite of the uncomfortable self-promotion, I was deeply excited about this opportunity. It not only allowed me to "do good," I thought, but also presented a unique opportunity to engage in social science research with a nonprofit organization. By virtue of my participation, I would be given access to a research field where, in most cases, participant observation had been highly problematic, if not impossible. In addition, I thought, it allowed me to "study up" in the nonprofit sector. Like many people—volunteers, employees, managers, and officers—involved in humanitarianism, I had conflicting motivations in "doing good." But for now, at least, they seemed too insignificant to dwell on.

Anthropologist, Laura Nader, issued one of the first calls to social scientists to rethink their approach to studying enduring social problems such as poverty. What if, Nader asked, "in reinventing anthropology, anthropologists were to study the colonizers rather than the colonized, the culture of power rather than the culture of the powerless, the culture of affluence rather than the culture of poverty?" (1972, 289). In effect, study up. By contrast, researchers' propensity to studying down, Nader (1972, 2008) argued, has been in the interests of the anthropologists, as opposed to the subjugated, in the interests of those in power, as opposed to the powerless, and continues to be a serious limiting factor in "the kinds of research we are weaving" (Nader 1972).

Two key aspects to Nader's challenge to studying up were of particular relevance to my research. First, was the need to see connections between groups involved in humanitarian policy and practice and, second, to link those groups and individuals to "larger processes of change," (Nader 2008). This approach to studying "up, down, and sideways simultaneously," Nader (2008) argues, will help to inform our understandings of patterns of production, distribution, value, and power within our field of inquiry. Also relevant to this research was Nader's challenge to question understandings of the research relationship taken for granted, thereby pushing researchers to address the interrelated issues of access, methodology, attitudes, and ethics in their research and scholarship (Nader 1972). I was seduced by both the opportunity and the challenge.

This, of course, was not my first experience with development work, international travel, or research methods. At the time, I had recently returned from fieldwork in the Alwar District in the state of Rajasthan, India. I developed a theoretical interest in the practices of nonprofits and how their practices "work" to produce legitimate knowledge and authority about various global subalterns and their humanitarian needs. However, my inability to write a "thick description" about the politics and location of development practice was due in part to the fact that I was unable to observe and participate in the actual practices of development practitioners. This research opportunity to study up seemed too good to pass up. Moreover, my teaching experiences in the fields of globalization and development, which included two study-abroad courses to India, had taught me that while NGOs maintain substantial influence and control over global humanitarian efforts, they have not opened themselves up to scholarly inquiry or critique. I saw this opportunity as a unique chance to do empirical research from the privileged and truly exclusive position of "inside" the nonprofit world—as opposed to outside, where most of the research happens.

Moreover, I told myself, this experience would be different from my participation in an expert forum to improve planning and policy development in aquaculture organized by the United Nations Food and Agriculture Organization (FAO) in Rome in 2008. I found the discussions at this stratospheric level of development policy rather discouraging, as high-level government advisors and private consultants competed to highlight their agendas over others, with little knowledge or acknowledgment of the practical and political implications of such policy. As I left Rome in the spring of 2008, and the report went to press, I wondered about the implications of this document on the people it was supposed to help (FAO 2008). I was determined that things would be different this time.

The strength of this type of "development" discourse, Gilbert Rist (2008) has suggested, comes from its power to seduce, in every sense of the term: to charm, to please, to fascinate, to set dreaming," but also to abuse, to turn away from the truth, to deceive. For example, the anthropologist Philippe Bourgois (2000, 205) has pointed out that "historically, inner-city poverty research" in the United States has "been more successful at reflecting the biases of an investigator's society than at analyzing the experience of poverty or documenting race and class apartheid." I was convinced that my seduction would not lead to this sort of abuse. My mistake was in thinking that I had control over this knowledge-producing exercise. Nevertheless, armed with epistemological questions concerning the politics and location of knowledge production, I was convinced that I could influence the people and practices of nonprofits to be more, well, humane. And with this belief in mind I boarded a plane in August 2010 for Kigali, Rwanda, to join a team of water research volunteers.

Our Biggest Goal Is to Train Individuals in Our Business

Like most nonprofit organizations, Water Water has steadily grown in both the number of projects as well as areas of influence. Water Water is currently operating in eleven different countries (Honduras, Guatemala, Nicaragua, Dominican Republic, Bolivia, Peru, Ecuador, Malawi, Rwanda, Uganda, and India) but claims to have worked in some capacity in over forty different countries in the past. Offices for Water Water are located in nine cities across the globe. Balancing out the centers of "bureaucratic" activity has kept a distributed powerbase at the global level as well as a sense of agility to respond to local emergencies. Total revenues for fiscal year 2012 were more than US$11.7 million, placing it among an elite group of transnational nonprofit organizations in the water and sanitation sector. The apparatus of locations, financial support, institutional networks, and communities involved ensures that Water Water maintains an interconnected transnational presence that is well positioned not only to serve local water crises and to build international support but also to influence the very character of humanitarian intervention in the area of water and sanitation.

Like many other humanitarian organizations, Water Water has also turned to the peer-review process and social science research, in an effort to build legitimacy and support for its specific interventions and long-term campaigns. A separate yet affiliated organization—Water Research—has been established as its research arm. Through Water Research, volunteers can participate in assignments such as scoping studies, baseline assessments, monitoring, and evaluations. In turn, Water Water maintains that this information is used in programming and resource allocation decisions. "Our biggest goal is to train individuals in our business," stated the director of the Water Research, "so that we can make sure that our program has this constant group of individuals that want to participate in" Water Research. The long-term vision for the Water Research program, the Director admitted, is that it might expand its services as an independent third party monitor and evaluator of water and sanitation programs worldwide.

This concerted effort to use and standardize data tools, assessments, and analysis by humanitarian practitioners, such as Water Research, is most often framed as a direct response to questions about the quality of both the data and the analysis, which continues to plague the nonprofit sector. NGOs, along with development banks, academic institutions, donors, and governments, have fully embraced this data revolution as an opportunity to reshape the character of humanitarian practice and policy. For example, the World Bank, the Inter-American Development Bank, and, in May 2014, the African Development Bank (AfDB) have all introduced online interactive platforms that map the location of their activities in different countries and regions. The AfDB says its data mapping tool will "provide transparent access to its work, . . . fast-tracking the implementation results."

The promise of big data, advocates such as the World Bank and the AfDB suggest, has yet to be fully realized in humanitarian aid. High-quality data remains a scarce and elusive resource for humanitarian practitioners, hindering poverty alleviation efforts everywhere. Moreover, the very notion of what constitutes accurate information is always difficult to establish and is usually fraught with methodological challenges that are deeply embedded in context-specific factors. However, better information and data systems, Jim Yong Kim, the president of the World Bank Group argues, is essential to empowering the poor. In effect, critics and advocates alike confirm that humanitarianism is drowning in data, but of the wrong sort! In an effort to obtain accurate and useful data, new online interactive forums such as MapAfrica have been developed, which the AfDB argues has the important and distinctive ability of linking open data from governments, other donors, researchers, and NGOs with specific indicators, such as population, poverty, and disease, in an effort to better target vulnerable populations and measure results better. Data, the AfDB claims, need to be presented in a simple way to demonstrate results, which brings the Bank and its stakeholders "closer to the people they serve." In effect, good data need to connect the There (what goes on in the field) of humanitarian practice with the Here (what goes on in the board rooms, offices, and classrooms of participating donors, governments, and research institutions) of humanitarian policy.

But for all the revolutionary zeal and humanitarian promise of using big data, little attention is paid to how data are captured in the field, whose expertise is relevant, who participates, how data are in turn interpreted, what goes to print, and so forth. Merely collecting data and writing reports are not enough to establish water and sanitation needs and programs or other humanitarian campaigns. One must first decide what counts as data and who the experts are before data can be collected and reports written. These choices about what to include and whom to omit are the culmination of many small and often unthinking decisions that create, maintain, and reinforce long-standing hierarchies, assumptions, and stereotypes and are rarely footnoted in the official reports. In an effort to explore this complicated process, we now turn to the practice of fieldwork to examine how assessments are conducted, paying close attention to whose participation counts and how that participation is counted (conducted). These two procedural matters raise deep methodological concerns that are of vital importance to both the validity and reliability of this disciplinary science as well as issues of legitimacy and representation in humanitarian practice and policy.

The Social Construction of Baseline Assessments

Like most of those who participate in humanitarian campaigns abroad, I believe wholeheartedly that "being there," in remote villages, talking directly to participants, and observing local conduct and customs was, and is, an essential phase in understanding the problem under study. Like other research practitioners and volunteers, I believed that NGOs' presence at the grassroots gave them a comparative advantage in conducting the type of research necessary to document and monitor the experiences of dispossession. In addition to enabling researchers to send home postcards from exotic places, this type of anthropological fieldwork, in which research practitioners leave the comforts of home (Here) to immerse themselves in a unfamiliar setting (There) over an extended period, has been a long-standing, albeit controversial, strategy for inquiry and a hallmark of empirical research. Clifford Geertz (1988) describes two sides of ethnographic research, which he calls "Being Here," and "Being There." "Being There" refers to time spent in "the field," while "Being Here" refers to time spent back home at the academy. This segmented strategy for inquiry is further elaborated by the sociologist Paul Atkinson (1990). Atkinson (1990, 61) has described time spent "in the field" as the "writing down" phase, and time spent back at the academy as the "writing up" phase, in which "writing down" serves as data for "writing up."

However, in the past two decades, emerging theories in qualitative research (Denzin and Lincoln 1994; Lather 2002; Segall 2001) and postcolonial studies (Bhabha 1990; Mosse 2005; Said 1979) have drawn attention to the complexities in the process in which research is conducted in the Global South. In particular, the unidirectional process of data compilation and analysis—with the particular field sites and beneficiaries at the beginning and donor agencies and governments as the end—obscures the complexity of this knowledge-making practice (Segall 2001). NGOs, like ethnographers, do not only write *for* a particular community; they also write *with* and *through* that community. Therefore, voices from this larger humanitarian community (the Here) inform the research process in the field (the There). That influence may extend to how the project is "conceived, shaped, explored, administered, analyzed, and reported," in addition to how it is funded (Segall 2001, 584). Nevertheless, navigating the problematics of mapping a baseline assessment when the ground upon which one paces—both the There and the Here—is constantly shifting ensures that incorporating voices from the There and the Here is always much more than simply a quantitative exercise. In effect, it is difficult to predict whose voices are heard and whose interests are represented prior to being both Here and There. In an effort to shed light on this multifaceted and messy process, we now turn to the more specific strategies of inquiry regarding data collection, analysis, and writing.

Data Collection

After arriving in Kigali, most of us had time for a meal and a quick shower ; we could work off our jet lag later. No sooner had we eaten lunch when I detected a hint of animosity between the in-country staff (one in particular) and the staffers from the head office, (see below). Moreover, the managing director of this baseline assessment campaign, an engineer on paid leave with no social science research experience, seemed to have little patience for the in-country people or their local ways. Standing over an unsteady steel table in the cramped and quasi-functional office, this white, Western-trained male, or what Rwandans called *muzungu*,[8] was keen to have this phase of the project begin.

> We should start, for those that don't have it, maybe I'll just read through the blurb. . . . The group will help Water Water-Rwanda understand the information that is missing, which the office would need to collect to better understand the water resources that are available in the district and those already exploited with respect to population and location in order to plan the most appropriate future interventions.

On the surface, the task seemed simple enough. The baseline assessment, another staffer explained, is an effort to "collect data" and "survey the existing infrastructure" to determine the level of coverage. This information would feed into high-level discussions regarding a hydraulic plan for the entire country. "Geographically, Rwanda is divided into 5 water districts, 450 sectors, 1,500 cells, and 15,000 villages. Our task would be to survey households in three of the seventeen cells in the Rulindo District."

But before demand and supply could be assessed and before water sources could be counted and infrastructure surveyed, we had to agree on what constituted a water source and water infrastructure. We needed to "get the set of observations that each group needs to make while we're out there, so you know what it is you're looking for, so you know what's going into your report section." This was the third baseline assessment in two years, and the Water Water crew, especially those from the head office, wanted to make sure they got it right this time. The head office staff wanted to ensure that, when researchers were in the field, they were making consistent observations with some level of reliability often referred to as intercoder reliability. In order for that to happen, researchers needed to be clear about what should be included in the survey and what should be excluded, what was acceptable and what was not. In effect, boundaries had to be constructed around variables before they could be counted; people had to be instructed in not only "what" but "how" to count. But as this conversation between in-country and head office staff revealed, it is exceedingly difficult to match the water reality (out there in the field) with people's representation of it (here at the office).

IN-COUNTRY STAFF: What is going on in a particular area, in a particular village, is hard to quantify . . . there are so many variables in what we're doing. Should we collect information at potential water points?

HEAD OFFICE STAFF: Unimproved [source], you mean? No.

IN-COUNTRY STAFF: Well, what if somebody goes to a marsh or a creek [for their water source]?

HEAD OFFICE STAFF: Well, it's a raw source

IN-COUNTRY STAFF: But it's a water source.

HEAD OFFICE STAFF: We survey, but I'm not sure if we sample it.

IN-COUNTRY STAFF: What happens [around here], you'll see, it's pretty dramatic, streams and rivers flow down [from everywhere], [gesturing with his hands], and the water is actually pretty good, and people use it.

HEAD OFFICE STAFF: Well, the other thing is, what are they using it for? Because if they're taking it out of the river, but they're not drinking it, we don't care.

IN-COUNTRY STAFF: But that is going to depend on the time of year.

The tension illustrated in this exchange between in-country staff and head office staff is palpable and stems from the disjuncture between what needs to be assessed from the head office's standpoint and what can actually be counted from the local perspective. The multiple water sources, many not known to volunteers and staffers, were proving to be difficult to explicitly demarcate, not only in terms of establishing what would be included in the survey and what was not but also in terms of whose knowledge and interests would be reflected in the survey. The few people in the room with intimate local knowledge about the complexity of water sources in the study area wanted a more inclusive definition because they thought it provided a more accurate description of local water resources. This local version not only included the diverse range of water sources—springs, rivers, improved, unimproved, ephemeral, catchment, tank, etc.—but also considered customary engagements and social relations within each watershed. Time in the field had taught them that where local people source water depends on many factors, including cost, distance, season, and use. Moreover, access to water among households was facilitated through a web of social relations that included informal arrangements, networks, and more formal associations that shaped the procurement, provision, and distribution of water within the community. However, these largely invisible social bonds and relationships around water access and water security were largely invisible to the outsider "looking in." In the few instances when these historical, social, and environmental relations became obvious—for example, the impact of the genocide in 1996 and its impact on rural land settlement patterns today—they seemed to have little relevance to our assessment of water and sanitation needs.

In contrast, those who were not familiar with the local context were far less willing to consider its influence, even after having it explained to them in detail by in-country staffers and local water specialists (fountaineers). They were more concerned with how the data collected would "fit" with the interests and programs of participating consultants, governments, and donor agencies. Their concern was not rooted in local conditions or concerns (the Here) but, rather, whether and how that data could be used to demonstrate and measure program efficiency and effectiveness. Data and information are critical to donors and governments (the Here), which are anxious to make lending decisions on solid empirical evidence and results-based programs. It was no wonder that the conversation became more animated as it went on.

HEAD OFFICE STAFF: You told me that probably the majority of the water points are springs.

IN-COUNTRY STAFF: Yeah, the improved water points. Yes.

HEAD OFFICE STAFF: All right, but do they have a well we can sample?

IN-COUNTRY STAFF: Not wells, not in Rulindo.

HEAD OFFICE STAFF: And are those springs covered? When you say improved?

IN-COUNTRY STAFF: Some of them are already pretty nice. Like, you know, I have pictures of some of them where there's some concrete there. There's a nice pipe coming out of it, and then some of them even have multiple basins downstream to wash clothes and all of that. I think they're absolutely gorgeous. Others it's just like on the hillside, there's an old piece of rusted pipe coming out of it, and that's all you have.

VOLUNTEER: If we see a water source that isn't used for drinking even though it might be improved, it's not part of the survey, right? Is that right? Because they're not taking drinking water from it?

HEAD OFFICE STAFF: You're right. Because they're not taking drinking water from it, you wouldn't collect information on it.

IN-COUNTRY STAFF: I don't like the idea of ignoring them. We need to address those if we want to move forward into hydraulic planning. As I said, you have a pipe that sticks out [of the hillside]. It's obviously not an improved water point, but it is a water point. Some people are using it. What do you do with this one? Do you survey it, or do you not survey it?

The real frustration for local staffers with activities deemed to be research by the head office and supporting agencies is that the knowledge about a particular form of dispossession—access to water, sanitation, health care, shelter, etc.—is generated, usually quickly, with little understanding of, or regard for, the specific, historical, temporal, and relational conditions in which that dispossession took, or is taking, place. The fact that a manager from the head office was oblivious to the local water conditions (springs, not wells) is striking. His lack of knowledge about the local water conditions, however, was not considered a necessary qualification for measuring it. For all the struggle "in the field," it is the head office staff who are able to convert their perspective into action. This is facilitated in part by head office's ability to choose who would participate in the baseline assessment. Volunteers included engineers from CH2M Hill and water-quality technicians from Nalco; both companies have and continue to contribute major financial support to Water Water, in addition to technical expertise. "We just have to do our best" was how one of the Nalco volunteers responded to ongoing questions about what should be counted. By extending the field site to include employees of engineering and water technology companies as "volunteers" on this project (and other projects), Water Water was able to focus its energies on how to count and shorten the debates on what should and should not be counted, effectively transcending local knowledge in the data-collection process.

As a consequence, what *counts,* as in what matters to local people, is not necessarily what *gets counted* by NGOs. More often than not, the biopolitical constructs used to measure dispossession rarely fit with the reality trying to be

Figure 1.1 Improved or Unimproved? You Decide. Photo by Michael Mascarenhas.

measured, let alone the interests of the targeted population. In this way, NGOs and their supporters continue to make humanitarian decisions based on incomplete information or nonknowledge about a particular area or community. This "on-the-ground reality" contradicts the claim made by the Asian Development Bank, the FAO, and other development-type institutions that NGOs, by virtue of being "over there" doing humanitarian work "behind the scenes" or "in the trenches of humanitarian crises," are more responsive to local needs or possess an epistemological advantage over government organizations and local authorities. Their presence at the grassroots may indeed give them an advantage in more closely monitoring and documenting the experiences of the poor and vulnerable. However, this knowledge and way of knowing, and the practices legitimated by them, are not disinterested, objective, or neutral (Segall 2001, 2013). In fact, such knowledge and ways of knowing are already positioned and positioning, embedded with ideologies, assumptions, and humanitarian values (Segall 2013). These positional and subjective preconditions construct and reify particular understandings and meanings about the poor and why they are dispossessed, limiting other constructions that do not easily fit with the dominant discourse and humanitarian worldview.

Moreover, "in the field," the dividing lines among data, information, evidence, and theory are not always clear (Dijkzeul et al. 2013). As this debate in the field office illustrates, the data one humanitarian versus another collects is not self-evident but, rather, is influenced or shaped by one's role in the project. These conditions help to shape, both epistemologically and ontologically, what humanitarian researchers see, limiting their consideration of the world in some ways and enabling it in others. Thus, in trying to do the right thing, it appears that humanitarians are collecting data that suit their positionality and fit their subjectivity, not necessarily collecting data *with* or *for* those they are trying to help. Yet NGOs continue to claim that the purpose of their research is ultimately to generate more data and information that will transform their (humanitarian) practice to the benefit of those in need. This contradiction is, in part, the reason that they always need more information. It should come as no surprise, then, that a lack of data and information has become a pressing point of contention for humanitarian practice and policy.

> Part of the exercise was really to have [you] look at what we are doing right now, the type of questions that are being asked, the type of data that is being collected and [ask] is this sufficient to . . . really be able to plan and program projects? And where do we do them and how do we execute them? Because one of the . . . struggles that we have in this country is that we do the baseline assessment, we collect data, and then we're supposed to program the projects. But I am not sure. What are you going to do with the data, what is the next step? It is difficult to take this data and really determine what kind of project are we going to do, where, and how. This was the purpose of bringing . . . you guys [here] . . . to examine the correct procedures, the methodology, the questions that are being asked, the type of response that we get. [And ask] is this sufficient for us to plan . . . a hydraulic plan, and if it's not, then what else needs to be done, is it feasible to collect this data? Does it need a separate crew? What kind of data is it? This is exactly the kind of observations that we need you guys to do.

The perspective offered here by a humanitarian practitioner who has spent much of his professional life working "over There" poses serious challenges to the assumption that big data are the panacea for poverty reduction and welfare reform in the Global South. According to this practitioner, more data and closer relations between NGOs (over There) and donor agencies (over Here) does not necessarily translate into programming efforts and policy reform. The frustration that he and others feel comes from the fact that the prevailing discourse of a lack of data and information alone will not determine what kind of projects will be supported. Moreover, a biopolitical consequence of not measuring what matters also further disadvantages the targeted population by making inaccurate inferences about the causes of, and the remedies for, their dispossession.

Several important observations can be made about this candid exchange concerning the process of data collection in the field. First, claims made by the FAO and the African Development Bank (and other sponsors working with or through nonprofit organizations) that an NGO's presence at the grassroots gives them an advantage in working with local populations does not seem to be borne out in practice. In listening to this and other discussions about the local water conditions in various in-country offices, I was struck by the lack of local knowledge. In fact, many of the staff rarely go out into the field, rarely do fieldwork, and rarely let fieldwork guide their programming. Conversely, it appeared that they spend much more time in the offices of government agencies, donors, consultants, and in the coffee shops of Kigali than they do in the villages of the people they supposedly represent and give voice to. The notion that they are somehow closer to the pulse of local concern and need is, in fact, idealistic at best and untrue in practice.

Second, the claim that NGOs can easily respond and develop appropriate and relevant programs/projects based on the specific needs of local people is also inaccurate. The assumption that those working at a particular office or on a particular campaign agree among themselves on a particular course of action is naive and misleading. Moreover, even if some form of consensus or coherence about a particular social problem is reached within the agency, there is no guarantee that it will, in turn, inspire external support.

As Heather Meyer admits,

> They always want us to do [something new]. Like here, [there has been] . . . a lot of discussion on urban population, vulnerable people: orphans, children, head of households, and handicapped. [Rwanda has] a lot of people like this. So, they want us to do water and sanitation for these people, and it's impossible to get a beneficiary contribution in these environments, and so it's very difficult: we want to tackle urban poverty [but we can't]. It's heartbreaking because you would do it. [I am here to help]. but there is no support or funding for these types of programs.

As this perspective clearly illustrates, although their office may be based in the Global South, their programs and campaigns are voiced in and by the Global North. And, in spite of the fact that they are there to help, they often, out of necessity—namely, their survival—ignore the most vulnerable people. In all fairness, this is what is asked of them. However, it is important to recognize that the mass of data and information being collected in the name of humanitarian practice and policy is based not on the needs of the dispossessed but, rather, on the needs of agents and agencies that are competing to define and manage worldwide water insecurity. If they were occupied with the social and material interests of the dispossessed, NGOs would be collecting different data. For many who are trying to help, this reflection, particularly if it is made after making personal and professional sacrifices to "do something very different for a period of time," is the cause of much heartache.

> We don't have local input! The questions [in the survey] haven't been designed with the locals [in mind], or the communities don't have really an input in what's important to them. We are asking questions in a formulaic [way]. Like this is what the questions are; we want these questions [answers] back. It's not like what is truly important to them, you know. And some of the questions that we ask are just kind of not getting to an answer that is going to be important to helping bring about change for a positive. And some of the questions create divisiveness, and kind of spread seeds of doubt and mistrust, I think.

Again and again, we see that this belief that NGOs are more attentive to local needs because they work more closely among the poor simply does not hold up in practice. However, it is equally important to recognize that this negotiated and contradictory knowledge-making practice does stop with data collection; data, once collected, has to be analyzed, and, in so doing, it again travels from the specific place it was generated (the There) to the place or places where it will be analyzed— the academy, the donor's office, the government agency (the Here). However, as my field work experience revealed, this knowledge-making process is also much more than simply counting the number of people and their urgent needs.

Data Analysis

After several days of surveying households in rural Rwanda, volunteers, including me, started to have concerns over the way in which we were compiling data and gathering information in the field: how that data was being analyzed in the offices (in Kigali and the head office) of Water Water and then how that data might later be interpreted. A real point of contention for many volunteers was that, to our disbelief, we were informed, after a week of fieldwork, that this baseline assessment was the third one that had been conducted this year. "There were two actual baseline assessments that occurred," a staffer informed us one evening, "one from January, one from February, both had conflicting information." So we had to "figure out what had been compiled" and "what was actually usable." We had "a lot of data . . . but it wasn't actually very usable." The original questionnaire was designed for South-Central America, which assumed each village had its own water point. Rural Rwandans, much to the surprise of those responsible for designing the questionnaire, had their own relationship and customary management practices with regard to water resources, which differed from villages in South America. "It was really the first time that we were doing it [a baseline assessment], in Africa besides Malawi," admitted another staffer. "We were going through growing pains, and it was a lot of things that we didn't get right in those assignments." Any fieldworker will tell you that qualitative research is messy, and "there is no easy way to tell when researchers did an exemplary job in the data collection and analysis or when they did a 'quick and dirty' job" (Lareau 2000, 187). Good writing can cover up poor research. However, the mistakes admitted here in the "inner workings" of these baseline assessments raise questions about the quality of the research and the conclusions that can be drawn from it. During this conversation, I could not help but look up at the shelves full of three-ring binders. It seemed like such a waste of time and money to repeat this process for a third time. A staffer explained, "There were questions that just didn't make sense or were not applicable" to this area. So we didn't know "what to do with this data" or "how to interpret this [it]. . . . It was impossible basically to illustrate the data [on our webpage] using the questionnaire that was used." To this frank admission, one of the volunteers responded,

> But you got enough data [from the last two surveys] that you actually summarized it on your webpage, right? I mean you knew from that data that there was good water coverage and that sanitation was really lacking, because that's what is summarized on the write-up in the webpage.

"Yes," was the immediate reply of one staffer, but it was "not necessarily done based on a very thorough [scientific] approach." That assessment was completed by "just like walking through the village." It was based on [anecdotal] "observation and what we know of the country." After hearing that response, a frustrated volunteer asked, "I just don't understand how you get from dealing with the kind of surveys we're doing to determine who is getting what. I mean we're going through each edge of the community, and some people are 300 meters from water, some people are few hundred meters, some people are 50. You're kind of just random sampling. I mean, it's not an accurate representation of what's going on in the community as far as water access, or sanitation."

This candid exchange raises some important epistemological and methodological concerns regarding the efficacy of activities that NGOs consider research. First, information is sometimes based on anecdotal knowledge (what a particular NGO believes to be true about a particular community or area) and not necessarily on empirical and systematic observation. Second, even when assessments are conducted "in the field," the way in which information—in this case, about water needs—is collected tends to have a tremendous amount of inconsistency. Numerous constraints, time being the most significant ("you're concentrating on 'how many households did we get today?'" recalls one volunteer) ensure that researchers adopt a multitude of convenient sample selection strategies, from showing up at the local market and staying on major thoroughfares to interviewing the local official's aunt (as I did on my first full day "in the field").

In addition to compromising reliability, numerous questions arise about what constitutes a valid measure of water access. "I'm not convinced that the best way to do it is to just go do household surveys everywhere," commented a volunteer. Having earned a Master's degree in Environmental Engineering, this senior water quality engineer was speaking from decades of experience in public health infrastructure. "You [may] decide . . . to go out and find your water points" first, and then "you decide where there is need, and then concentrate the surveys there, as opposed to just doing the widespread survey" of the population. Given the fact that water sources are so variable, and water scarcity so specific in this region, limiting surveys to households also limits the inferences that can be made for other regions and contexts.

All these epistemological and methodological concerns can prove overwhelming at times to the unseasoned volunteer researcher. After much debate about the sampling strategy, one volunteer admitted, "I guess I don't know what I'm supposed to be doing [here]." "This really infuriates me," said another volunteer, "the first baseline survey on paper wasn't useful and now I question the usefulness of this data." A local staffer agreed:

> We all admit that the survey instruments and methods are far from being good, and if you don't feel like this, it is because you haven't spent enough time in the field! So there is a huge room for improvement in our baseline assessment methods, as well as monitoring and evaluation techniques. And because of this, there is just so much we can extract out of the data collected. Poor methods equal poor results, no matter how much time we spend looking at the data.

This staffer recognizes all too well that more data alone cannot and will not solve the problems associated with water inaccessibility in rural Rwanda or Malawi. In many ways, she is a lone voice against the chorus of big-data evangelists who continue to believe that it alone will provide the solution to water access and poverty reduction worldwide.

Decisions have to be made about whose voices to include *as data*, and these decisions have more to do with who was counting than what was counted. Reflecting on the role of identity politics and how it plays out in fieldwork, the scholar Avner Segall writes, "our varied layers of positionality—the very essences and lenses through which we see and hear—are also those which obscure, preclude us from seeing and hearing 'otherwise'" (2001, 586). This positionality would, in turn, be inscribed into the final report. However, as we entered the writing stage, no one, including myself, was sure what would emerge.

Writing

At the end of our fieldwork, we began to reflect, both individually and together, on how our research efforts would contribute to the lives of rural Rwandans. It was now time to turn our attention to "writing up" our results. Like data collection and analysis, this phase of the research would prove to be much more than a mechanical exercise of putting pen to paper. Laura Richardson (1994, 516) points out that writing can no longer be thought of simply as "a mopping-up activity at the end of a research paper" or project. Writing, too, is an integral step in "giving voice," and, as in the data collection and analysis phases of this baseline assessment, decisions about writing, specifically what and whom to include and what and whom to leave out, had to be "worked out" in practice. In addition to writing, some of us took this opportunity to go on a safari. Others, including me, visited the genocide memorial. Yet others sought out restaurants and souvenir shops that catered to the throng of Western tourists—nobody was leaving without some exotic photographs and cultural artifacts. During this *reflective* "writing up" process, I was struck by the observation of scholars Martyn Hammersley and Paul Atkinson (1995, 255) that "*how* we write about the social world we observe is of fundamental importance to our own and others' interpretations of it." Our interpretations were not only couched in what we observed or what we decided to collect but also were reflective of deep and unconscious cultural and racial assumptions—assumptions that mirrored the discourses of the dominant cultural/racial order, making the written text, like the data and analysis on which it is grounded, anything but a "transparently neutral medium of communication" (Hammersley and Atkinson 1995, 255).

Lost in information, location, language, not to mention politics, how does some write one report amid a plurality of voices? How does one choose? "Even if we spend a lot of time phrasing questions properly with a clear purpose in mind for each question," the program advisor explained, "the survey is first translated into the local language—Kinyarwanda—by someone who does not comprehend at all the importance of phrasing the questions properly." These "someones" were Generation Rwanda (GR)[9] students hired by Water Water to accompany their Western volunteer researchers as translators. The GR student translated every question from English into Kinyarwanda and every answer from Kinyarwanda back into English. This was no simple task—particularly because French, not English, was the colonial language of choice for many young Rwandans.[10] Until a few years ago, English was taught as a foreign language but was not mastered by many. However, "none of [the] survey creators can check after the translation is done because too often we [white Western researchers] don't speak the local language," a staffer reflected. In effect, we had no way of verifying whose voice was being heard and written into the official text.

For example, a local staffer explained that, while translating the survey, she changed the way in which some of the questions were asked because she did not like them. Similarly, a volunteer complained, "It just embarrasses me that we're asking a lot of those questions," such as "when do you wash your hands with soap?" (after defecating, before eating, after cleaning a baby's bottom, before cooking). "Do we really need this information?" As part of our assessment, we were required to take pictures of household toilets. This was required, we were told, to determine whether households were using unimproved (open-pit latrine) or improved (covered and ventilated-pit latrine) sanitation facilities. Some volunteers found this request so offensive that they refused to ask the participant whether they could inspect their toilet. Those who did were asked to observe and note whether they observed urine or feces on the floor/walls/seat of the latrine. They also had to look for soap or other cleansing agents for washing hands available near the latrine. "We all know that they need sanitation, and I am surprised that they were as much into sanitation as they seem to be now. I thought it was just water . . . they . . . be doing. But do we really have to take pictures of their toilets to post of the web? How embarrassing." Moreover, feeling the obvious stigma associated with being asked about such an invasive matter, some participants also refused to let us take pictures.

As it turned out, Water Water's recent interest in the sanitation habits of rural Rwandans was motivated by a $5.6 million grant from the Bill & Melinda Gates Foundation to support its innovative Sanitation as a Business program. "The program will combine profit incentives for small local companies and income generation programs for poor households and schools, demonstrating a shift from unsustainable, subsidy-based sanitation programs toward sustainable, profitable sanitation services . . . in multiple locations worldwide" (Bill & Melinda Gates Foundation 2014, 1). Yet as NGOs use funding from grants, such as those from the Bill & Linda Gates Foundation, to enforce market access rights in water and sanitation in rural Africa and elsewhere, it is unclear to what extent, in their efforts to enhance access, transparency, and accountability in water and sanitation, they are also bolstering subtle and not-so-subtle mechanisms of surveillance into every facet of life of the poor and dispossessed. Of all the questions we asked and observations we made in the field, these questions about people's hygiene had to be the most degrading and patronizing. The narrative we were constructing was one that pathologized communities and individuals in rural Rwanda for having backward attitudes toward personal hygiene and public health. The goal became "saving" Rwandans from themselves with little reflection on the root causes of extreme poverty in the community or without looking at how global poverty is connected to white supremacy and colonialism.

GR students also had their own version of the questionnaire and the text. These urban, educated, Tutsi students were also making their own intercultural interpretations about rural, poor, and predominantly Hutu Rwandans. "You have the problem that these people are human," noted the program advisor, "and will not ask the questions [or give answers] the same way to everyone." We have no way of knowing but most assume that the racism between these two groups influenced the data we gathered and the report we wrote.

Another voice that was unofficially written into the official text was that of local government. "We need to be accompanied by an official of the local administration," explained the program advisor.

In the 2009 survey, one of the drivers was interested in what we were doing, so instead of sitting in the car and waiting for us, he accompanied us one day. At some point, I saw him getting mad at the official because the official was not asking the questions correctly and was forcing answers from the people! He obviously had a private agenda! In other circumstances, the presence of the official may discourage people from "telling the truth" because they may not want to "complain" in front of the official. This is certainly true in Rwanda and any other more dictatorial administrations. So the impacts [of what gets filtered from the official text] by the presence of this guy are largely unknown and un-measurable, but very significant.

And then there "is the fact that we are white people arriving in a big white truck," asserted a cynical staffer. "Right away, the story that people will tell us will be worse than it is in reality."

"Again, and again," the advisor concluded, more biased voices get in, and "at the end of the day, the whole story may be completely distorted." Of course, there is no "real" story to be accurately captured or distorted, but as this advisor correctly observes, what is recorded in the official text is more often reflective of the power relations and forms of privilege and subjugation embedded in every interaction.

Yet while we acknowledged that no voice should be treated as politically innocent, we somehow still choose to innocently incorporate some voices in the text while problematizing others. For example, before we went out into the field, we were instructed to "talk to the [GR] students before they disappear for the day, . . . not in a group . . . [but in] person and say, 'listen, did we hear the truth today on all fronts or what?' "

"Exactly," added a staffer to this instruction, "develop that relationship right away with your students and talk to them about this and say, 'you're going to be my ears and my eyes, if you see that the questions are not answered properly [please let me know]." To which another staffer added, "I can't emphasize enough the importance of interacting with the student and government official as much as possible, especially with the student."

As researchers, NGOs cannot separate themselves from the societies and their social problems that they seek to understand; like other observer/researchers, NGOs participate in shaping and representing the society in which they operate (Lee and Lutz 2005). By contrast, we, as researchers, were instructed to be vigilant about the true motives of the villagers, the poor people we were supposed to be helping. We were instructed that they were not to be trusted, and their involvement in the project was continually problematized. In effect, in our efforts to map and understand the context of the water and sanitation conditions of rural Rwandans, we carefully scrutinized the motives and meanings of their participation. However, the question "Did we get the truth today?" was never asked of the GR students. They seemed to mean what they said, and we had no misgivings about using their voices and appropriating their words into our text.[11] Although we repeatedly asked ourselves "Did we get it right?" for those for whom we spoke for, were never applied the same set of rigor to those we spoke with, namely, government, donors, and other supporters. Words and voices from the World Bank, the AfDB, and the Bill & Melinda Gates Foundation, for example, seemed to mean what they said. They were to be trusted. Moreover, for some of us it did not seem to matter with whom we were speaking (or working). "I don't remember if it's the World Bank or the African Development Bank or the Asian Development Bank that is funding this project," admits the program advisor, about the supporting agency for the hydraulic plan. When the World Bank says it wants to reduce extreme global poverty in one generation, we believe what it says. Conversely, when Tabu Anastasie tells a fieldworker that her improved water source is located 200 meters away, but she uses a community-shared water source instead, we choose what to believe. We probe further and ask where is it located, how often does she use it, why does she use an unimproved source, and is she sure? Her voice, which is representative of local water practices, was consciously amended and systematically eliminated from the official record.

Similarly, questions regarding the Rwandan government's motivation for relocating 2 million people from the hillsides, which is predominantly used for subsistence farming, to villages was met with little reservation. Government officials, a staffer informed us, "are the authority on the ground, and people respect them." And we were instructed to "have officials suggest households to be interviewed" in spite of their not-so-innocent political agenda. Conversely, resistance voiced by many participants to this involuntary resettlement program was received with skepticism and cast aside, using the discourse of cultural racism and essentialism that has come to dominate much of Rwanda's postgenocide period. According to the program advisor,

> "Rwandans are followers." . . . If the government says you have to do this, they will do it. If [the government says] you have to kill your neighbor, that's okay: you're going to go and kill your neighbor. So it's going to be interesting to see what's going to happen over the next two years [or so]. Of course, they're not going to be able to move 2 million people in two and a half years. But that's the plan at the moment, and they are very ambitions with it.

"Getting them in group settlements is going to be important if we are going to quickly be looking at providing services to everybody," admits a staffer about the organization's real interest in this ambitious development project. "If that doesn't succeed, then there is a portion of the population that stays scattered on the hillside," and "these people will not get this water supply. . . . So the idea [sponsored by development banks and supported by the Rwandan government] of moving them in [to] group settlements is going to become important to providing water and sanitation."

One thing is for certain: writing, too, is an integral part of "giving voice." As with the data collection and analysis phases of this baseline assessment, decisions about writing—specifically what and whom to include and what and whom to leave out—had to be "worked out" in practice. The politics of this knowledge-making practice comes from the different ways in which NGOs treat the voices they weave, separate, and assemble. Despite the overt commitments to use participatory practices and grassroots approaches, Northern NGOs increasingly scrutinize voices collected "from the field" compared to the largely unproblematic treatment of voices "in the field" (banks, donors, government, etc.). Additionally, how these humanitarian researcher/analysts represent and interpret the observations they make "in the field" is a consequence of how they reconstruct the social worlds they observe. In the case of forced resettlement, these humanitarians-turned-analysts invoked an unsubtle form of cultural racism to silence the concerns of those who are about to be dispossessed from their land. In fact, what was expressed in a conversation about resettlement was a deep and highly problematic cultural bias between the Self (white, Western, elites) and the Other rural Rwandans (brown, global, poor). In this instance, we have a chance to fully appreciate how the question of representation, about whose voice matters, is shaped by deep-seated and likely unconscious assumptions about race. In effect, the implication of treating voices asymmetrically, effectively drawing out debates about whose knowledge and authority matters, will ensure, methodological speaking, that the continent of Africa and the African people, together with other subaltern places and people, will remain a "living laboratory" for this new humanitarian science for years to come (Tilley 2011).

At the heart of this knowledge and knowing debate is whether the data collected represents the construct—in this case, access to water and sanitation—that these humanitarian researchers are trying to measure. When new humanitarians tell you and me that they are just trying to help, what is it that they think "helping" is? Theoretically, the question remains: can more or bigger data solve the pressing social problems of our time, as so many fourth paradigmers claim it can and will? After all, for them, it is "simply a matter of time." But as this fieldwork has illustrated, it is not simply a matter of whether the criterion or content is valid (e.g., "unimproved" verses "improved") but, more importantly, whether the data collected represents the construct itself (access to water and sanitation). Questions of construct validity are germane to whenever a test (research measurement) is to be interpreted as a proxy of some attribute or quality that is under investigation. I have tried to illustrate that debates about construct validity are actually debates about meaning, representation, and ultimately identity and therefore is always more than simply matching constructs to measurement.

Conclusion, or Where Is the Accumulation in the Dispossession?

NGO-led research carries profound implications for human health, democratic civil society, and environmental well-being (Mosse 2005; Phadke 2005; Rist 1997). NGOs continue to claim that the purpose of their research is ultimately to generate data and information that will transform the degree to which a growing ethics of care will spread globally. Open and big data, advocates insist, will transform the way in which the world tackles poverty. NGOs, such as Water for People, Water for Life, Living Water International, and WaterAid, with the firm support of international banks and donor governments, are constantly revising and reframing programs or introducing more sophisticated measuring and monitoring techniques to shore up their legitimacy in a quickly changing humanitarian environment. However, as this chapter has tried to illustrate, the mass of data and information being collected in the name of humanitarian practice and policy is not necessarily based on the needs of the dispossessed. What becomes striking from this analysis is that the constructs used to measure dispossession rarely fit the reality being measured, let alone the interests of the targeted population. Time and time again, what *counts,* as in what matters to local folks, is not what gets *counted* by NGOs.

As the local program advisor reflected,

> When I first have the chance to look at it [the survey], I basically sent it back with a gazillion comments. Some questions were poorly asked, answer choice did not make sense, some questions I would just remove. I mean the way they're structured [it didn't make sense]. I sent it back [to head office] with comments, and then I was told, "well, the board has already approved it, we cannot change anything." I mean I was screaming I was so frustrated.

These knowledge-making practices about humanitarian needs can no longer be seen as an "unproblematic, objective, value free enterprise" but, rather, as constructed, motivated, and contested (Geertz 1973; Hermes 1998; Lather 2002; Segall 2001, 579). The politics of this knowledge-making practice comes from the different ways in which NGOs treat the voices they weave, separate, and assemble. Despite the overt commitments to use participatory practices and grassroots approaches, Northern NGOs increasingly scrutinize voices collected "from the field" as opposed to the largely unproblematic treatment of voices "in the field" (banks, donors, government, etc.). If this is, in fact, the case—that what matters (to the dispossessed) is much more than what is counted—then we need to pay attention to the way in which the politics of humanitarian representation (specifically assumptions about race, gender, culture) are performed and experienced.

Put slightly differently, given the fact that all empirical research, including this one, produces "partial truths" and serious fictions, as anthropologist James Clifford (1986, 1988) has recognized, even powerful "lies," as Vincent Crapanzano (1986) and Gary Allan Fine (1993) have suggested, the question remains as to which partial truths about the hidden abode of inequality and dispossession are revealed and which are concealed in the knowledge-making practices of humanitarian actors, as they try to do massive social good.

The paradox of the fourth paradigm approach to humanitarianism is that it continues to ignore the plain fact that construct validity and research discourses are motivated by beliefs and commitments, influenced by explicit ideologies and tacit worldviews, and shaped by political and economic systems, (Cherryholmes 1988; Geertz 1973; Segall 2001, 2013). Moreover, what can and cannot be said, as well as what can and cannot be known, is often a matter of who is doing the analysis (Bourgois 2000; Lather 2002; Van Maanen 1988). I remember clearly how frustrated one of the home office managers became at repeated epistemological questions from thoughtful volunteers. On one occasion, he took me aside after an intense group meeting, which went horribly wrong from his perspective, and explained to me that the volunteer who had been asking him critical questions "clearly came with an attitude." In another conversation, he described another volunteer as "not getting on board" with the project.

I, too, was frequently forced to reflect on my own role in this knowledge-making practice. To whose voice was I giving priority and whose was I silencing in my efforts to help? One particular example comes to mind. It began with a simple question from a participant, delivered in a somewhat stern demeanor: "What are you doing here?" This question was only asked when I was not accompanied by the local official. The first question was often followed by another: "What are you going to do for us?" At the beginning of my fieldwork, the answers were easy enough: "I am here as part of an international nongovernmental effort to compile a baseline assessment—I am here to help. I am here to measure and qualify your environmental problems—water scarcity." However, the suspicion of the "outsider wanting to help" expressed by this research "participant" was surely justified and explains the cautious reception that greeted this and other field interviews. This, of course, was not the first time an outsider had come to their village asking similar questions in an effort to help them. This is not the first time that they had been objects of research with little or no real participation or control in the research process. This was not the first time that they would reveal themselves to "us" for our benefit, not theirs. This was not the first time a researcher had come and gone, never to be seen again. In other words, this was not the first time they had been exploited by research. From these, and many more, moments of self-reflexivity, I began to raise similar questions about the difficulties and limitations of the methods and practices we use in humanitarian work. I

Figure 1.2 Privatization by Other Means. Photo by Michael Mascarenhas.

also began to wonder about how I might be contributing to or perpetuating the relations of dominance and uneven development that characterize North-South relations in spite of my liberatory intentions. Was I part of the problem rather than the solution?

When I was asked about the recent privatization of the improved public taps, and our role in this, I was less confident that I was "doing good." It was explained to me that until three months earlier, the taps had been run by a local water collective or fountaineer, and the cost to fill each jerrycan under that form of water management was 5 Rwandan francs. However, the district government, under duress from the World Bank, entered into a contract with a private purveyor to manage all the improved water systems in the region. The price was instantly raised from 5 to 10 Rwandan francs, with no notable improvement in the quality or quantity of water, according to the households I interviewed. As a result of this price increase, many households were unable to procure the water they needed. In Kiyanza, Kelly Myers reflected, "they're paying 50 [francs for each jerry can], so they get like, they need eight jerry cans a day. That's 400 Rwandan francs. They can't afford that, and they're not going [to the nearby improved sources that we installed]. They're walking huge distances [to get water]." Some do without by

Figure 1.3 Look Closely at the Locked Tap. Photo by Michael Mascarenhas.

sourcing local ephemeral springs or the river, while others decided how to lever-age their farming practices to pay for the increased cost of drinking water. For the first time in these villages, some people were going into debt to pay for access to drinking water while others were growing cash crops, coffee in particular, and some were moving. Somehow I had become a part of this process—a fragmented and particular process of dispossession—a privatization, a corporatization, and a financialization of water provision in rural Rwanda

Postcolonial intellectuals often complain about the woefully "underdevel-oped" epistemology of those in the Global North to understand and reflect on the systemic causes of poverty and dispossession, let alone one's complicity in that which one critiques (Escobar 1995; Harding 2012; Mohanty 1988; Said 1979). These scholars point out that the Northern epistemologies do not possess the appropri-ate lens to enable them to recognize their own location in either the history of human knowledge production or in natural and social relations on the planet today. Consequently, they are not well equipped to engage in informed participa-tion about debates around global inequality and poverty or even what massive

Figure 1.4 Commodification by Other Means. Photo by Michael Mascarenhas.

social good means in an era of structural adjustment, neoliberalism, and, most recently, austerity.

The attraction of the data narrative, acutely exemplified in traditional quantitative survey methodologies used by NGOs to document water poverty and dispossession—collected by white, upper-middle-class, Western-trained humanitarians who swoop through communities in their chauffeur-driven SUVs, like seasonal monsoons, leaving behind both short-lived tumult and a sense of eternal hope—represent a significant dimension of those practices through which power is exercised in today's humanitarian world. As a result, humanitarian research has been more successful at reflecting the biases and priorities of their donors and NGOs than at analyzing the experiences of poverty or documenting racial and class apartheid. In effect, the state of humanitarian research into poverty and social marginalization in any given country not only serves to pathologize the poor and dispossessed but also reinforces contemporary racial attitudes toward inequality and social welfare—namely, that poor brown-skinned people of the Global South are incapable of saving themselves and can break free of their poverty and subjectivity only by becoming developed, using Western standards as the benchmark for evaluating their emancipation. This is why few people in the embattled margins of the Global South trust outsiders, particularly well-meaning Westerners, when they are asked invasive questions about their water access, hand washing, and toilet routines.

However, hope springs eternal in this humanitarian governing mentality, and many people committed to doing massive social good argue that the problems encountered in this and other baseline assessments were more indicative of past practices and policies than they are of new humanitarian efforts. The rapid expansion of educational and training institutions in humanitarian policy and practice in the Global South today, advocates argue, is a testament to righting the wrongs of past humanitarian efforts. The staggering growth of humanitarian departments and programs in the Global North is just one example of its increasing credentialism and professionalism. How these new humanitarian professionals *choose* to represent and interpret the observations they make "in the field" is a consequence of how they are trained and educated. However, the extent to which this now global educational complex trains its students to cultivate both a critical and reflective understanding of poverty and dispossession in the Global South remains unclear and is the subject of the next chapter.

Notes

1. This invitation to move away from the noisy sphere of the market and enter the hidden abode of production was first advanced by Karl Marx in volume 1 of *Capital* as a way to empirically examine how surplus value, "the secret of profit-making" (Marx, 1976 [1867]), was produced from the labor process of England's industrial factory floors. For Marxist scholars, the labor process marked the contested terrain, where struggles over the conditions of labor, including workers' rights, managerial privileges, state involvement, and workers' resistance to exploitation, were constantly fought out.

2. Devex is an internet based media platform for the global development community. See devex.com for more information.

3. Critiques of this assertion—particularly those working in this area—may argue that is it unfair to burden NGOs with such a task as institutional reform. I am not suggesting that this be so, nor am I suggesting that such an analysis would reveal a definitive approach one way or another. This effort, like much human activity, is much more ambiguous than definitive. However, it is important to analyze the degree to which NGOs acknowledge that the historical, political, and social causes and contexts (that they are now championing) may have contributed to the very problems they aim to solve, in an effort to examine how they navigate this ambiguous humanitarian space.

4. Pseudonym.

5. Pseudonym.

6. It was estimated that my trip would cost $3,000. World Research agreed to pay $1,000 of my expenses and the remaining $2,000 was approved by the acting dean of the School of Humanities, Arts, and Social Sciences at Rensselaer Polytechnic Institute.

7. I am constantly reminded of this observation when asked by family, friends, and colleagues what I do. When I answer "development," they often reply with pleasurable comments, fascinating acclamations, and, even personal stories of "doing good."

8. The verb *muzungu* come from *kuzungura*, which means "to replace, to take over."

9. An organization and scholarship fund for Rwandans orphaned as a result of the 1994 genocide (www.generationrwanda.org).

10. In 2008, French was dropped as one of Rwanda's three official languages. However, this sudden linguistic change has created many challenges, among them establishing a teaching force fluent in English.

11. One of the lead volunteers took offense over the fact that a few Generation Rwanda students used the smartphones meant to be employed to administer the survey for personal surfing on the Internet.

2 Educating the Global Humanitarian Citizen

"Columbia [University] touts a lot of diversity, but at the end of the day, it's still largely a rich, white [student body] population."[1]

"And so, in this great question of reconciling . . . vast and partially contradictory streams of thought, the one panacea of Education leaps to the lips of all."[2]

IN THIS CHAPTER, we examine the impact and growth of a central meaning-producing institution within the global humanitarian assemblage: the education system. In particular, the rapid growth of institutions involved in humanitarian training and education not only has aided in the professionalization of the global learning experience but also has been integral to shaping the means and methods by which humanitarianism is practiced and understood. The rapid rise of volunteer and study-abroad programs has allowed more students to take advantage of cross-cultural learning experiences in an effort to influence career aspirations and personal worldviews in a global age. This practice is occurring during a period when state programs concerning global citizenship have diminished in size and importance. Today, the majority of students studying abroad are not doing so on a Commonwealth Scholarship, in the case of UK citizens, or volunteering with the Peace Corps, like so many US citizens have done previously. Today, most Western youth and young at heart interested in a life-changing international experience are searching the Internet for innovative companies such as Frontier, Global Glimpse, and Cross-Cultural Solutions for a personalized global learning experience. The majority of international volunteer programs today are facilitated by nonprofit organizations operating in an unregulated and nonaccredited industry eager to sell an "adventure of a lifetime for people of all ages and walks of life" (Cross-Cultural Solutions 2015). Moreover, this rapidly growing informal-academic educational complex is increasingly merging with and influencing the curricula of more formal academic institutions. For example, Global Glimpse is partnering with public high schools to offer summer immersion programs in which high school students are introduced to a wide range of global issues, including poverty, politics, human rights, and aid and development (Global Glimpse 2015).

Colleges and universities, as well as nonacademic programs, present themselves as a model for (re)making society better, a place where students learn the skills to adapt to the grand challenges of their time. I often tell my students "the key to a healthy democracy is an educated citizenry" and try to make the classroom a place in which they can cultivate the skills and knowledge to realize their hopes and ambitions. Schools, the sociologist David Labaree (1997, 41) suggests, "present themselves as a model of our best hopes of our society and a mechanism for remaking that society in the image of those hopes." From a Geertzian perspective, schooling helps to establish social practices and rituals that reinforce a culture of global social solidarity, in spite of obvious global tensions and unprecedented inequities. What is important to ask in this analysis is: as students and institutions "go global," to what extent can these practitioners and institutions of change bridge the divide between what they hope society will become and what they think it really is? Put slightly differently, to what extent are the ideas and practices of global education and citizenship fostered in institutions of higher learning not only based on notions of compassion, charity, and a "shared humanity" but also attentive to issues of power and economic realities—in effect, connecting local manifestations of dispossession and injustice with global systems of uneven accumulation?

Doing Good and Doing Well

The tension between doing good and doing well underscores an old struggle over the role of education in civil society and is markedly illustrated in a recent Oxfam report. Education for global citizenship, according to Oxfam (Oxfam GB 2006, 1), "helps enable young people to develop the core competencies which allow them to actively engage with the world, and help to make it a more just and sustainable place." For Oxfam, education for global citizenship is essential for cultivating a sense of shared humanity and solidarity in Western youth. In addition, Oxfam (Oxfam GB 2006, 1) claims, "education for global citizenship gives them [students] the knowledge, understanding, skills and values that they need if they are to participate fully in ensuring their own, and others,' well-being and to make a positive contribution, both locally and globally." In effect, education for global citizenship, according to Oxfam (Oxfam GB 2006, 1), not only "encourages children and young people to care about the planet and to develop empathy with, and an active concern for, those with whom they share it"—in effect, to do good by compassion, charity, and a "shared humanity"—but also to do well by "ensuring their own well-being."

Oxfam, of course, is not alone in extolling the virtues of global education and citizenship and its ancillary practices of studying and volunteering abroad. Nor is it unique in its insistence on having things both ways—doing good and doing well—through "the magical medium of education" (Labaree 2012, 143). Yet for all its enthusiasm, Oxfam, like so many other centers of humanitarian education, struggles to define what the concept of "good" global citizenship entails and how it should be practiced. The essential problem posed by this tension, David Labaree (1997, 2012) suggests, is the extent to which education is defined as an institution that, on the one hand, promotes democratic equality and justice while, on the other hand, fulfilling its mandate of credentialism and social mobility. This inherent contradiction, Labaree (1997, 41) concludes, has led to "a tale of ambivalent goals and muddled outcomes" over the history of modern education.

Today, new beliefs and meanings about humanitarian government and governmentality—like all cultural practices—are learned and cultivated in an education system that continues to reform its curricula, extend its boundaries, and change its business model. Yet it remains unclear in what ways recent reforms in education, including the corporatization of public colleges and universities and the increasing popularity of private and venture-type schooling, and recent trends, including the decline in government funding, rising tuition fees, and the demands of student life, have influenced the subjectivity of newly minted humanitarians. For example, a market-based logic of education, scholars argue (Arum and Rosksa 2011; Labaree 1997, 2012), encourages students and educational practitioners to focus on its instrumental value—that is, as a credential—and to ignore its academic meaning and moral character. Yet it remains unclear how this market-based logic of education and training directs the field of global and humanitarian studies to attend to questions of power, politics, and identity when teaching about global poverty and dispossession. Put slightly differently, to what extent are students who aspire to do good also taught to critically reflect on the legacies and processes of their cultures and contexts?

Students today are increasingly defined as consumers and clients, as schools become more responsive to articulated individual student needs and demands at the same time as presenting themselves as a model of good social behavior and moral development. In this chapter, we examine the experiences and practices of both the consumers (students) and practitioners (teachers, administrators, and institutions—academic and nonacademic) of higher education in an attempt to examine the role of this global educational complex in fostering an ethos of a global moral community upon which humanitarian solidarity is based. In particular, we look at recent changes in the core practices and structures around which this institution is organized, including the rapid rise of international and global curricula, programs, and schools and the ever increasing corporatization of the academy. In particular, we examine the explicit, the implicit, and the null curricula of these teaching and learning institutions in an effort to elucidate the inner workings of a cultural system that simultaneously prepares students to be global citizens and local consumers. We begin with the experiences of students participating in the fasting growing sector of the tourism industry: voluntourism.

The Transformative Student Experience: The Explicit, Implicit, and Null Curricula

"I originally got interested in community service when I was in high school," recalls Ashley Smith. "I actually traveled to Nicaragua when I was a junior in high school with Global Glimpse," a nonprofit organization that offers study-abroad programs to high school students from all socioeconomic backgrounds (globalglimpse.org). "I know friends who went to Africa. I know friends who went to Mexico, and I know friends who went to India, and places like that on this program." Global Glimpse is one of many nonprofit organizations that are part of a rapidly expanding educational sector of volunteer organizations and programs directed at the teaching, learning, and practice of contemporary humanitarianism. Corporate funding partners include Goldman Sachs, Morgan Stanley, Staple Street Capital, HealthCor—venture and growth equity health-care investors— United Airlines, and a variety of foundations and trusts whose primary goal is to support opportunities for young people. For its part, Global Glimpse offers needs-based scholarships on a sliding scale to high school students in the United States for study abroad in an effort to develop "a new generation of young Americans who think and act as responsible global citizens" (Global Glimpse 2015). This "transformational experience" is rooted in Global Glimpse's commitment "to building a new generation of diverse young leaders who are equipped and inspired to tackle the social, political, and economic challenges of their generation" (Global Glimpse 2015). "It was a life-changing experience," recalls Ashley.

> Being there really exposed you to the really poor poor urban areas in Nicaragua. . . . I've never been exposed to poverty like that, and when I was there it was first hand, right in my face. You couldn't really ignore it, and you couldn't blame them either because they didn't have any other options. It was challenging.[3]

Ashley's story is not unlike that of many other youth who are inspired to be good global citizens by what they saw and experienced on study-abroad programs. Other Global Glimpse alumni offer similar testimonials of their transformative experience:

> It was a life-changing experience and one of the few programs that actually changed my life. I will never forget the memories, smiles, hardships, and people I met in Nicaragua. This program makes you realize the reality of life and prepares you for it. I never expected that I would be able to experience something so great and mind opening, while meeting new friends. Global Glimpse did not just help me help others, but it also helped me find a purpose for myself.

In 2008, the year that Ashley and her high school classmates went to Nicaragua, it was estimated that more than 1.6 million global tourists, specifically rich white students from the Global North, spent about $2 billion to use their so-called vacations to work in orphanages, build schools, engineer drinking water and sanitation systems, and teach English in the Global South. This number, however, does not include a rapidly growing group of self-proclaimed Samaritans, such as Adrian Roberts (introduced in chapter 1), who decided to put his life on hold and volunteer "on the ground" in Thailand in the aftermath of the South Asian tsunami. Global Glimpse has also been able to share in this swiftly growing humanitarian wave. In 2008, Ashley was one of eighty-five Global Glimpse students. In 2014 the Global Glimpse cohort grew to 584 students, supported by over $1 million in need-based scholarships.

Moreover, Global Glimpse is not alone in its use of an experience of a lifetime to sell travel programs. For example, Cross-Cultural Solutions' webpage has an artfully designed carousel featuring a video and photos. The centerpiece of one photo was a smiling white youth with at least four smiling African boys ringing his neck (it is unclear where in Africa the picture was taken, and in terms of representation it does not matter to the Western gaze). The caption below the image reads, "A volunteer trip abroad with Cross-Cultural Solutions will change you. Change the way you see other cultures. Maybe even change how you live your life. All while you change the lives of others for the better. Ultimately we're changing the way volunteering is done, making it a safe, exciting adventure of a lifetime for people of all ages and walks of life" (Cross-Cultural Solutions 2015). In addition to individual opportunities for volunteering, Cross-Cultural Solutions offers high school volunteer programs, family volunteer opportunities, group volunteer trips, gap-year options, international internships, and faculty-led groups. Cross-Cultural Solutions matches roughly 4,000 volunteers per year with civic service opportunities in 12 countries (Caprara, Quigley, and Rieffel 2009). The rise of organizations selling the "experience of a lifetime" guarantee or formulation—individual, group, family, institutional—that will bring about this change has contributed not only to its substantial growth but also its professionalization, rendering this humanitarian education as something that everyone, regardless of socioeconomic standing, can and must do.

The American education scholar Elliot Eisner theorized that all schools "teach" three curricula: the explicit, the implicit, and the null curricula. Curriculum here is defined broadly as an opportunity to learn that can occur in any structured learning environment (Cherryholmes 1988). The explicit curriculum simply refers to publicly announced programs that an institution provides—"an educational menu of sorts" from which students, at least in principle, can choose (Eisner 1994, 88). The implicit curriculum, by contrast, comprises values and expectations generally not included in the formal curriculum but nevertheless learned by students as part of their school experience. Lessons learned from the implicit curricula, Eisner (1994) has suggested, are among the most important ones that students learn. For example, students quickly recognize the importance of a particular subject by how much time is devoted to it or when in the day or in the term it is taught. In effect, Eisner points out, "schools teach far more than they advertise" (1994, 92). The null curriculum, according to Eisner (1994), is simply that which is not taught in schools. Eisner reflected on the fact that "there is something of a paradox involved in writing about a curriculum that does not exist." Yet he suggests that "if we are concerned with the consequences of school programs and the role of curriculum in shaping those consequences," then we must "consider not only the explicit and implicit curricula of schools but also what schools do not teach" (Eisner 1994, 97). For example, "what students cannot consider, what they don't know, processes they are unable to use, have consequences for the kinds of lives they lead" and want to live (Eisner 1994, 103).

With regard to the humanitarian education experience offered by Global Glimpse, Cross-Cultural Solutions, and many other volunteer-abroad-type programs, we can identify certain publicly explicit goals, such as international experience, cultural immersion, and leadership development, which are offered via many programs, including, but certainly not limited to, literacy, child nutrition, and global health. Cross-Cultural Solutions informs potential students that "whether you're teaching English and the ABC's, leading students in a song, or giving a math lesson, your service will make a difference" (Cross-Cultural Solutions 2015). Its website features a twenty-something white male attentively hunched over seven brown children in what is described as an overcrowded classroom. This teacher, we are informed, is "a role model for children" and an "inspiration to local educators" (Cross-Cultural Solutions 2015).

The iconic image of brown and black children surrounded by one young Westerner also projects a powerful implicit message about humanitarian-oriented volunteer tourism. First, their smiling faces and affectionate embrace intimate to the viewer not only that these boys desperately need your help but, more importantly, that they welcome outside intervention. In effect, this, and numerous other images that populate the webpages of all humanitarian-orientated volunteer organizations, reinforces an implicit curriculum that is consistent with Western values and beliefs about the subaltern—namely, that "the South is or has a problem and the North is and has the solution to this problem" (Andreotti 2006, 41).

The Third World child, Mary Mostafanezhad (2013) suggests, has become the primary object of Western volunteer tourists' compassion and the dominant iconography of the Global South. This imaginary of vulnerable, poor, uneducated, and otherwise sick children, depicted on webpage carousels, is then intimately

Figure 2.1 A Life-Changing Experience. Source: http://www.crossculturalsolutions.org.

experienced by the Western moral consumer, eager to act out a sense of moral responsibility and social solidarity with those less fortunate. "One memory has stuck with me to this day," recalls Ashley, a Global Glimpse graduate:

> We went to a dump, and there were a lot of people there, a lot of kids there, collecting plastic because that was how they made a living; that was how they survived. I was talking with some of the kids, and I tried to teach them the alphabet. But the kids had no education! They didn't even know what the alphabet was. I'm talking about kids that were my age at the time, fifteen and sixteen . . . and it was really eye-opening.

Ashley's construction of self and other—in this case, Nicaraguan youth—is also consistent with that of other students, who believe that they can only affect "poorer" people in positive ways—in this example, teaching poor children the alphabet. Ashley's reflection also upholds an implicit Western assumption that locals are ignorant. In this case, Ashley's assumption that childhood poverty was due to a lack of formal education among Nicaraguan youth (and not opportunity) and that she could, in fact, make a difference in their life chances (by teaching them the alphabet) is consistent with a deep-seated belief that those in the Global North can help improve and promote the welfare of those less fortunate in the Global South. While in Nicaragua, Ashley, a Spanish-speaking American, also volunteered her time to translate museum documents into English in an effort to help generate local tourism.

> It was a gross, nasty environment [to grow up in]. We went to rural communities that didn't have running water and had to travel miles and miles to get safe drinking water. It was a very hard experience for me to process at the time.

But these reflections become more telling when one considers what is learned and what is ignored about "the others" they encounter during their global learning experience. Those participants, like Ashley, who speak of the abject poverty they encountered most often frame this form of dispossession as simple unlucky happenstance. Children, in particular, Ashley reflects, cannot be blamed for their life situation "because they didn't have any other options." Reducing "the reality of life" for many Nicaraguans to simply being unlucky, however, not only leads to an inaccurate understanding of the causes and consequences of global poverty but also reinforces the belief that those in the Global North are simply innocent bystanders to the unfortunate life experiences of those in the Global South.

Moreover, in learning that gross material differences are a matter of luck, the focus quickly turns to how those fortunate individuals in the Global North can help those less fortunate in the Global South in dire need of assistance. After "graduating from Global Glimpse," Ashley heard about Engineers without Borders in her freshman year. "It really looked cool," Ashley recalled. "You get to build things and you get to help people. It went well together." Moreover, this un-lucky "reality of life" understanding also "prepares" students to conclude that the root cause of their newly found friends' poverty and dispossession lies "over There." The lesson learned is that "those" people and "their" institutions are lacking—lacking health care, lacking teachers, lacking water, and lacking educa-tion. And, in this particular case, the obvious solution for Ashley and her study-abroad classmates to this personal crisis is to teach them—teach them the alphabet, teach them English, teach them how to read and how to write. These banking methods of humanitarian education, however, where the skills suppos-edly lacking are first identified and then deposited in the deficient individual, the Brazilian educator Paulo Freire (2011, 73) argues, "serves the interests of the oppressors, who care neither to have the world revealed nor to see it transformed."

This type of pedagogy, which reinforces a limited critical engagement at best and simple ignorance at worst, with regard to global poverty and oppression, is in part a reflection of what study-abroad programs neglect to teach: the null cur-riculum. A sample itinerary from Global Glimpse's Nicaraguan program includes a history lesson—in which students spend time talking with former revolution-ary fighters—and lessons in cultural immersion—in which students are intro-duced to local food, artisans, and traditional dance. In addition to taking several adventure outings, students engage in various community service projects, includ-ing a visit to a local dump, to better understand the challenges of business, labor, and poverty in a developing-country context. Conspicuously absent from the formal curricula is any mention of the efforts by the United States in the 1980s to "democratize Nicaragua" by providing financial aid, weapons, and military training—in violation of international law—to various rebel groups, referred to as the Contras, to oppose the democratically elected Sandinista government. The rebel Contras, together with devastating US economic sanctions, debilitated the Sandinista government by forcing it to divert scarce resources to the war rather than desperately needed social programs. The cost of this unabashed American-style of democracy resulted in the death of 30,000 Nicaraguans, and another half-million were uprooted from their homes (Chomsky 1992).

Also conspicuously absent from the formal curricula presented to Global Glimpse students is any mention of structural adjustment programs in the mid-1980s by the International Monetary Fund (IMF), the World Bank, and the Inter-national Development Bank (IDB), which forced Nicaragua and all other Latin American countries to denounce a state-led strategy of economic policy-making in favor of a neoliberal free-market approach in return for future debt refinancing. The journalist Naomi Klein pointed out that, in some cases, these "reforms" involved military coups and the rise of dictatorships throughout the region (Klein 2007). This form of economic shock recovery was found in government austerity measures, trade liberalization policies, currency devaluation, and the privatization of publicly held assets, which together, scholar David Harvey (2003, 2005) has suggested, constituted the cutting edge of accumulation by dispossession. The fact that Global Glimpse students will see, study, and help "Nicaragua" without ever hearing the words "Contras," "structural adjustment," or "neoliberalism" is a stunning testament to the impact of the null curricula on humanitarian-orientated volunteer organizations.

It may be instructive to recall that, not so long ago, these places were noted for their stunning beauty, wealth, and resources. It was, and still is a major reason the Global North remains so interested in the Global South, in spite of all "its" problems. It is equally instructive to get a sense of the depth and breadth of this expansive and diverse educational complex in which humanitarian government and governmentality have become a part of the very fabric of modern-day living and learning (see Figure 2.2). And as much as I have tried to be comprehensive, I also recognize that I am simply scratching the surface of what and who constitutes this rapidly expansive and widely linked global educational complex.

The Universe of International Volunteer Programs

I wanted to "have a purposeful travel experience, and go somewhere, and do something that's helpful," explains Jessica Richards, about some of her personal reasons for volunteering with international nonprofit organizations. Jessica first got bitten by the travel bug as a volunteer with the Peace Corps. "I was in the Peace Corps in the early 1980s in what is now the Democratic Republic of Congo. I enjoyed that. It was a challenge. . . . More recently I wanted to combine my traveling with a purpose." Jessica has a bachelor's degree in environmental science and a master's degree in environmental engineering, so her interest in finding "an organization that did drinking water projects" made sense. This decision, however, did not come easily to Jessica. "I have found that the majority of the organizations are faith-based," and "it didn't quite interest me as much." Nevertheless, her drive to travel combined with her passion to do social good has taken Jessica to counties in Central and East Africa as well as South America.

Volunteer tourism, or "voluntourism," remains the most rapidly growing segment of the tourism industry. The number of students alone does not aptly describe the extensive institutional assemblage that shares in providing the popular, and, as I explain later, increasingly necessary, ritual of global civic service. In addition to nonprofit volunteer-sending organizations, such as Global Glimpse, can be added a long list of for-profit volunteer-sending organizations and programs such as Global Crossroads, Frontier, Atlas Corps, United Planet, and Projects Abroad, which, according to Global Crossroads (2015, 1), provide "professional, need-targeted assistance to the world's most deserving people in some of the world's most exotic travel destinations" (see Table 2.1). A Brookings Institution report identified more than a hundred for-profit and nonprofit programs in the

United States, which together send more than 40,000 paying volunteers to work in foreign countries every year (Caprara et al. 2009).

Government volunteer-sending organizations, such as the US Peace Corps,[4] as well as nongovernmental volunteer-sending organizations, such as the United Nations Volunteers, can be added to this list of global civic service providers. In 2008 the US Peace Corps placed around 8,000 volunteers in more than 70 countries. However, 2014 was a record-breaking year for this government agency as "17,336 Americans applied for two-year service positions in fiscal year 2014," a twenty-two-year high for this fifty-three-year-old government agency, and an increase in applications of more than 70 percent over the previous year (Peace Corps 2015, 1). The only other international volunteer program funded by the US federal government is Volunteers for Prosperity (VfP), a program managed by the US-AID that seeks to connect Americans who wish to serve abroad with private-sector programs (Caprara et al. 2009).

Faith-based volunteer-sending organizations not only constitute the longest-standing form of international service but also are responsible for the largest number of people volunteering abroad. In fact, a recent survey on international volunteerism reported that about half of all international service placements from the United States were sponsored by faith-based organizations (Lough 2012). Catholic Volunteer Network, established in 1963, is a nonprofit membership organization of more than 200 domestic and international Christian-based volunteer and lay mission programs. American Jewish World Service (AJWS) is another faith-based organization dedicated to alleviating poverty, hunger, and disease among people in the developing world.

Another, albeit boutique, segment within the global civic service industry comprises volunteer vacation organizations and programs. These types of programs are typically offered by for-profit organizations. Hands Up Holidays, for example, promises luxury travel and lasting impressions through tailor-made volunteer vacations in twenty-six countries, ranging from a two-week animal rescue adventure in Costa Rica that would make the Kratt Brothers cringe (starting at US$6,990, not including airfare) to a ground-breaking environmental conservation project in New Zealand to help save native birds, including the kiwi, in between heli-hiking, whale watching, and wine tasting (starting at US$34,990, not including airfare). Another growing segment includes study-abroad organizations and service learning programs affiliated with institutions of higher education, which combines learning with volunteer service (explored below). Language programs, in which students can both volunteer and learn a new language while in another country, offer students another way to experience a sense of global citizenship. Lastly, multinational corporations, organizations, and agencies are increasingly seeking to facilitate opportunities for their employees to volunteer in communities around the globe. A short list of frontrunners in this sector includes

Table 2.1 Volunteer Organizations and Programs

Volunteer Organizations and Programs	Examples
Nonprofit volunteer-sending organizations and programs	VSO, WorldTeach, Cross-Cultural Solutions, United Planet, and Global Volunteers.
For-profit volunteer-sending organizations and programs	Projects Abroad, i-to-i, ProWorld Service Corps, Global Crossroad, and Volunteer Adventures
Government and nongovernmental volunteer-sending organizations and programs	The Peace Corps, Volunteers for Prosperity (VfP), Volunteering for International Development from Australia (VIDA), Deutscher Entwicklungsdienst (DED), Voluntary Service Overseas (VSO), European Voluntary Service, and UN Volunteers.
Faith-based volunteer-sending organizations and programs	Catholic Network of Volunteer Service, American Jewish World Service, Mennonite Central Committee, and the United Methodist General Board of Global Ministries, Catholic Medical Missions Board, Catholic Volunteer Network, Christian Peacemaker Teams, CRISAPZ (Christians for Peace in El Salvador, Habitat for Humanity), Hope Corps, Jesuit Volunteers International, Lay Mission-Helpers Association, Mercy Ships, Mission Discovery, Projects Overland, Viatores Christi, and Christian Aid.
Volunteer vacation organizations and programs	Hands Up Holidays, Globe Aware, Bike & Build, and Voluntouring
Volunteering and study organizations and programs	International Partnership for Service-Learning and Leadership (IPSL) and World Learning
Volunteering and language programs	AmeriSpan and BridgeLinguatec
Volunteering via an Employee Engagement Program	Nalco, CH2M Hill, Timberland, IBM, General Electric, IBM, Boeing, and Shell
Volunteering and Education programs	Teach for America

IBM's Service Corps, Pfizer's Global Health Corps, and General Electric's employee volunteering councils (Caprara et al. 2009; Idealist.org 2015).

The way in which individual organizations and programs are funded, structured, and implemented, of course, have important differences. Volunteer-abroad programs range from long weekend adventurers to two-year service positions. Volunteers have the option to build classrooms in a Berber village while staying in a nearby luxury hotel. The young and the young at heart can choose from among meaningful custom-made adventures. Additionally, ethical consumers can decide how they want to help. Some programs involve construction, repair, and renovation of needy schools, orphanages, or clinics. Others include teaching, medical care, water infrastructure and solar energy installations, and helping with environmental conservation, such as caring for elephants or planting trees.

Moreover, these organizations and programs have not only increased in number and taken on new functions but have also forged innovative and increasingly complex links with government agencies, international development agencies, and corporate and philanthropic donors. For example, the Peace Corps is beginning to collaborate with UN Volunteers, NGOs, and faith-based and corporate volunteering initiatives in an effort to scale up its efforts in HIV/AIDS prevention. Similarly, the United Kingdom's leading volunteer-sending organization, Voluntary Service Overseas (VSO), has recently multilateralized its program to include volunteers from Canada, other Commonwealth countries, Ireland, the Netherlands, India, Kenya, and the Philippines (Caprara et al. 2009). Together the growth and interconnectedness of this global civic service has provided the practical and ideological means for realizing and supporting a global moral community. In a matter of a decade or two, this institutional assemblage has turned what was a radical and antiestablishment, yet certainly elitist, practice of traveling abroad into a professional and mass participation event. For Ashley, Jessica and the millions of other students who leave the comfort of their hometowns and school environs to travel thousands of miles to a foreign country and often remote community, this usually short experience is not only eye opening but life changing.

In many ways voluntourism has become a rite of passage for thousands of young people, one of many rituals—like getting a driver's license, being accepted to college, drinking, and being able to vote—that mark a person's transition from adolescence to adulthood. These messages of doing good and mutual support—changing your life and their lives for the better—have contributed to this rapid rise of volunteer tourism as a cultural artifact. For example, Cross-Cultural Solutions, which was founded in 1995, has tripled the number of volunteers it sends abroad since 2000 (McGray 2004). However, it is not only a deep sense of empathy, which this burgeoning industry seems to tap into so well, that has fostered the practice of doing massive social good to become mainstream. Generally, the growth of international travel and tourism is a direct response to the continued rise in real income and leisure time of mostly white well-to-do people in developed countries (Brandon 1996). And while no reliable estimates are available on worldwide expenditures on voluntourism alone, the World Travel & Tourism Council (WTTC) estimates that, in 2011, travel and tourism directly employed 98 million people and generated $2 trillion in direct gross domestic product (GDP) (World Travel & Tourism Council 2012). Put simply, paid voluntarism is not cheap. For example, a two-week trip to Lima with Cross-Cultural Solutions costs approximately US$3,300. However, for those wanting a little more tourism and a little less volunteering Hands Up Holidays promises luxury travel and lasting impressions on tailor-made volunteer vacations in twenty-six countries, costing from about US$7,000 to $35,000. "For an adventure that counts," Anita Roddick, the founder of the Body Shop, says, "I recommend Hands Up Holidays." The latter example is clearly more tourism than volunteering. Nevertheless, this increasingly popular cultural practice is indicative of this modern form of humanitarianism, one in which individuals seek social solidarity with, and social and environmental justice for, vulnerable populations, wildlife, and environments, through conscientious consumptive habits (Bryant and Goodman 2004).

The Galaxy of Study Abroad

Some might suggest that is it unfair to saddle volunteer organizations and their programs with the encumbrance of democratic equality and global social justice. Perhaps it is unfair to hold them to the same "social change" standards as university-based programs and curricula, which often present themselves as models of our best hopes and ambitions. The scholars Joanne Benham Rennick and Michael Desjardins (2013) argue that, if done right, international learning is consistent with cultivating a global citizenship by fostering an extraordinary perspective and understanding of ourselves (both students and educators in the Global North) and the Other. However, they acknowledge the lack of agreement on what the concept of global citizenship entails or how one might recognize a study-abroad program that is "done right." Similarly, Allan Goodman, the president and chief executive of the Institute of International Education, and the career consultant Stacie Nevadomski Berdan (2014), co-authors of *A Study Guide to Study Abroad,* claim that this rapidly expanding transnational educational complex is the most effective and accessible way for students to develop needed skills to interact with people from other countries and cultures, training future leaders in all sectors to address urgent issues—from curing diseases and finding energy solutions, to fighting terrorism and hunger—shared across borders. But they warn that study abroad has to be done correctly. It cannot be a separate or tangential part of education but, rather, an integrated part of the curriculum. If done right, advocates say, study abroad enables future leaders to do good and to do well by credentializing their unique skill set in the service of humanity.

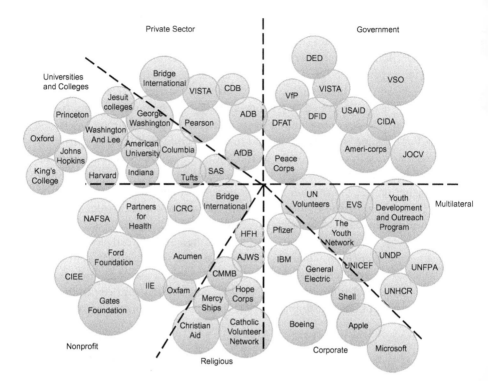

ADB   Asian Development Bank
AfDB   African Development Bank
AJWS   American Jewish World Service
CDB   Caribbean Development Bank
CIDA   Canadian International Development
        Agency
CIEE   Council on International Educational
        Exchange
DED   Department of Education
DFAT   Department of Foreign Affairs and Trade
DFID   Department for International Development
EVS   European Voluntary Service
HFH   Habitat for Humanity
ICRC   International Committee of the Red Cross
IIE   Institute of International Education
JOCV   Japan Overseas Cooperation Volunteers

NAFSA   National Association for Foreign
        Student Advisers
SAS   Semester at Sea
UNDP   United Nations Development Programme
UNFPA   United Nations Population Fund (formerly
        United Nations Fund for Population
        Activities)
UNHCR   United Nations High Commissioner
        for Refugees
UNICEF United Nations International Children's
        Emergency Fund
USAID   United States Agency for International
        Development
VfP   Voluntary Filing Program
VISTA   Volunteers in Service to America
VSO   Voluntary Service Overseas

Figure 2.2 The Galaxy of Study Abroad.

Moreover, proponents suggest, it has never been easier to do good. For example, in addition to, or while, earning a degree in international relations, law, finance, public health, or information science, students can volunteer with a nonprofit organization, enroll in study-abroad and foreign-exchange programs, participate in leadership conferences, join a "without borders" society, compete for internships with government, think tanks, or consultancy groups, or apply to a growing number of fellowship programs offered in the private sector. Some passionate individuals with great ideas have chosen the entrepreneurial route, trying out novel avenues and innovative approaches to "doing good" by themselves (most often referred to as DIY [do-it-yourself]). And for those needing assistance and willing to pay, companies such as CharityFolks.com and CharityBuzz .com represent the tip of the proverbial iceberg of internship placement programs ready to jumpstart future humanitarian careers.

"I went on a semester to Semester at Sea, and, after that, my whole world got flipped upside down," recalls Anthony Sampson, now a consultant working in the water quality and water resource sector. Semester at Sea is a 100-day study-abroad program in which students leave the United States on a cruise ship and circumnavigate the globe, visiting from eight to eleven countries in Asia, Africa, and South America, while taking university-accredited courses.

> I was exposed to all types of cultures and I realized that I had a gift of some sort to not only appreciate these cultures but really immerse myself as much as possible. . . . I really enjoyed interacting with different groups of people on a constant basis. That [trip] changed my way of thinking.

Upon returning to the United States, Anthony recalled, "I switched my major [to] economics with a focus on economic development." After graduating with a master's degree in international development, Anthony was hired by a large US-based nonprofit organization working in the provision of drinking water and sanitation. He is currently a consultant working in the water quality and water resource sector in Colombia.

On the surface, the opportunities to learn, work, and live a purposeful life seem endless, as a growing group of participants, such as Anthony, join this expanding humanitarian complex. The nonprofit sector alone has more than 19 million paid employees and is rapidly becoming the career of choice for many college graduates, from engineering and the social sciences to lawyers and MBAs. Moreover, charity workers' salaries have started to rise rapidly in recent years, with those in executive positions often making sums of more than six figures, making humanitarianism an attractive career choice (Canadian Broadcasting Corporation 2011). In addition to rising donations and employment opportunities, more than one-quarter (27 percent) of adults in the United States alone volunteered with an organization, according to the 2012 Urban Institute report (Blackwood, Roeger, and Pettijohn 2010).[5] Other than volunteer opportunities with NGOs and other CSOs, a wide range of employment options among the ranks of the global humanitarian complex are available: government agencies such as Australia's Department of Foreign Affairs & Trade, the United Kingdom's Department for International Development, the US Agency for International Development, and the Canadian International Development Agency; international finance institutions such as the World Bank, the African Development Bank, the Asian Development Bank, the China Development Bank; and thousands of consulting firms—global, national, and local—specializing in international development and humanitarian efforts that work alongside NGOs, governments, and international organizations. In fact, it is often hard to differentiate between an NGO and a consulting firm, as many play similar roles in the global humanitarian complex, often partnering and also frequently competing for similar resources. This growing amalgam of nonprofit organizations, government agencies, and consultants work alongside international and multilateral organizations, such as the United Nations Children's Fund (UNICEF),[6] the United Nations Development Programme, the United Nations Population Fund, and the United Nations High Commissioner for Refugees, mandated to lead and coordinate international actions to protect the rights of subjugated and displaced peoples and populations.

Lastly, multinational corporations are now working alongside these state and international organizations and humanitarian consultants, in an effort not only to expand but also to reshape what it means to do good—giving charity and donating the time and talent of their employees. In addition to charitable donations, corporations such as Pfizer, Nestlé, ExxonMobil, Dow Chemical, Syngenta, Unilever, Coca-Cola, Pepsi, Walmart, and Goldman Sachs, are also including corporate social responsibility programs and more general philanthropic work as part of their global strategy to alleviate poverty, combat disease, and build local partnerships and markets with the world's 4 billion poorest people—two-thirds of the world's population.

Humanitarians, such as Ashley, Jessica, and Anthony, in search of an elusive career in the fight against poverty and injustice can now turn to a burgeoning array of global studies and international relations schools and programs. American University's School of International Service, for example, offers an online executive master's-degree program in international service. This accelerated program is designed for experienced professionals working full-time while earning a master's degree. At the other end of the student spectrum, the Association of Jesuit Colleges and Universities provides online higher education to refugee camp residents in Kenya and Malawi, as well as urban refugees in Aleppo, Syria, and Amman, Jordan (Ladika 2012). Providing education to refugees, however, is also transforming the lives of American students. "Through this [study-abroad] experience, I've learned to question stereotypes and celebrate diversity, feeling empowered by the strength of our refugees," recalls an undergraduate student at Washington and Lee University in Lexington, Virginia (Ladika 2012, 16).

Harvard University's Kennedy School of Government, Georgetown University's Edmund A. Walsh School of Foreign Service, Johns Hopkins University's School of Advanced International Studies, Princeton University's Woodrow Wilson School of Public and International Affairs, Tufts University's Fletcher School of Law and Diplomacy, and George Washington University's Elliott School of International Affairs continue to rank among the top international relations programs for bachelor's degrees, master's degrees, and PhDs, according to a recent survey (Maliniak, Peterson, Powers, and Tierney 2014). The University of Oklahoma's College of International Studies, founded in 2011, and Indiana University's newly created School of Global and International Studies (SGIS), which opened in 2012, are indicative of the latest collegial effort to prepare students in "global competencies of the 21st century" (Indiana University 2014). "I really do want to change the world," declares an undergraduate featured in an SGIS brochure, "I want to do everything I can to make the world a better place. The School of Global and International Studies really allows you the opportunities to do that" (Indiana University 2014). An administrator gave a more behind-the-scenes interpretation of the newly created school:

> Indiana University has always been recognized for its international academics, its foreign languages learning, and its area studies programs. I think it really prides itself on being one of the more internationalized universities in the Midwest, if not in the entire country. And I think there was also a recognition that even though we are so international we might not be. We might not have the connective tissue that is necessary to build on all those resources and that expertise. In many ways I think the school is an attempt to have that infrastructure, to align all of our strengths into a new school. I think also, and everyone needs to be honest, but it is also about competing with some of the other international affairs schools in the country. About three or four years ago there was a task force put together by the University about new directions. It was called the New Academic Directions Report. That is where it was first suggested that a school for global and international studies be created. And I believe our president thought it was a fantastic idea, and everybody agreed that it was the right thing to do, and from that point on it went very quickly to a reality.

It appears that the success of college presidents these days is measured not only by their million-dollar compensation packages but also by their strategy, intentional or not, of further internationalization of both the institution and its programs. "And like a lot of universities," an Indiana University administrator revealed, "we're thinking about how to innovate and internationalize curriculum."

> And not resting on degrees like international business or international development or international studies [but], rather, how you integrate global learning

outcomes and global perspectives, and global learning into a variety of different disciplines from nursing to engineering to policy schools and humanities, and throughout the academy.

Like other programs, Indiana University's SGIS offers thematic concentrations, minors, majors, and certificates in global and international studies and is committed to having all students pursue a study-abroad experience. However, as indicated above, schools are also pursuing other avenues for internationalizing their institutions by offering globally enriched learning experiences on campus, in addition to, or as a substitute for, sending students abroad. The internationalization of curricula across traditional disciplines is one example of these efforts, which involves global learning outcomes and intercultural perspectives in course content and teaching methods.

In the academic year 2012/2013, 289,408 US students studied abroad for academic credit, 46,090 students earned full degrees abroad, and 15,089 students participated in noncredit work, internships, and volunteer study abroad (Institute of International Education 2014). Participation in study abroad has more than tripled over the past two decades but remains a small percentage (1.5%) of US students enrolled in higher education. Less than 3 percent of Canadian university students gain study-abroad experience for credit in a given year (Toope 2012). One effort to address this shortfall has been advanced by the Institute of International Education's (IIE) Generation Study Abroad initiative, a five-year strategy, in conjunction with 450 partnering institutions, including Indiana University, intended to double the number of US students studying abroad by the end of the decade (Institute of International Education 2015). For its part, Germany has made significant investments in internationalization, including the equivalent of more than 36 million euros in funding for study-abroad scholarships in 2010 alone (Toope 2012).

The Association of Universities and Colleges of Canada (AUCC)-led visit by fifteen Canadian university presidents to India in November 2010 signaled another strategy in the pursuit of internationalization by Canadian universities. The most important benefits of internationalization for students, according to a recent AUCC survey of university presidents, are (in descending order) the development of a global perspective and values (global citizenship); second, the development of international competencies, and increasing employability; and third, access to job opportunities in the international marketplace (Association of Universities and Colleges of Canada 2014). In effect, university leaders ranked the broader and more democratic goal of global citizenship ahead of the more private goal of social mobility via increased credentialism, when defining their motivation for internationalization. This public-good perspective shared by university and college leaders suggests that the benefits of internationalization, for them, are, first and foremost, collective, in that they accrue to everyone.

The impact of this perspective, which ranks doing good ahead of doing well, on schools is profound, particularly given the increasing corporatization and the recent emphasis on a consumer approach to education (Labaree 1997). The emphasis on global citizenship training as the principal learning outcome of internationalization, however, not only offers students intercultural experiences, innovative instruction and curricula, and potential employment opportunities but also signals to students what academic content, knowledge, and expertise are necessary to make the world a better place. Students learn which global and cultural competencies are necessary by virtue of what is emphasized and ignored, taught and not taught, in their supposedly innovative and increasingly international curricula. Like most schools, Tufts University's Fletcher School of International Affairs offers a variety of degree programs (master's degree, PhD, dual degrees, and exchange programs) that allow students to tailor their education to meet specific international interests or career goals. In addition to degrees, students can choose from six certificates[7] to further specialize in their area of concentration. Similarly, Tuft's Friedman School of Nutrition Science and Policy offers a three-course online graduate certificate in evidence-based humanitarian assistance. This online program teaches students to carry out needs assessments in the food security and nutrition fields, design and carry out field research programs to measure the effectiveness of programming, and assess the impact of programming in both short- and long-term humanitarian crises. At the end of the course, students will be prepared to conduct their own fieldwork and assess the value of others' field research. Tuft's approach to internationalization is that global competency skills, such as needs assessment and measurement, can be learned online. What is implicit in this curriculum is that students do not have to spend time in "the field" to be experts in fieldwork. In effect, students are implicitly taught that granular and cultural-specific knowledge is irrelevant when doing good.

"I'm in the process of finishing up my master's of public health and in environmental health science [at Columbia University]. I'm also getting a graduate certificate in health and human rights," explains Sofía Rodriguz, a first-year master's-degree student. The Columbia University Mailman School of Public Health, like Indiana University and the University of Oklahoma, launched a full review of its program and in 2012 launched a two-year interdisciplinary master of public health (MPH) program and an accelerated one-year master's degree. And, like the program at Tufts University, Columbia's MPH program offers a certificate in a second, more-focused area of expertise that can lead to a New York State–recognized credential. The year this program was initiated, the school offered certificates in over twenty areas.

> I think Columbia's environmental health sciences program is really great, especially with its ties to the Earth Institute, because you just have so many people of different disciplines that you have access to. But at the same time, it's still a very basic sciences [degree]. . . . Everything is very lab science oriented.

So I really wanted a certificate that was more sociological based, population level, health based. I thought health and human rights would be a great way to do that, because it's broad, but it's important. And it really complements that basic science education really well.

Like Tufts and other schools, Columbia uses certificates as a way to internationalize its curricula and credentialize expertise and knowledge in international studies. "The certificate kind of allows you to branch out past [the MPH] and past your requirements in your department," explains Sofía. "It's the only way to complete a really interdisciplinary kind of master's degree." She continues,

At Columbia, for instance, we have a whole certificate in global health and a certificate in humanitarian action. For both [certificates], you have to go to developing countries for either six months or three months, depending on the certificate. But I think it's kind of weird that this very prestigious institution in the United States . . . send[s] a bunch of very privileged, majority white kids to go to Africa and sub-Saharan Africa and work on humanitarian issues. I don't think it does much for those communities and I think a lot of times it's a little harmful. I have heard kids from Global Health come back and say, I saw what was happening [over] there, and I felt like I was almost a detriment to them. Like, I don't know enough about the culture to just go in for three months [and help them].

Sofía points to a growing critique about study abroad, whether enabled by degree-granting academic institutions or private volunteer tourism organizations—namely, that they are doing more harm than good. "I followed second years [on social media] who were abroad," she recalls, "and they were just having a good time putting photos on Instagram. . . . It was like, all they were doing was riding elephants and posting photos of [themselves], saying 'look how much fun I'm having'! . . . How are we supposed to be helping people when we are not a part of that community, when we aren't making an effort to understand that community?"

In effect, the inability to cultivate a global perspective consistent with global citizenship, at least for these students, is not about geographic distance, as suggested by advocates of study-abroad programs but, rather, pedagogy. The Brazilian educator Paulo Freire (2011, 95) argues, "Such a program," which fails to reveal how social and economic structures cause injustice, "constitutes cultural invasion, good intentions notwithstanding." In effect, Freire concludes, "the oppressors use their humanitarianism to preserve a profitable situation" which "must be maintained in order to justify that generosity" (2011, 73, 60).

Paradoxical to public and well-meaning efforts to integrate and promote internationalization at their universities and colleges, students are returning from far-off places and leaving prestigious educational programs without developing the cross-cultural communication skills or global competencies necessary to cultivate a sense of global citizenship. "I kind of see the Humanitarian Action

Program at the Public Health School as more of a credentialing kind of thing," asserts Sofia. "Something really cool to put on their resume, but I think ultimately they want to work domestically. They just want to say that they have been [abroad]." The students who end up leaving Columbia, Sofia continues, "end up going into high positions in the UN, in Geneva or New York. A lot of kids go on to work in banking and finance, and they all work on Wall Street now. Most of them have no intention of going back into the field."

This form of humanitarian education brings affluence and poverty together in a way that hides the causes of both. For many students graduating from these prestigious programs, gross material differences are still a matter of luck, not structure. In effect, this wall between the rich and the poor is reinforced not by brick and mortar but, rather, by pedagogy, as the skills and subjectivity of a growing surplus army of humanitarians, ready to serve and save, are cultivated by an education system that has become highly professional, ambiguously credentialized, exceedingly hierarchical, and increasingly profit driven. Moreover, deepseated beliefs and meanings about what is good and right for the world's poor and dispossessed are learned and cultivated by an "education" system that consists of numerous actors—public, private, and civil society—that are increasingly influenced by factors other than the goal of doing massive social good. At many campuses, *New York Times* reporter Diana Jean Schemo (2007, A1) writes, "study abroad programs are run by multiple companies and non-profit institutes that offer colleges generous perks to sign up students." These include "free and subsidized travel overseas for officials, back-office services to defray operating expenses, stipends to market the programs to students, unpaid membership on advisory councils and boards, and even cash bonuses and commissions on student-paid fees" (Schemo 2007, A1). This money, Schemo (2007) suggests, generally goes directly to colleges, and not always to the students who take the trips. This cozy relationship came under some scrutiny in 2007, as fifteen colleges and universities (ten in New York and five elsewhere), including Harvard, Columbia, and Brown, were investigated by the New York attorney general for allegedly taking bribes and other kickbacks. For many players in this rapidly expanding education assemblage, Schemo (2007) writes, study abroad has become a prized credential, creating a competitive, even cutthroat, industry, with an army of vendors vying for student money and universities moving to profit from the boom.

Today, the discourse of humanitarianism—doing good, being fair, social justice, human rights, and so on—has become mainstreamed into the policy framework of states, the objectives of nonprofit organizations, the principles of the United Nations, the directives for multilateral lending agencies, the accountability of corporations, and the curricula of schools. This growing education assemblage, as with poverty and dispossession, is conditioned by the same structures of economic, political, and cultural dependence of the Global South on the Global

North, the latter enjoying not only knowledge and power over the former but the ability to use this form of hegemony to further their individual and collective interests, profiting from the very system they decry.

Conclusion

Colonial countries have had a long history of sending young people "overseas" under the pretense of spreading democracy, goodwill, and charity. Most often these young people carried guns and other colonial tools indicative of an expanding military-industrial complex. However, with the recent upsurge in voluntourism, study abroad, and programs in internalization, young people today are carrying knapsacks or backpacks, depending on their colonial origin, on their humanitarian mission. Armed with good intentions we jump on planes to be driven in jeeps to secluded mountain villages in the Himalayas, or remote rainforests in the Congo to save people we have little in common with. The real question to ask about this postcolonial mission is whether a new generation of organic intellectuals can emerge from this educational system, and become integral members of the next revolutionary wave to challenge common sense notions of global poverty and dispossession? Colleges and universities, as well as the non-academic programs, continue to present themselves as a model for (re)making society better, a place where students learn the skills to adapt to the grand challenges of their time. However, the effects of this educational experience, Sofia submits, is exceedingly limited on how students imagine themselves, and the world in which they want to change for the better.

> I think we need to have the really uncomfortable conversation about this white savior complex. I don't think any class [course] I have taken has talked about that. Like, what are the dangers of sending American white boys and girls over to the developing world to fix something? I think that this is the kind of conversation we need to have. I think my program in the core course work, there were some socio medical sciences based courses, where we did talk about power structures and the dynamics of those power structures, but [that was it]. . . . Instead of talking about it in the abstract, we need to talk about what do you actually risk? And what you are actually doing? If you are really going to do humanitarian work or international development work, you have to have that conversation. I think even for me, it's something I have to remind myself. I am not the best person for this job, probably. There is probably someone in the community who would do a better job than me at this. I need to ask them for their input and help, rather than coming in and saying, here you go, problem solved.

Such an education, Sofia believes, would encourage and enable students to think critically about the mechanisms and systems of uneven development, and avoid the temptation to pathologize the poor and dispossessed. Such an education would underscore the interdependence between luck and opportunity, poverty and wealth, and global citizenship and social mobility that are conspicuously absent in humanitarian curricula. Our uncomfortable conversation must begin with a pedagogy of, and for, the oppressed that attends to questions of power, politics, identity, and culture, where the Global North is as much a part of contemporary forms of epistemic violence as it is a part of creating a more just and sustainable world. "Pedagogy which begins with the egoistic interests of the oppressors," Freire maintains, "and makes of the oppressed the objects of its humanitarianism, itself maintains and embodies oppression (2011, 54)." Without this critical understanding of contemporary humanitarian moral sentiments the argument for global citizenship is left to rest on notions of compassion, charity, and a "common humanity" that fails to recognize the new relations and disposition of power that are emerging as a result of this new humanitarian government. However, schools are not alone in their commitment to solving the "defining moral issue of our time." Today corporate responsibility and venture philanthropy are two rapidly expanding strategies for doing massive social good, and with that thought in mind we now turn to the business of humanitarianism.

Notes

1. Research participant.
2. Du Bois, W. E. B. (2014 [1913]), 44.
3. Later, in her freshman year of high school, Ashley heard about Engineers without Borders "It really looked cool," she recalled. "You get to build things and you get to help people. It went well together. And when I came to Rensselaer Polytechnic Institute, I signed up to join the Engineers without Borders Chapter at the students fair."
4. President John F. Kennedy created the Peace Corps in 1961.
5. Volunteers contributed 15.2 billion hours, worth an estimated $296.2 billion.
6. Formally, the United Nations International Children's Emergency Fund.
7. Certificates are offered in diplomatic studies, human security, international development (political and social change, economic analysis, trade & investment, or sustainable development), international finance & banking, and strategic management & international consultancy.

3   The Business of Humanity and the Humanitarian Business

SPEAKING BEFORE A crowded audience at the Framing the Global Conference at Indiana University, the plenary speaker, Yasmina Zaidman, director of communications and strategic partnerships for Acumen Fund, began by describing a vision of how Acumen "wants to bridge the gap between rich and poor in an interconnected world." The idea of interconnectedness, Zaidman explained,

> is not just about how economies rely on each other, for commodities, for labor, or for capital; it is about a more fundamental truth, that we have a shared destiny. That the challenges by those with the least of everything are all of our challenges and that the opportunities enjoyed by the most privileged to fully express their humanity are opportunities that should be enjoyed by all.

Acumen Fund, a nonprofit venture capital firm founded in 2001 by Jacqueline Novogratz, a former investment banker and Rockefeller Foundation fellow, has been heralded by many as a maverick for doing good. Combining charity and traditional investment, Acumen accepts donations and then invests them, either by lending to or taking stakes in products or services of private venture firms, whose goal, in addition to making a profit, must also be to serve the poor. Profits from their investments, in the form of loan repayments or dividends, are then reinvested in other entrepreneurial ventures. This market-based approach to humanitarianism earned Novogratz a distinction as one of *Foreign Policy*'s 100 Top Global Thinkers in 2009. And in 2010, then US Secretary of State Hillary Clinton applauded the fund for creating an "innovative approach [that combines] philanthropy and capitalism" (Batavia et al. 2011, 2).

In 2013, Acumen raised $15.7 million in philanthropic capital, an increase of 57 percent over the prior year, and accrued total assets of $107.2 million. These sums may seem trivial compared with the billions of dollars lent by banks or spent by governments and big charities such as the Gates Foundation to help the poor. Acumen, however, does not seem intimidated by this comparison in its efforts to tackle the inefficiencies and other problems that often afflict traditional humanitarian efforts. "The real question that has driven me," Zaidman mused, "is what will it take to create the new systems that will allow people to live out their full human potential? At Acumen, we . . . leverage the best of business to achieve lasting and meaningful change in the lives of low-income people, with the heart and ethos of charity and philanthropy, to actually create change for everyone and not only for the elites."

This humanitarian society, Acumen, Zaidman explained, can be achieved by

looking for ways to partner with corporations in creative ways . . . using the tools of business and partnering with corporations to change the way the world tackles poverty. . . . Our work at Acumen has shown us the power of forging connections between some of the world's poorest communities and some of the most affluent through our partnership model, where we use philanthropic donations primarily from individuals but also from foundations and corporations to invest in businesses that serve the poor.

Acumen claims to be responsible for assembling a global network of philanthropists from the United States, Europe, South Asia, and Africa based on a shared passion for building innovative business models that address poverty from the ground up. "We have learned so much from the companies we invest in," Zaidman explains.

Sanergy is a sanitation company in Kenya that is partnering with Unilever to provide access to sanitation, hand-washing education, and soap. Virtualcity is a company in Kenya that links small holder farmers to markets, and they are working with Marks and Spencer to develop transparent supply chains for a product that Marks and Spencer's offers. Water Health International . . . has been partnering very closely with Dow Chemical, and it has opened up the door for us to look at Dow Chemical as a potential partner because they really recognize the value of innovation happening in this social enterprise space

The notion of applying business methods to philanthropy, Zaidman explains, is nothing less than contagious.

So since then we have found that through either our own partnerships or the partnerships of the companies that we invest in, some of the world's biggest corporations are now reaching deep into this social enterprise space. They are looking to engage small holder farmers, something that Unilever does extensively. ExxonMobil provides critical material for the production of antimalaria bed nets in Africa. Goldman Sachs invests in women enterprises throughout the developing world and is in support of our global fellows program. Syngenta partners with one of our seed companies in Kenya to provide improved hybrid seeds, and Google has been a real pioneer in helping to improve energy access around the world including through its work with Acumen. So this seems to me just the tip of the iceberg.

To date Acumen has invested, in the form of loans or equity, $90 million[1] in eighty companies in the water, health-care, housing, energy, agriculture, and education sectors in the Global South, specifically in Ghana, India, Kenya, Nigeria, Pakistan,

Rwanda, Tanzania, Uganda and Ethiopia. Those companies, Acumen claims, have served about 150 million people and created over 60,000 jobs.

However, doing massive social good may not be the only motivating factor behind the contagion of social venture capital (SVC), outlined by Zaidman, as nonprofit organizations, foundations, corporations, and banks have the potential to achieve double-digit annual returns on their investment. In effect, Acumen's donors (called "partners") contribute tax-deductible capital to the nonprofit fund for robust returns. Acumen's network includes notable investors such as the Bill & Melinda Gates Foundation ($13 million donated), the Aman Foundation, the Skoll Foundation, the International Finance Corporation (IFC, the World Bank's private sector arm), the German Development Bank, and Industrial Promotion Services (the private equity arm of the Aga Khan Foundation) (Batavia et al. 2011). Moreover, board members such as Nobel Prize–winner Joseph E. Stiglitz, Andrea Soros Colombel (the daughter of billionaire financier George Soros), Naveed Riaz (the chief executive officer for the Africa Division for Citigroup), and billionaire Michael Novogratz (former partner of Goldman Sachs Global Securities Division and current principal and director at the investment firm Fortress Investment Group) constitute a powerful cadre of global elites in the service of the poor.

Moreover, other SVC funds are quickly joining this elite and powerful global humanitarian assemblage. The Tandem Fund, Venturesome Fund, Bridges Ventures, and Gray Ghost Ventures, share some similarities with Acumen but differ in geographical and industry focus, and range widely in terms of social and financial returns (Batavia et al. 2011). Two recent superstars to enter this growing humanitarian assemblage are worth mention here. First is the Africa Health Fund, launched by the London-based private equity firm Aureos Capital in June 2009, with backing from the International Finance Corporation, the African Development Bank, DFG (a New York–based Securities and Exchange Commission–registered asset management firm specializing in structured and alternative credit products), and the Bill & Melinda Gates Foundation. This $105 million fund will focus on improving access to finance for African health-care companies by investing in African clinics and other health-care providers (Bill & Melinda Gates Foundation 2015). Going forward, investments will focus on late-stage health-care delivery enterprises in Africa that have the potential to achieve an annual return of 10 percent to 15 percent (Batavia et al. 2011).

The second recent and notable entrée into this social enterprise space is the Global Innovation Fund (GIF), launched in September 2014 and supported by the Department of International Development in the UK, the USAID, the Omidyar Network, the Swedish International Development Cooperation Agency, and the Department for Foreign Affairs and Trade in Australia. To date, these partners have pledged over US$200 million over the next five years and will distribute money through grants, loans, and equity investments to creative, pioneering social innovations that aim to improve the lives and opportunities of millions of people in the developing world (Global Innovation Fund 2015).

Like Acumen, the Tandem Fund and the GIF are experimenting with new approaches to aid delivery. As Zaidman explains, these social venture capitalists see their role as much greater than simply the capital conduit of massive social good.

> We also realize we have [to] provide more than just capital. We also invest in supply management support, we play a role on the board[s] [of the companies we invest [in], and we think about how we can leverage networks to support these companies.

This insight became apparent to Acumen after early efforts to simply bankroll good intentions, such as a low-cost point-of-care diagnostic for dengue fever, which incurred cost overruns and other local barriers and ultimately never reached its intended audience. Much to Acumen's disbelief, it turned out that local conditions really did matter. "And so we moved into a whole new business model that was very much informed and educated by early failure," Zaidman reflects. "It is not enough to have a great gadget. . . . You have to think about distribution, you have to think about maintenance of products, marketing of products, [and] really building that whole [humanitarian] infrastructure."

But Acumen, of course, is not the only nonprofit organization who claims that the barriers to poverty alleviation and the limits to their philanthropic efforts are rooted in local conditions, such as supply chains or the culture of local management. Nowhere is this captured more clearly than in a YouTube video of Ned Breslin, former CEO of Water for People.[2] Standing (naked) in front of an improved water source project that Water for People supported in western Uganda, Breslin declares that he is "offended by the fact that this" five-month-old "project is not sustainable." He goes on to say that "the construction is spectacular" and that "the engineer . . . did a beautiful job." "Everything looks great," Breslin continues, "but the naked truth [the title of the video] is, this project is going to fail." For Breslin, the reason for failure is simple:

> The reason is not because of the quality of the construction, not because of the great work that our [engineering] partner did, it is because the financing for this system is not in place. That is the story of hand pumps throughout Africa. . . . The biggest problem in Uganda is functionality. Hand pumps get put in, tariffs aren't collected, management is weak,[3] and the systems fail.

For this CEO the "biggest problem in Uganda" and "throughout Africa" is not the virtuous non-human hand pump but, rather, local government officials, who, according to Breslin, are unable to manage this new infrastructure. Also for Breslin, the solution to these local problems is equally clear:

We have come back, and we've seen that this system, though beautiful, is not sustainable. So we need to turn this around; we need to finance in different ways to support our partners, so that they can continue to work long after the project is finished, and only then will this community truly emerge from water poverty.

Like Acumen, Water for People has begun to recognize that investments alone are not sufficient to guarantee successful returns in emerging markets. And again, like Acumen, Water for People has turned to financial innovation in local markets as a solution to transcending or even bypassing local blockages and barriers that might arise, whether customary, bureaucratic, or illicit—a reason often expressed by many do-gooders in the West (Nordstrom 2007).

Working in ten countries, and with revenues of over $14 million, Water for People is a major player in the water aid world, and it, too, is now experimenting with innovative ways to engage in venture philanthropy in emerging markets in the service of the world's poor and dispossessed. "We are now looking into bigger roles in business," stressed a Water for People manager during a conversation over drinks after a long day of fieldwork. "We're now bringing in more folks in finance because they know this [humanitarianism and charity] better than anything, especially folks that work in international markets." Water.org, another major player in the water aid world, is also looking at financial innovation as a way to increase and stabilize its water aid programs. An employee expanded on the importance of proper finance for its projects:

> Water.org has water credit where they loan community share households money so they can build the water project and then they pay [it] off. We have something similar, which is sanitation loans for folks in India. They do it for folks in India, some in the slum areas, but most of them in the rural areas, and we are working our way into more densely populated areas.

In many ways, what sets one nonprofit organization apart from another is its ability to achieve and secure financial independence and returns, for themselves, their partners, and their new customers—the poor. And, like Acumen and Water.org, Water for People also works closely with donors, supply chains, and other partners in the service of the poor. For example, in addition to distributing financial aid, many partners have taken on a definitive role in the management and direction of their humanitarian ventures. For example, under Breslin's tenure, of the eight "global sponsors"—companies that had donated between $100,000 and $999,999 each—three of them also had executives who served on their board of directors. Similarly, executives from two of the five "continental sponsors"— companies that had donated between $50,000 and $99,999—were also members of Water for People's board (Table 3.1). Many of those on Water for People's board of directors also occupied managerial and executive positions in other water

Table 3.1 Water for People (WfP) Global Corporate Sponsors (donated between $100,000 and $999,999)

Sponsor	Type of business	Additional ties to WfP
CDM Smith	A private consulting, engineering, construction, and operations firm in water, environment, transportation, energy, and facilities	Senior vice president—member of WfP Board of Directors.
AECOM Technology Corporation	A public company providing technical and management support services to a broad range of markets, including transportation, facilities, environmental, energy, water, and government.	
American Water	The largest public water and wastewater utility company in the United States	
American Water Works Association	A nonprofit organization that provides water quality and supply information and other water industry resources to its members.	Founded WfP in 1991
CH2M HILL	Engineering consulting and service provider.	Managing director—member of WfP Board of Directors. Employees "volunteer" in the regional operations
Green Mountain Coffee Roasters	Producer of coffee and coffee-brewing devices	
Nalco Company	A public company involved in water treatment and process improvement services.	Chief marketing officer and VP of sales, Americas; member of WfP Board of Directors. Employees "volunteer" in regional operations
Xylem	A public company involved in water and waste water treatment and process improvement services.	

technology and service sectors, including engineering consulting and banking (see Figure 3.2). Some corporate donors also supplied the volunteer labor force required to carry out program work. For example, in one of Water for People's baseline assessments, the project manager was an engineer from CH2M HILL. He was intensely involved in the planning, data gathering, and reporting phases of the project. In-kind technical support and guidance for the baseline assessment were provided by three employees from Nalco, one of five "continental sponsors."

In addition to working closely with corporate donations, humanitarians wanting to change the way in which the world tackles poverty have also sought out foundations that share an equally entrepreneurial vision to combating poverty and other social problems. In 2010 Water for People received a $5.6 million grant from the Bill & Melinda Gates Foundation to support its Sanitation as a Business program. The goal of this program is to introduce profit incentives to the improvement of sanitation in households and schools in "developing" countries. According to Water for People, this program will transform "unsustainable, subsidy-based sanitation programs" into "sustainable, profitable sanitation services" by "merging business principles of market research and segmentation" with community involvement and program monitoring (Water for People 2010). This grant, according to an employee, has put Water for People "on the [humanitarian] map." "That just lifts us to a whole new category of nonprofit." "People [subsistence farmers] in developing countries," a Water for People employee explained to me, "understand composting; they just don't know [or] understand the business side of it. So, what Water for People is trying to do is branch out of sanitation and make it lucrative for business."

For Acumen, Water for People, and others joining this mushrooming cadre of transglobal humanitarians, "partnering with corporations" and "using the tools of business . . . to finance in different ways" are not about simply helping the poor but about empowering them as consumers as well. The poor are not merely dispossessed or victims; they are also customers, self-interested individuals who should be able to choose and not be told by, say, governments, what is in their best interest. "As we have progressed," Zaidman explains, "we have begun to define dignity not just as a lack of income but also as a lack of choice or opportunity." In effect, choice and opportunity equal free people. This belief in the morality of the marketplace is so strong that there is little room for other considerations. For these new humanitarians, providing individual freedom and choice in the marketplace of humanitarianism is the only way to design "a world that works for everyone."

Capital Is Not Enough

If Africa represents the laboratory in which to test modern technologies of empire, as the historian Helen Tilley (2011) has argued, then Acumen is the studio where experiments in humanitarianism are devised, conducted, and recorded.

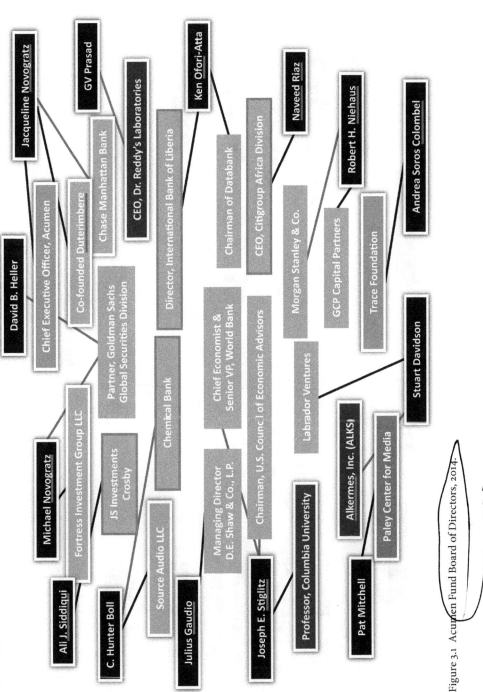

Figure 3.1 Acumen Fund Board of Directors, 2014.

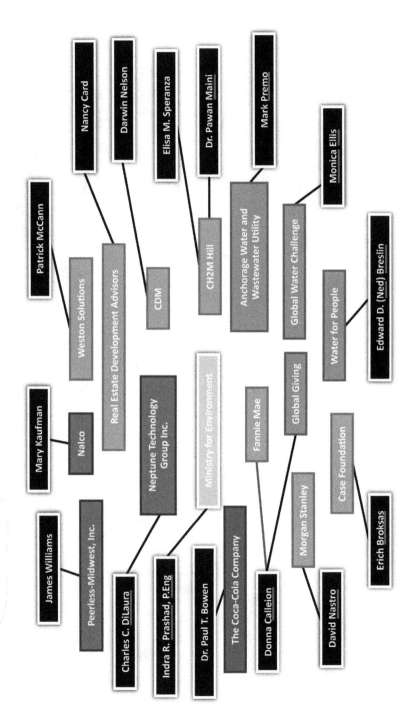

Figure 3.2 Water for People Board of Directors, 2013–2014.

These trials of humanitarianism call not only for new types of governing apparati but also for new kinds of knowledge and expertise—in effect, Zaidman asserts, "a new vision for the world."

> We also know that it is not enough to have a diverse, exciting, dynamic pool of social enterprises, that we [also] need a new leadership model that goes beyond the [social enterprise] space and penetrates global institutions and global corporations. So in some way our leadership work has opened up to us the notion that for Acumen changing the way the world tackles poverty begins with our portfolio but really goes much further into the space of leadership, and really changing the way people think.

Operating like a true multinational, Acumen has offices around the world. "In each place where we have an office," Zaidman explains, "we are working to build a local community of donors, partners, entrepreneurs, and more and more young people who are eager to be a part of this. We have chapters in many of these geographies, and we are now offering a global curriculum . . . that we share now through our global fellows program, [and] through regional fellows programs in each of the countries that we invest [in], as well as an online leadership curriculum."

The Acumen Fund Fellows program has become one of its most valuable and sought-after credentials among aspiring do-gooders. In 2010 the Fellows Program attracted more than 600 applications from 60 countries for 10 spots. The fellowship involves eight weeks of leadership training at Acumen's New York headquarters and ten months in the field with an Acumen investee (Batavia et al. 2011). For many young aspiring entrepreneurs who cut their humanitarian teeth at prestigious global studies schools, like Columbia, Princeton, and George Washington University, being chosen as a Acumen Fellow signifies that they are among the chosen few to have obtained not only the necessary competencies and expertise but also an open-ended license to do massive social good. "We need a whole new universe of these entrepreneurs making change," admits Zaidman, "and our dream is that alumni from these programs will go onto create significant social impact by building sustainable innovations and initiatives that can solve some of the world's most pressing problems."

A recent PBS documentary, "The New Recruits," followed three business students—Heidi Krauel, Joel Montgomery, and Suraj Sudhakar—who were chosen as Acumen Fellows in 2009 and assigned to work with startups selling drip irrigation in Pakistan, LED [light-emitting diode] lights in India, and toilet service in Kenya. The documentary portrays the deep hubris of these highly educated, well-intended, and naive do-gooders and casts reasonable doubt about the ideology and realism of solving the problem of global poverty with the same mind-set and institutions that created it, namely, competition and capitalism. The documentary scratches the surface of numerous tensions and contradictions of treating the poor primarily as consumers keen to accept Western technology, know-how, and products. And for all the rhetoric about giving the consumer voice and choice, many of the practical efforts illustrated in the documentary were spent on securing markets and supply chains for the products of Acumen's investees. In effect, shifting the risk of humanitarian research and development away from the financers and onto the local community.

Of course, Acumen is not the only organization to offer internships, fellowships, and other educational opportunities to change the way in which the world thinks about and tackles poverty and other social problems. The London-based multinational Pearson, the world's largest for-profit education business and owner of the *Financial Times*, with adjusted operating profits of £720m or approximately $1.1 billion[4] in 2014, continues to blur the line between government services and business opportunities when it comes to education policy and practice. Taking on the role of a quasi-government agency, Pearson has continued to expand its influence over all aspects of education, including assessment, pedagogy, curriculum, management, funding, certification, and policy, to the point that it is difficult to determine what part of education Pearson and its subsidiaries have not influenced. Moreover, while the United States and the UK continue to be Pearson's two largest markets, evidence of the firm's global education strategy can be seen in its publication of textbooks in South Africa and Brazil, in digital learning products in Australia, in English-language schools in China and Saudi Arabia, and in online university partnerships in Mexico. Pearson Schools, a subsidiary of Pearson PLC, educates more than 130 million students worldwide in over 60 countries. According to its parent company, Pearson Schools is the fastest-growing chain of schools in India, with 27 schools in 17 cities, educating over 15,000 students across the country. And because schools are so much more than brick and mortar, Pearson also provides textbooks, digital content, teacher training, and clinical assessment to help educate India's aspiring middle class. Many people might disagree with my labeling of a multinational corporation such as Pearson as humanitarian, but its efforts to provide education to poor families can be viewed as an attempt to do massive social good, albeit while making a hefty profit.

In Kenya, Bridge International Academies, founded by the American entrepreneur Jay Kimmelman, is merging the power of information and communication technology, the spirit of entrepreneurialism, and the acumen of business to revolutionize primary education for the world's poorest of the poor. To date, Bridge International Academies has set up more than 200 private for-profit primary schools in Kenya, where students learn a standardized and scripted curriculum developed by Bridge International, which is delivered on an e-reader tablet. The advantage of a standardized curriculum, Kimmelman suggests, is that all students in all schools in a particular grade are learning the exact same content at the same time. It is also a tremendously efficient and cost-effective way to provide education to the poor, claims Kimmelman. It currently costs a Kenyan family $5 a month on average to send their child to a Bridge school. Bridge was scheduled to open its first schools in Nigeria and Uganda in 2015 and planned to enter India by 2016. Its goal is to educate 1 million preschool and primary-school children by 2017 and 10 million by 2025.

Moreover, Kimmelman is not the only entrepreneur who believes that the for-profit education model will "disrupt the way the world learns." Some of Bridge's major backers include Bill Gates; JPMorgan; Omidyar Network, a nonprofit venture philanthropist organization established in 2004 by eBay founder Pierre Omidyar; the CDC Group,[5] the UK's Development Finance Institution, whose mission is to support the building of businesses throughout Africa and South Asia, to create jobs, and to make a lasting difference in the life of people in some of the world's poorest places; the International Finance Corporation (IFC) of the World Bank; and Facebook's Mark Zuckerberg. Bridge has also attracted the support of venture capital firms New Enterprise Associates (NEA), Khosla Ventures, and Learn Capital, in which Pearson is a limited partner.

However, in July 2016, almost a year after they opened their first schools, Bridge International was ordered by the Uganda's High Court to close their sixty-three schools over widespread concerns about poor sanitation, inadequate infrastructure, unqualified teachers, and not following the national curriculum. Moreover, the school has courted controversy elsewhere. In Kenya, for example, the teacher's unions and nongovernmental organizations have publicly called for the closure of Bridge International schools, saying that the schools were compromising teaching standards. To its accustions by the Uganda High Court, Bridge International, along with its major backers, have decided to go to court to fight the High Court's decision (British Broadcasting Corporation 2016).

In addition to Bridge International Academies, Pearson is also an investor in Omega Schools, another private low-cost chain located in Ghana with 38 schools and over 20,000 students. According to Bridge cofounder Shannon May, low-fee private schools in sub-Saharan Africa alone make up a virtually untapped $14.5 billion market (Sulaiman 2014). Bridge International, along with its investors, believes that low-fee private schools can help increase access to and improve the quality of education in developing countries and be profitable—in effect, doing good and doing well. However, the recent controversy in Uganda might seem to indicate otherwise.

But when we consider the generosity and ambition of the latest crop of superrich, we gain a better understanding of the true magnitude of this new humanitarian movement. Saudi Prince Alwaleed bin Talal, for example, is one of the more notable to recently announce a personal donation of $32 billion to philanthropic causes. In his announcement, Prince Alwaleed stated that his gift "is a commitment without boundaries. A commitment to all humankind." This "groundbreaking gift" will be administered by the prince's Alwaleed Philanthropies foundation and will focus on finding impactful solutions to some of the most pressing humanitarian issues of our time, without regard to gender, race, or religious affiliation (Alwaleed Philanthropies 2015). Since starting his foundation in 2000, the richest man in the world—Bill Gates—has spent more than half a billion dollars on educational causes, including $150 million in grants to establish Common Core standards in the United States. In an increasingly unequal country and world, the Gates Foundation has signaled that philanthropy can and should be a central mechanism in educational reform and, by default, the remaking of society.

King's College London received a £20 million ($31 million) gift for its School of Law from Dickson Poon, a Hong Kong–based philanthropist, in an effort to redefine transnational law. Poon is among the latest crop of billionaire humanists who have decided to use their wealth to influence elite academic institutions. Oxford University is now home to both the Blavatnik School of Government, supported with a £75 million ($116 million) gift from the metal and oils baron, and newly turned philanthropist, Len Blavatnik, and the Said Business School, founded with a £20 million ($31 million) gift from Wafic Said, a Syrian-Saudi financier, businessman, and philanthropist (Freeland 2012). Many of these gifts, however, are not really free. For example, the Walton Foundation, backed by the family that founded Walmart, has spent more than $1 billion supporting various charter schools and voucher programs that seek to establish alternatives to the current public school system in the United States (Sorkin 2014). This form of educational philanthropy, however, is rarely directed at programs, services, and institutions that might directly benefit the poor or dispossessed.

Whereas institutions of teaching and learning were formerly rooted in national economies and state-based direction and funding, today education, like the capitalist production process itself, has become increasingly expansive, transnational, and interlinked with circuits of accumulation, finance, and commodity trade in differentiated world markets. In the so-called developing world, education itself has become a growing sector of emerging markets. However, the ambition of these "educational" institutions and the latest crop of millionaire and billionaires committed to solving the "defining moral issue of our time" does not stop at helping the poor. They want to use their wealth and influence to reshape not only the way the world governs poverty but also how it thinks about (governmentality) poor people. Effectively transforming how the welfare of the majority of the world's population is to be understood and managed.

Feeding this new humanitarian movement of "educational" institutions and people committed to solving the "defining moral issue of our time" is the disquieting relationship in which humanitarianism is now embedded: crushing poverty and unprecedented wealth. Today, eighty-five people control the same amount of wealth as half the world's population. In the United States, the wealthiest 1 percent have captured 95 percent of post-financial crisis growth since 2009, while the bottom 90 percent became poorer. This pattern is repeated throughout the world as the richest 1 percent increased its share of income in twenty-four out of twenty-six countries (for which data exist) between 1980 and 2012 (Oxfam International 2014). It appears that the astute observation of Andrew Mellon—the US Treasury secretary during the Great Crash of 1929, and one of America's richest men at that time—that in a financial crisis "assets return to their rightful owners" (namely, the rich) appears to hold as true today as in the past.

For the latest crop of millionaire and billionaire humanitarians who have decided to use their wealth and influence to change the way the world governs poverty, the favorable solution to rising global inequality—if, in fact, they acknowledge this disquieting trend—is one rooted in innovative, definitively measureable, and readily scalable humanitarian gadgets and systems. What is notable about this new class of superrich philanthropists is that finance capital, social entrepreneurialism, and business management principles (i.e., the market) remain reliable allies in creating new possibilities for the prosperity of the rest of humanity. Moreover, this belief in the morality of the marketplace is not only shared by those who have amassed their fortunes from them. For example, Julia Gillard, former prime minister of Australia and chair of the Board of Directors of the Global Partnership for Education, an international nongovernmental organization focused on educating children in the world's poorest countries, argues that the business community—not schools, teachers, the local community, or even education researchers—must be engaged in a more meaningful way to lead global education efforts. However, the fundamental weakness of this and other educational strategies of the business-minded and the affluent, as Robert Arnove (1980) and other scholars have pointed out, is that, first and foremost, it helps to reinforce a stratified economic and political order that benefits the ruling-class interests of philanthropists, not change it. For all their elaborate efforts to find a solution to "the way the world tackles poverty," and "a new vision for the world . . . that works for everyone." Those leading this humanitarian crusade spend very little time and effort asking another relevant question: why is the gap between the rich and poor continuing to increase in the face of unprecedented humanitarianism?

Accumulation by Dispossession

In seeking answers to the problem of rising rates of poverty and inequality in the face of unprecedented wealth, it is important to remember that the crises conditions of the world's poor—mostly located in the Global South—is the direct result of the management and manipulation of crises by those in the North. Moreover, it is equally important to recognize that the major advocates for, and beneficiaries of, this form of "disaster capitalism" (Klein 2007), many of them identified above, are also the major supporters of humanitarian aid around the world today. At first glance, this observation may seem contradictory. However, in his analysis of the rise of British imperialism, Karl Polanyi (1944, 132) observed that the destructive tendencies inherent in the expansion of the market system in the late nineteenth and early twentieth centuries inevitably called for demands for social protection by those most affected. This planned expansion of the market system, Polanyi (1944, 139) maintained, "was synonymous with the simultaneous spreading of international free trade, competitive labor market and [the] gold standard." So devastating were the effects of the self-regulating market, Polanyi (1944, 132) insisted, that not only human beings and natural resources but "also the organization of capitalistic production itself had to be sheltered from the devastating effects of a self-regulating market." This contradiction between the tendency of capital to relentlessly transform geographical landscapes and communities into commodities, on the one hand, and the tendency of those communities embedded in those landscapes to resist such relentless transformations, on the other, is fundamental to the workings of global capitalism (Arrighi 2007; see also Marx 1976 [1867]; Polanyi 1944). Resistance, for Polanyi (1944, 132), relied "on the varying support of those most immediately affected by the deleterious action of the market—primarily, but not exclusively, the working and the landed classes—and their ability to bring forth "protective legislation, restrictive associations, and other instruments of intervention." What is notable from this historical perspective is that resistance to the devastating effects of a self-regulating market did not come from those profiting from a system of uneven development but rather from those most immediately affected.

And yet, as Polanyi's (1944) double movement seems to be unfolding before our very eyes, two important conjunctural distinctions need to recognized. First, demands for social protections today are largely in the form of market solutions, as opposed to protective legislation as in the past. Second, calls for social protection, particularly for increased humanitarian aid and charity, are increasingly coming from the mouths of NGOs, philanthropists, and foundations in the Global North and not necessarily from those alienated by the workings of global capitalism, as suggested by Polanyi—in this case the dispossessed mainly living in the Global South. This leaves us with yet another paradox of humanitarian government: the very methods and institutions responsible for causing unprecedented global inequality also form the preconditions for its relief.

In order to more fully understand this paradox, we need to place the present conjuncture in its historical context. The dynamic history of these opposing tendencies, as Marx (1976 [1867], 876) pointed out long ago, "assumes different aspects in different countries, and runs through its various phases in different orders of succession, and at different historical epochs." In effect, reflecting the particular historical conditions (or conjuncture) of its time—in Marx's case, late nineteenth-century capitalism. The expansion of Britain's empire to different parts of the world, Marx (1976 [1867]) argued, occurred through a process he called primitive accumulation. But Marx (1976 [1867]) was careful to preface this label with the descriptor "so-called," so as to insist on its particular historical conditions and preclude the idea that this transition to capitalism was somehow natural or idyllic. "In actual history," Marx (1976 [1867], 874) writes, "it is a notorious fact that conquest, enslavement, robbery, murder, in short, force, play the greatest part." For Marx, the combination of a newly created government-sanctioned system of public credit, and its "brood of bankocrats, financiers, rentiers, brokers, job-seekers, etc." (1976 [1867], 920), an international credit system, the modern system of taxation, and the slave trade, among other causes, created the "artificial means" (1976 [1867], 937) that the British empire used to widen and deepen its hegemony over global affairs. In his analysis of how the geographic expansion of capitalism has also contributed to its survival, Neil Smith (2008, 128) points out that the colonies (or the Global South) provide a special function for capital, namely, "through the relations of foreign trade, and economic and geographic expansion, the contradictions at the heart of capital can, to a greater of lesser extent, be displaced toward the periphery of the system (i.e. the poor)," allowing this transnational system of uneven development not only to survive but to expand. Smith (2008), like Marx (1976 [1867]), also noted that the realities of the system became more vivid and apparent at a distance than from the center (see also Harvey 2005, 2006).

By contrast, the conjunctural character of this historical moment varies greatly. The United States and the Soviet Union, not Britain, shaped a mutually reinforcing conjunction during the last decade of the twentieth century. On the one hand, the collapse of the Soviet Union opened up entirely new markets to Western power and interest. To many, the fall of communism signaled both the triumph and legitimacy of Western capitalism and its apparent connection with democracy. On the other hand, the opening up of these new territories to Western capital interests represented a new form of primitive accumulation, one that scholar David Harvey (2003), has called "accumulation by dispossession." What makes dispossession different from primitive accumulation, Harvey (2005, 178) argued, is that dispossession is "fragmented and particular—a privatization here, and environmental degradation there, a financial crisis of indebtedness somewhere else." This peculiarity and specificity makes it difficult to recognize and even more difficult to systematically oppose. This form of accumulation by dispossession was triggered by a major and rapid restructuring of the international system, under the not-so-direct supervision of the United States, United Kingdom, and other core states, keen to take advantage of this unique opportunity (i.e., the Group of Seven). Above all, Harvey (2011, 16) noted, was the restructuring of a new global financial architecture that facilitated the easy international flow of liquid money capital to wherever it could be used most profitably. "The deregulation of finance that began in the late 1970s," Harvey (2011, 16) concluded, "accelerated after 1986 and became unstoppable in the 1990s." In effect, the legacy of this global and political conjuncture, which began with the debt crisis of the late 1970s and subsequent restructuring of Third World economies in the 1980s, morphed into demands by the West (from the World Bank, IMF, and later the WTO, all supported by Washington) for the privatization, deregulation, and cessation of government spending everywhere (Rosenberg 2005).

In this context, in the 1990s international flows of private finance increased more than sixfold (from $44 billion at the start of the decade to $256 billion by 1998), as limitless sums of money were able to circumnavigate the globe at great speed, betting on everything from cocoa to currencies and resulting in enormous volatility wherever it touched down (Thomas 1999). Over the same period (1990–1998), public flows of overseas development assistance dwindled by 40 percent to its lowest level in fifty years. In 1998, the figure stood at $33 billion, equivalent to 0.25 percent of the GDP of First World countries (Thomas 1999). Poor countries were left with few alternatives to this form of shock therapy but to accept the West's recipe to remove or reduce state regulations, privatize common resources, and defund social programs.

The human costs of the past decade of such social engineering are simply immense. Systematic data on dispossession is always difficult to gather, and linking *this* policy with *that* dispossession is often impossible, if not futile. However, in 2003 the United Nations Human Settlements Programme (UN-Habitat) released a report titled "The Challenge of the Slums: Global Report on Human Settlements," which may represent the first truly global audit and chilling assessment of urban poverty (UN-Habitat 2003). The report (UN-Habitat 2003, xxviiii) is about the astonishing prevalence of slums—"the places where poor people struggle to make a living and bring up their families, and the places where about one third of the world's urban population live." Moreover, while the "Washington Consensus" types (World Bank, IMF, etc.) have insisted on defining the problem of global inequality as a result of bad governance or failed states, this report broke with traditional UN circumspection and self-censorship to squarely indict neoliberalism, especially the IMF's structural adjustment programs, as the chief cause of the rapid increase in urban poverty (Davis 2004).

Slums may have been around for centuries, yet they still lack an agreed-upon definition. As a result, an enumeration of slums has not yet been incorporated into mainstream monitoring instruments, such as national population censuses, demographic and health surveys, and global surveys (UN-Habitat 2003). Actual numbers, then, may be much higher than reported. An operational definition used in the UN-Habitat report included any area that combines, to various degrees, the following characteristics: inadequate access to safe water, inadequate access to sanitation and other infrastructure, poor structural quality of housing, overcrowding, and insecure residential status (UN-Habitat 2003). The report (2003) estimated that about 924 million people lived in slums worldwide in 2001, about 32 percent of the global urban population. The incidence of slums in African cities and many smaller cities in other parts of the developing world is over 50 percent. Asia has about 60 percent of the world's slum dwellers. Africa has about 20 percent, but this is growing quickly. Latin America has 14 percent (UN-Habitat 2003). The world's highest percentage of slum-dwellers live in Ethiopia (an astonishing 99.4 percent of the urban population), Chad (also 99.4 percent), Afghanistan (98.5 percent), and Nepal (92 percent) (Global Urban Observatory 2003). In Delhi, planners complain bitterly about "slums within slums" as squatters take over the small open spaces of the peripheral resettlement colonies from which the old urban poor were brutally removed in the mid-1970s. In Cairo and Phnom Penh, recent urban arrivals squat or rent space on rooftops: creating slum cities in the air (Davis 2004).

Moreover, in the majority of cases, slum dwellers exist outside the law of the country where they live and work. As a consequence, they are often unable to access social services, such as subsidized health care or education, which are largely used by the middle class and more affluent. Governments, in many cases, refuse to provide them with services on the grounds that their settlements are not legal, even though many may have been in place for over fifty years and comprise a majority of the population (UN-Habitat 2003). This form of double dispossession—first "pushing" people out of the countryside, where they most often had access to some custom of entitlements in the form of land, labor, and social institutions, and then forcing them to live in a state of permanent insecurity and illegality, with no opportunities for decent employment, let alone access to health care, education, or other social services—is nothing short of a crime against a mass of humanity. The specific artificial crises or means of dispossession vary significantly: mechanization of local agriculture in Java and India, food imports in Mexico, Haiti, and Kenya, civil war and drought throughout Africa (Davis 2004; UN-Habitat 2003). Nevertheless the end remains the same all over the Global South: immense global inequality. Those elites who could get out left for the oil-rich Arab countries and the Western world, further eroding local capacity and decisively hindering any chance of organized resistance (Odun Balogun 1995). Regardless of how one counts, this dispossession of the majority of humankind represents a watershed in human history.

The Business of Humanitarianism

Why are the nouveau riche so interested in helping the world's poor? Before answering this question, it might be informative to return to the great recession of the twenty-first century, a moment that turned out to be deeply profitable for many of them, and consider their actions during a time of grave financial crisis for the world's majority. Shortly after Lehman Brothers declared bankruptcy in September 2008, David Harvey (2011) writes, a few Treasury officials and bankers, including Treasury Secretary Henry Paulson, a past chairman and chief executive officer of Goldman Sachs, emerged from a meeting with a document that requested a $700 billion bailout of the banking system. And a few weeks later, Congress, and then-President George W. Bush provided a life preserver to financial institutions that were deemed "too big to fail." Left to float away, however, were over 2 million people who lost their homes, as housing values plummeted across the United States, with many owing more on their asset than it was worth. These events marked the worst US economic crisis since the 1930s, resulting in foreclosures on millions of homes, the shuttering of businesses, and large-scale unemployment. European economies were in equally serious difficulty, though unevenly, with Spain, Greece, Ireland, and some countries in the former Eastern Europe Bloc hardest hit. We should also remember that in the United States, big banks targeted blacks and Hispanics by charging them higher interest rates and fees than equally qualified white customers. As a result, African-American and Hispanic borrowers were more than twice as likely to be placed in subprime loans as non-Hispanic white borrowers who had similar credit qualifications. No life preserver was given to these families of color in the United States, and many lost their homes between 2005 and 2008.

In the last three months of 2008 alone, Merrill Lynch lost $21.5 billion, forcing a US Treasury–backed takeover by Bank of America worth $20 billion. However, as bad as 2008 was for Merrill, the discredited financier paid out an estimated $3 billion to $4 billion in bonuses in December 2008, a month before the takeover. The total compensation bill paid to top executives at Merrill in 2008 was said to have been around $15 billion, a sum reported to be only 6 percent lower than in 2007 (*Telegraph* 2009). Similarly, the insurance giant American International Group (AIG), which suffered the largest corporate loss in history, $61.7 billion in the fourth quarter of 2007, received a bailout from the US Treasury and Federal Reserve of more than $170 billion, $85 billion in the form of a two-year loan from the Treasury. And, like Merrill Lynch, it paid its top executives handsomely, $165 million in bonus payments, in addition to $121 million in previously scheduled bonuses for the company's senior executives and 6,400 employees (Andrews and Baker 2009). Of course, banking executives were not the only financiers to profit heavily during the financial crisis. In 2007, the top three hedge fund owners—who essentially made money by hedging their bets—made almost $10 billion. John Paulson of Paulson & Co. earned $3.7 billion, George Soros, the chairman of Soros Fund Management, earned $2.9 billion, and James Simons of Renaissance Technologies earned $2.8 billion. Goldman Sachs had its most profitable year to date in 2007, earning $17.6 billion pretax, including

$4 billion from its hedge funds. In 2009, a year after the crisis "ended", Goldman did even better, earning almost $20 billion pretax.

In April 2010, the Permanent Senate Subcommittee on Investigations held official hearings after conducting a year-and-a-half–long investigation of the role of investment banks and credit rating agencies in the financial crisis of 2008. Speaking at the fourth hearing, Chairman Carl Levin (D-MI) said:

> Investment banks such as Goldman Sachs were not simply market-makers, they were self-interested promoters of risky and complicated financial schemes that helped trigger the crisis. . . . They bundled toxic mortgages into complex financial instruments, got the credit agencies to label them as AAA securities, and sold them to investors, magnifying and spreading risk throughout the financial system, and all too often betting against the instruments they sold and profiting at the expense of their clients.

Internal emails from company executives revealed how they used residential mortgage-backed securities and collateralized debt obligations (CDOs),[6] financial instruments that were key in the financial crisis, to profit from the mortgage mess. One email in particular, from David Viniar, the chief financial officer of Goldman Sachs, explained that, in one day, the firm netted over $50 million by taking short positions (i.e., betting on a downturn) that increased in value as the mortgage market cratered (United States Senate 2010). In effect, they made decisions that put their needs ahead of those of their clients. For its transgressions, Goldman Sachs settled the Federal Housing Finance Agency's lawsuit for about $1.2 billion. In total, the Federal Housing Finance Agency (FHFA), which oversees the secondary mortgage market of the Federal National Mortgage Association (FNMA), commonly known as Fannie Mae, and the Federal Home Loan Mortgage Corporation (FHLMC), commonly known as Freddie Mac, filed lawsuits against 18 banks and over 130 executives for their involvement in misleading the public about the quality and riskiness of the loans underlying the securities they sold to Fannie and Freddie. The world's largest banks are still wading through a thicket of legal and regulatory proceedings that are the result of their self-serving actions in the years leading up to the worst financial crisis ever in the United States. The Goldman payment comes on the heels of a settlement with the Bank of America that totaled $16.65 billion. JPMorgan Chase paid $4 billion as part of its bigger $13 billion settlement, and Morgan Stanley settled its FHFA suit for $1.25 billion (Baer and Light 2014).

What this litany illustrates is that these "best of business" leaders—as Yasmina Zaidman describes them—clearly put their own affairs and interests ahead of others, even clients. So the question remains, if these folks are more concerned about helping themselves than others when financial push comes to personal shove, then how are we to understand why this very same group cares so much about those less fortunate, when evidence overwhelming contradicts such an idea. I am not particularly interested in the psychology of these new humanitarians, as plenty has been written about that subject, but I am interested in the sociology of trust as it pertains to doing massive good. Here I am struck by Zaidman's comments about Acumen's rigorous anticorruption policy:

> We work with entrepreneurs who share our zero-tolerance policy for corruption because corruption is the biggest tax on the poor. They are always the ones that suffer the most . . . so we think there is no other pathway forward then to confront it head on, and if it means that we have to walk away from a company [then] we will do so.

This mantra that the poor suffer the most from corruption is constantly repeated among social enterprises and their partners, most often attached to the management and manipulation of those in the South—people, businesses, and governments. Jim Yong Kim, the president of the World Bank, has repeatedly advised that corruption is the biggest obstacle in the fight against poverty: "it is simply stealing from the poor." Recall that Kim cancelled the bank's $1.2 billion loan in support of the Padma Multipurpose Bridge project in 2012 in an effort to hold corrupt Bangladeshi officials accountable. Like the World Bank, Acumen is "willing to hold up, suspend and even cancel projects if they cannot be done in some sort of ethical matter."

"Going through the list of companies," Zaidman explains, "Goldman Sachs [and] other companies that we have worked with—Dow Chemicals having the most infamous legacy, "[including] Coca-Cola, [all have] huge issues in India." However, she continues, "I think the moment we decided to engage with the global corporation, we knew that we were going to be working with companies that have messy histories [and] that they have made poor decisions again as part of a system that I think is broken." In effect, Zaidman believes, partners—Western-based transnational corporations—can and should be trusted, regardless of their past and present transgressions. The fact that a company such as Union Carbide—and its present parent company Dow Chemicals, a company "proud of the contributions chemistry has made to humanity"—is also responsible for what is considered the world's worst industrial disaster (when chemicals leaked from its pesticide plant in Bhopal, India, and swiftly killed thousands in December 1984) does not seem to register on Acumen's moral compass. Over thirty years later, Dow's legacy lives on in Bhopal, as more than 25,000 people have died and over 500,000 have suffered a variety of ailments—cancer, tuberculosis, and birth defects, among others—from long-term exposure to methyl isocyanate. Coca-Cola is currently accused of causing water shortages, pollution of groundwater and soil, and exposure to toxic waste and pesticides from its fifty-six bottling facilities in India, where approximately 70 percent of the population depends on agriculture (water and land) to make a living, yet this is not enough for Acumen to "walk away" from a valued partner, either.

Moreover, in her terse assessment of enduring poverty, Zaidman plainly points to the destructive tendencies inherent in the expansion of the market system—transnational finance, international free trade, and competitive global labor markets—as the main obstacles to ending enduring poverty and injustice. "The system," as she plainly describes it, is the problem. Yet in spite of this profound observation, Zaidman explains that Acumen will continue to find ways "to better create inclusive business models that look at low-income people, not just as a liability [that cannot be trusted] but as a real source of talent, as partners, [and] as customers, and I think that is where we are going to be doing a lot of our partnerships work moving forward." In effect, these new humanitarians are not only willing but eager to use the same tools and techniques that have made them rich and powerful, and everyone else marginalized and poor, even while recognizing that they are in part responsible for rising rates of poverty and inequality, to supposedly create new possibilities for the prosperity of the rest of humanity.

Part of what makes this current humanitarian conjuncture so extraordinary is the way in which the convergence of finance capital, corporate philanthropy, and social entrepreneurialism have converged and been reconfigured to solve the most pressing problem of modern society. But as this chapter has tried to illustrate, entrepreneurism, no matter how social, is not charity; rather, it is business as usual. And those who want to either sell or invest in markets that serve the poor in the Global South are not about to question the system that is responsible for generating their recent wealth and influence. As in the case of education, other sectors of humanitarian need, such as water and sanitation, health care, housing, energy, and transportation, emerging markets themselves are the future, not only for new humanitarianism but also for Western capitalism itself.

Today financial institutions awash in credit are now looking to the world of philanthropy to expand and explore, but they want to do it in a way that is familiar to them, where their risks and returns can be managed and guaranteed. The biggest profits do not come from buying or selling actual things anymore (such as houses, wheat, or cars) but rather from the manipulation of ethereal concepts such as humanitarian risk and collateralized debt. Wealth flows from financial instruments that are truly fictitious commodities (Kaufman 2012). Investing in a water index is now more popular than ever, and today more than 100 indices track and measure the value of stocks of companies in water-related businesses, such as utilities, sewage treatment, and desalination (Moyo 2010). Most offer healthy returns on investment, if done right. As a result, financiers such as Goldman Sachs, AIG, the World Bank, and the IMF, always on the lookout for market-based security for the billions of dollars of credit they extend to poor people worldwide, have been pushing countries to privatize their water services and other publicly owned resources as collateralized debt. In the water sector, these include the lakes, streams, reservoirs, and hand pumps throughout Africa and India. And Acumen, Water for People, Nalco, Water Health International, and Dow Chemicals, among other so-called social entrepreneurs, are only too happy to help. However, for many of these new humanitarians, the crux of their moral imagination and compassionate capitalism is not only about finding the right proposal to "serve people in the developing world" but also about finding the right technology.

Notes

1. At the end of June 2010, approximately 70 percent of Acumen's health investment portfolio was equity and about 30 percent was debt (Batavia et al. 2011).
2. See http://www.youtube.com/watch?v=EJmnFEkZDRs/.
3. I am particularly intrigued by the use of the word "weak." Here we have a partially naked white man referring to local water management systems, which are typically collectively managed and also have a women's constituency or presence, as "weak"—in need, I suppose, of making it more competitive and masculine, of course. Such talk only perpetuates the stereotype that competition is an essential feature of good (strong) governance.
4. Based on 1.55 exchange rate on December 31, 2104.
5. It is worth noting that the CDC Group was originally called the Colonial Development Corporation, which then changed its name during the so-called postcolonial period to the Commonwealth Development Corporation. Today it simply goes by CDC Group.
6. A CDO is a promise to pay investors a certain amount over a certain period of time based on the cash flow the CDO collects from a pool of bonds or other assets, including mortgages, it owns.

4   Failure Is the F Word

STANDING ON A well-lit TED (technology, entertainment, and design) Talk–like stage, Fraser Moore, a charismatic host and organizer, welcomes a cheering audience of 400 to "[another] year of failure." Moore is referring to Fail Festival, an annual public event or, as Moore describes it, "a celebration," where development practitioners and other "do-gooders" use a combination of satire, comedy, and musical parodies to share their latest experiences with one another about how their technological innovations, platforms, or other devices failed to perform according to their humanitarian plans. "Failure is the 'f word' of international development," Moore says, "unspoken in polite company, but a reality in our work. . . . We are on a mission to make failure acceptable in development discussions." Using a combination of humor and sarcasm that is rare in humanitarian circles, the enigmatic Moore takes the stage and begins the evening by declaring to an energetic audience, "It's okay to fail. It's *good* to fail. In fact, you know, that failing is positive. Because that means we are pushing the envelope or changing things or making new things happen." When the audience burst out in laughter, he responds, "Right?" After the laughter subsides, Moore continues, "And theoretically this [means we are] improving the lives of people we're trying to help." Right? To which another woman responds, "Right," followed by even more laughter from the audience. The striking ease with which Moore seemingly applauds individuals, development organizations, and donors for their efforts and ambition to improve the lives of others while, at the same time, questioning their belief and actions strikes at the heart of the debate and ambiguity surrounding the practice of contemporary humanitarian government. The use of comedy and laughter in the face of much needed social justice projects and governance, however, is particularly revealing, as it seems to smooth over an otherwise disturbing fact about the way the world is and the way we would like it to be—and the glaring reality that, for all our promises to help, we continue to fail. This weighty paradox defines the conflicted social space in which the contrite humanitarian works and lives. Those who listened deeply to Moore's message might also hear the infamous words of Karl Marx (1978 [1852]), "that all great world-historic facts and personages appear, so to speak, twice . . . first as tragedy, then as farce." In this chapter, we examine the nature of this two-step marvel as it applies to contemporary humanitarian government and governmentality.

Because of this grave irony, Fail Festivals have become all the rage in the media seeking forerunners of the humanitarian assemblage. The World Bank alone hosted three Fail Faire events in fifteen months. UNICEF has also hosted several themed Fail Faire events, including "Fail to Scale" in November 2013. According to UNICEF (2013, 1), Fail Faire aims "to encourage shared learning from collective failures and to inject a 'failure-friendly' culture into the work that we do." Featured speakers from leading nonprofit organizations, the private sector, and international agencies share their stories in five- to ten-minute "fail slam" talks. The atmosphere is always electric, the audience is completely engaged, the food and libations are always lavish, and the waiting lists are always long (based on my experience). Many humanitarian organizations, in the public and the private sector, have started their own internal Fail Faires in response to this growing cultural norm.

Ariel Fiszbein, the World Bank's chief economist in human development, wrote, "publicizing what doesn't work is a fundamental part of any approach to evidence-based policy. Lack of results is a likely outcome of any innovation. We should remain open and even celebrate those that bring us the bad news as they are helping us stay honest." Similarly, beating on the failure drum, Jim Yong Kim, the president of the World Bank Group, advises, "if we 'fail fast and learn fast,' we will have a much better chance to end extreme poverty, and build shared prosperity in every corner of the world." It would appear that, like "big data" supporters, the failure advocates also seem to believe that more is better in doing good.

Equally revealing in Moore's introduction to Fail Festival is his steadfast trust in the civilizing mission of Information and Communications Technologies for Development (ICT4D), a civilizing mission that continues to fall into spectacular disfavor. The idea that science and technology were among the gifts that Western imperial powers brought to their colonies, the historian Suman Seth (2009) writes, was an integral part of the discourse of the "civilizing mission," one vaunted by both proponents and critics of the methods of colonialism. Moore's postcolonial turn at the microphone, then, can be seen as an opportunity to rally the troops who continue to work hard in an effort to recover the ideological basis of their missionary work, while also recognizing ICT4D's messy, political, and power-laden effects. The questions that lingers, well after the open bar has closed, however, is not why we continue to fail in the face of great effort but, rather, how does one account for the rise in the discourse of failure as an organizing concept for understanding contemporary humanitarian government, and how does this discourse shape practice?

On stage, much of the discussion about failure is rooted in technical terms and expressions, such as design, scale, and even finance. However, upon closer examination, failure can also be interpreted as a political outcome that is largely shaped by the interests and priorities of powerful, usually donors and supporting agencies. Fail Faires offer a poignant ethnographic moment because they bring together humanitarian organizations that, on the one hand, have diverse, incompatible, and, in some cases, competing interests and, on the other hand, need to maintain relationships with one another for the sake of their own existence and legitimacy. However, Fail Festivals also reveal that humanitarianism's tools and techniques rarely work counter to existing patterns of power. Moreover, the stories shared at these events also reveal that many practitioners recognize this fact and try to profit from it, aligning their ideas and projects with the agendas of powerful donors, willing to give lottery winnings to those lucky practitioners holding the right ticket (or proposal). In fact, failure to do so results in their failure to exist (Latour 1996, 2005; Mosse 2005).

The Discourse and Practice of Failure

For Moore, and other techno-evangelists, comedy has become an effective vehicle for dealing with the glaring fact that the gap between the rich and the poor, and the developed and developing countries, continues to widen at an increasing rate in spite of massive efforts to the contrary. "We need to get beyond that [focusing on failure]," Moore proclaimed, "because you know the reality is, technology is *hard*, right?" To which the audience once again responded with laughter. "Even if you try," Moore continued, "sometimes you really screw that shit up!" To which the audience responded with more applause. "I know they fail in health, they fail in education, and agriculture and economic development and whatever sector or silo, or thing that we wanna dream up, right." Again, the hall explodes with laughter, cheers, and applause in agreement.

But Moore is not alone in his mission to "get beyond" failure and make it acceptable in development discussions. During his talk he referred—with the use of much profanity—to a report produced by World Bank (Zall Kusek, Görgens Prestidge, and Hamilton 2013) titled "Fail-Safe Management: Five Rules to Avoid Project Failure." This performance review of the World Bank Group, undertaken by its Independent Evaluation Group, revealed that almost a quarter of World Bank–funded projects and programs have failed, and the remaining "76 percent had satisfactory outcome ratings" (Independent Evaluation Group 2011, xix). This analysis, of course, does not begin to account for the impacts of structural adjustment programs promoted by the World Bank and the IMF on the countries and people in the Global South. Conditional loans were given to poor and cash-strapped countries to encourage economic growth in return for removing "excess" government controls and promoting market competition as part of the neoliberal agenda followed by the Bank and the IMF. Many borrowers were required to restructure state agencies, reform national budgets, rewrite tax systems, and open up markets in finance, property, health, and natural resources—in effect, subordinating national laws to WTO standards and regulations (Goldman 2005). Two decades of development failure and zero net growth on entire continents have produced much devastation, insecurity, and discontent—culminating in widespread popular protests in the early 1990s (Craig and Porter 2006; Goldman 2005). However, in spite of a long list of abysmal failures and destructive effects, the sociologist Michael Goldman (2005) argues, the Bank remains hegemonic, successfully controlling the parameters and frameworks in which we speak and act in the name of development, notwithstanding its ineffectiveness.

The recent and somewhat successful shift to a softer, more humanitarian agenda by the World Bank is a testament to its immense power and permanency, not to mention its flexibility. Today, the World Bank claims that "problems are inevitable in any development program; failure is not" (Zall Kusek et al. 2013, vii). And while acknowledging that some failure is rooted in factors outside a particular project's direct control—generally confounding effects endemic to local government and ownership—the Bank highlights what it sees as a recurring pattern of failure within the control of the project manager, such as poor setting of objectives, overambitious designs, weak results frameworks, and weak implementation capacity. To minimize the possibility of failure, the Bank generated a "fail-safe" system— five rules—not only to plan for success but also to anticipate the possibility of failure. "Like a fail-safe system in the engineering world," the report (Zall Kusek et al. 2013, 9) explains, the Bank's "goal is to introduce strategies that will allow the project manager to anticipate points of failure and to have a plan for compensating for possible failure, if it does occur, in a way that causes the least possible disruption to the project." Planning for failure, the Bank concludes will ensure success.

However, the apparent epiphany that the World Bank has come to pride itself on having learned from its past is not what I want to dwell on. Rather, I want to draw attention to the striking incommensurability of a humanitarian system that, on the one hand, encourages the management of failure—its predictability, its calculability, and its regulation—while, on the other hand, encourages a culture of risk-taking, entrepreneurialism, and innovation—in effect, unpredictability and change. This humanitarian system encourages a gambling culture in which caring subjects can concurrently celebrate both their failures and achievements while also denouncing the conditions of its organization. This new humanitarian subjectivity, at least according to the Bank, must place its faith in the magic of the market, its conviction in modern technology, and its hope in Silicon Valley–type entrepreneurialism to change the way in which the world tackles poverty. However, the deep reflections, albeit comedic, shared by Moore and other new humanitarians at Fail Festivals seem to suggest that the making of this new subjectivity is never fully complete and always a work of malleable social construction. A *subject* that not only learns from repeated failures at saving the world's dispossessed but is also able to celebrate this achievement as a mark of leadership, innovation, and risk-taking virtue in pushing the boundaries of what is possible,

Figure 4.1 Fail-Safe Management. Source: World Bank, 2012.

yet highly improbable. An entrepreneurial *subject* who should be respected for taking the race against poverty and dispossession on, knowing that, in order to win, one must be ready to lose.

Of course, the process of engineering social systems to fit contemporary systems of accumulation is hardly new. In volume 1 of *Capital*, Marx (1976 [1867]) outlined various preconditions, what he characterized as secrets of primitive accumulation, that must first be fulfilled before the process of accumulation could occur. "For the conversion of his money into capital," Marx (1976 [1867], 272) wrote, "the owner of money must meet in the market with the free laborer, free in the double sense, that as a free man he can dispose of his labor-power as his own commodity, and that on the other hand he has no other commodity for sale, i.e. he is rid of them, he is free of all the objects needed for the realization [*Verwirklic-hung*] of his labor-power." "One thing, however, is clear," Marx further explained. "Nature does not produce on the one hand owners of money or commodities, and on the other hand men possessing nothing but their own labor-power. This relation has no basis in natural history, nor does it have a social basis common to all periods of human history." Marx (1976 [1867], 1991) pointed to a variety of preconditions and prerequisites, including a legal system, an international credit system, the modern system of taxation, and the slave trade, among other causes, which created the "artificial means" for the capitalist mode of production.

Similarly, Taylorism, pioneered by mechanical engineer Frederick Taylor, introduced a series of scientific management techniques and incentive systems that transformed factory labor organization at the end of the nineteenth and the beginning of the twentieth centuries. According to the Italian Marxist Antonio Gramsci (2000 [1935]), Taylorism provided the preconditions and prerequisites for Fordism in the United States, a hegemonic system of mass industrial production. For Gramsci (2000 [1935]), the system of coercion and consent in which Fordism flourished, included the exclusion of free labor unions, "high wage" incentives and a surplus army of labor, the hiring of workers of "good moral standing," and the "policing" of worker's lives both inside and outside the factory. Fordism, Gramsci (2000 [1935], 278) concluded, "has determined the need to elaborate a new type of man suited to the new type of work and productive processes."

Fraser Moore and his class of new humanitarians personify "a new type of man" suited to both the exceptionally creative and incredibly destructive tendencies inherent in the workings of modern global capitalism yet, at the same time, remaining highly critical of its so-called charitable intentions. They are free to choose! This version of capitalism, according to the anthropologists Jean Comaroff and John Comaroff (2000, 292), presents itself as "a gospel of salvation . . . a capitalism that if rightly harnessed, is invested with the capacity wholly to transform the universe of the marginalized and disempowered." This is a system of both coercion and consent in which humanitarianism has flourished and thrived.

One only has to listen to Moore describe the importance of "failing often, and failing big" as a marker of humanitarian innovation and risk-taking to get a sense of how humanitarianism has become akin to an immense game of speculation and luck. Moore has referred to this strategy as "a moonshot," in which "you propose a really unique or crazy idea" to a funder, drawing big grant money, "with the knowledge that you have a 1 in 10 chance of it working." "Hey, everybody makes mistakes," Moore explains, "and when working with new technologies and approaches, we should *expect* lots of failures." Moonshots are a popular response among new humanitarians, who comfortably propose radical solutions that address a huge problem, such as extreme poverty, using innovative science and technology. These humanitarian entrepreneurs have become accustomed to a culture of failure, explains Moore, "10 bad ideas that sink before one gets to its multibillion-dollar initial public offering." So it makes sense to Moore and other new humanitarians that one should risk it all to compete in the transnational market of moral intervention and civic virtue (Dezalay and Garth 1998; Hardt and Negri 2001).

This culture or risk taking, speculation, indeed gambling, is not only symptomatic of the emerging global market of civic virtue but part of the Western fiscal order and capital markets in which they are embedded. George Soros, with a net worth of $28.2 billion, is the model subject of a burgeoning class of entrepreneurs willing to bet the farm to strike it rich. "I'm only rich because I know when I'm wrong," he explained to *Wall Street Journal* reporter Greg Ip (2008), "and I would say that I basically have survived by recognizing my mistakes." Indeed, Soros, is best known as the speculator who made his fortune by betting against Britain's currency in his short sale of US$10 billion worth of pounds, giving him a one-day profit of $1 billion during the UK currency crisis in 1992 (and then again with the Thai baht in 1997). Soros, of course, is just one of many entrepreneurs and beneficiaries—hedge fund managers, commercial and investment banks, and pension funds—who created and used innovative financial technology to accumulate money by betting against a debt issuers' ability to pay, expanding financial markets to levels unimaginable before the financial crisis of 2007–2008. The market for credit default swaps (CDS), for example, grew from $920 billion at the end of 2001 to more than $62 trillion by the end of 2007. Similarly, the market for CDOs totaled $275 billion in 2000 and skyrocketed to $4.7 trillion in 2006 (Salmon 2009). Together, this organized and innovative techno-financial practice of turning failure and risk into success created one of the largest markets, albeit of entirely fictitious commodities, in the world.

The point I want to emphasize here, however, is that this culture of hedging bets and high-risk dealings is not the province of just the financiers and the superrich (although these two groups often go hand in hand). Today, lottery life and casino culture have seeped into all strata of life and subjectivity, including humanitarianism. Gambling, the commentator George F. Will (1999) writes, is the fastest-growing industry in the United States, increasingly operated and promoted by financially strapped governments that consider taxes an anathema, and lotteries and gaming levies have become a favored means of raising funds for the provision of all sorts of social services from education and pension funds to drinking water and sanitation (Comaroff and Comaroff 2000). To build on the observation of Jean and John Comaroff (2000, 297), it appears that the defunct machinery of a growing number of welfare states is being turned by the wheel not only of fortune but of misfortune as well.

Helping Us Stay Honest

Yet, for many new humanitarians, risking it all is an uncomfortable wager that they are forced into by the World Bank and other donors. In this bet, they believe that they take on all the risk, and consequent blame, for failure associated with this type of venture philanthropy, while the donors get all the credit. At risk in this humanitarian assemblage is not only the lives of the dispossessed but also the life and death, at least in terms of career and livelihood, of humanitarian practitioners as well. "[In] 2006," a Fail Festival speaker recalls, we were actually able to earn enough money so it could be our sole source of income . . . and 2007/2008, we actually hired people, we had health care. That to me was the sign of being a real business . . . and I believed the hype—social entrepreneurialism, do good work get everyone to know what you do and don't worry about profit, don't worry about the bottom line; it'll just come . . . and that was great . . . then this year we fell off a cliff . . . suddenly I had no money, and I had to fire everyone . . . I'm gonna lose my shirt this year.

Among new humanitarians, this all-too-frequent phenomenon has come to be known as "the non-profit starvation cycle" (Gregory and Howard 2009). This vicious cycle leaves nonprofit organizations so hungry for decent infrastructure, including sturdy information technology systems, financial systems, skills training, fundraising processes, and other essential overhead, that they can barely function as organizations—let alone serve their beneficiaries. The cycle starts, according to practitioners Ann Goggins Gregory and Don Howard (2009, 49), "with funders' unrealistic expectations about how much running a non-profit costs." This systemic underfunding leads nonprofit organizations to misrepresent their costs while skimping on vital systems. These survival strategies however, fuel donors' doubts about the nonprofit organizations they support, doubts that in turn require greater internal demands in the form of detailed metrics and reporting requirements. To break the nonprofit starvation cycle, Gregory and Howard (2009) argue, funders must take the lead.

Practical experience has engendered much cynicism in a humanitarian assemblage that forces the hand of the new humanitarian practitioner and, in effect, undermines (what they see as) legitimate personal attempts to "make a difference." The collective frustration directed at the recent World Bank handbook, "Fail-Safe Management. Five Rules to Afford Project Failure," comes from the fact that practitioners remain highly critical of the Bank's real intentions. Moreover, being told that they can fail safely with the introduction of five simple rules, and requisite metrics, not only smacks of condescension but also disingenuousness for many practitioners. "WHAT THE FUCK IS THAT?!" is one presenter's on-stage response to a slide showing the cover page of the Bank's report. "This actually comes from a World Bank slide. I shit you not."

Most notable in the eyes of practitioners, however, is how the recent managerial turn by the World Bank and other major donors has helped to push the donor agenda further down into their organizational practices. This forces practitioners to frame their activities in ways that are suitable to donor's priorities, which can then (again) be used to further audit and control their organizational efforts. This sort of audit culture, Michael Power (1997) argues, is almost impossible to criticize in principle—after all, it advances values that are generally held dear by everyone, such as responsibility, openness about outcomes, and widening access. The real frustration for many practitioners, however, is that they have found themselves subject to new and more intensive accounting and audit require-

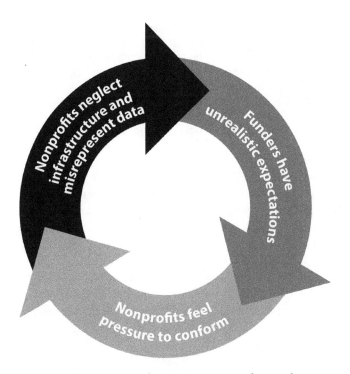

Figure 4.2 The Nonprofit Starvation Cycle. Source: Gregory and Howard, 2009.

ments that are far from contributing to greater transparency or more reasonable accounts of why they continue to fail. For many nonprofit organizations, this contradiction has become a major source of concern and ridicule.

"I'm not here to talk about failure," Thomas Reynolds explains. "I'm here to talk about success. I am going to present to you a fail-safe method to make sure that all of your projects end up a success."

> First of all, the most important thing, to make sure your projects do not fail, make sure that all of your projects are a success, rule number one: do not ever fail. [audience bursts out in laughter.] Failure is for losers. If you fail you won't get any funding. If you fail, you will lose your job; you will not be loved; why did you ever want to fail? Do not ever fail. Second rule . . . don't ever talk about it. Your funders don't need to know that, they don't wanna know that because they have to tell their superiors . . . just tell them what works, what's working, and brush everything else under the rug. If you have trouble with that, if people start asking questions about, well, didn't you say, well, I thought this was about, well, the next rule comes into effect . . . stick to your performance measures. And if you're smart, you will set up an evaluation criterion in a manner that is failsafe. Use the most obscure statistics you can. Don't talk about the number of visitors to your site, talk about hits—hits are much better. And look like a

much bigger number than the visits. Don't talk about whether or not people are actually using the skills they learned in your training; talk about the forms they had to give in, in evaluating your training before you hand them their transportation site license; use those as your criterion. The fourth rule of my failsafe method—unclog the pipes;[1] . . . [And, finally,] remember those people that you're actually there to help. . . . Remember that those people don't have a voice, and that is why they are a great group of people to work with. When all else fails, talk about the indigenous conditions and how they've changed since you initially wrote the proposal.

These reflections by another Fail Festival participant, although delivered for enter-tainment effect, suggest that this most recent demand for new and more intensive accounting and audit–type reforms by the World Bank and other donors is pro-ducing the opposite result. What is seen as a form of coercive accountability by Reynolds and other new humanitarians—forcing them to post metrics and report measures that have little practical or performative value—has not only failed to discipline this practitioner, or "helped" them "stay honest," but, rather, encouraged the opposite behavior among practitioners, namely, deviance. "Please, please," concludes the CEO of a medium-size SMS (short messaging service) management nonprofit organization at another Fail Festival, "can we all lie a little bit less so we can all get a little more?"

This custom of deviance or nonconformity expressed on stage stems directly from the audit-type culture imposed on practitioners by donors. Moreover, in-creasing numbers of new humanitarians are finding ways to adopt novel and more intensive accounting and audit requirements under the guise of innovation. Water Water "prides itself in being an innovative program," explains Adrian Roberts, a program manager, to a group of volunteers involved in Water Water's most recent baseline assessment. "This year," Roberts explained, "we have shifted the way we measure success or progress [to be more compliant with donor de-mands]. . . . We're implementing . . . entire databases that we've designed specifically for our work, it's a game changer. . . . No other water and sanitation organization is doing it." "Evaluation now has become a special project" for Water Water, eager to profit from being a leader in the audit culture that has permeated new humani-tarian practice and support. "It's fraught with all kinds of problems," Roberts admits to a group of weary volunteers, "but [with] each assignment, we get better and better at this." "This really is accountability to ourselves as well," proclaims an enthusiastic intern. "I mean this is one of the things that we're trying to do as an organization as well; we're trying to say, we promised to uphold our end of the bar-gain." "This information," Roberts continued, is "going to go into . . . this global monitoring program . . . to help donors and the general audience . . . verify the data."

However, as previously mentioned, whether these performance measures actually translate to greater transparency is unclear. Even more opaque is the relationship between the use of these types of methods of verification and humanitarian reform. In fact, Power (1997) has suggested that these contemporary rituals of verification come at a cost, not only economically, but also at the expense of other forms of knowledge and practice. In forcing a narrow understanding of what humanitarian thought and action should be, these audit-type practices threaten "to become a form of learned ignorance" (Power 1997, 123). In effect, these accounts of verification pose a real threat to the integrity of the nonprofit humanitarian enterprise, apparently ready to say and do anything—even misrepresent data—their funding partner wants to hear and see, in order to keep the funding pipeline constantly flowing. If these recent rounds of reforms were intended to engender trust and more accountability between humanitarian practitioners and donors, then they, too, have failed.

A Culture of Failure

Equally informative is the fact that, although all those involved in doing good unanimously agree that failure is a cultural norm of sorts, they likewise disagree as to what, where, and who are responsible for this recurring pattern. The World Bank, for example, places blame squarely on the shoulders of project managers and their inability to set appropriate objectives or to design appropriate technologies (among other attributes of being unsuccessful). However, as the following vignette illustrates, practitioners place equal blame on donors' unworkable expectations.

Returning to another Fail Festival stage, a presenter, after the introductory jokes and sound checks, turns to a story about MAVC, a woman he identified as being from the land of don-or. "And I don't know if you've met a woman from the land of don-or, but, God damn, they're hot! They've got a giant wallet—I mean they are just so beautiful and smart!" The speaker describes how MAVC showed him her request for proposals (RFPs):

> I thought this would be the moment where I see the millions. This is going to be the moment where moolah is going to rain down from the land of don-or. It was gonna change me, it was gonna change my company, it was gonna change my industry, it was going to change the world! Right?

But after looking at MAVC's RFP, the speaker asked in theatrical indignation: "How could MAVC do that to me? . . . That's not enough money to change my industry. That's not enough to change my company! That's not enough to change my career. That's not even enough for me to get change for a coffee in this town, right? Uh, how could she! How could MAVC desert me? . . . I mean . . . I'm [a] cool, international implementer, I know what I'm doing, right? And she's just a woman from don-or; all she's got is the money." And then the speaker asked the audience, "[Do] you know what she does? She tells me . . . 'I want to work with people in local organizations who are doing real things.' And that's when I realized, right, shit, the whole time I was thinking about me, and how I was going to be cool because there would be millions, and I would get to fly around on planes [and do other cool things] but really, it wasn't me but those people in the countries we were supposed to help, right?"

It is then that the speaker revealed the true moral lesson of this story, with some coaxing from the audience, of course. The imaginary women from the land of don-or, MAVC, he revealed, was Making All Voices Count, an organization that makes grants available to support the development of new, ideas, technologies, and initiatives that help recipient governments become more effective and accountable. This story was a somewhat sensationalized reflection of a recent interaction with one of their program officers from MAVC. A heart-rending video on its website for mainly Western users declares, "Solvable problems need not remain unsolved" in the Global South. The video clip goes on to suggest that enduring social problems remain unsolved because governments are not transparent, accessible, or accountable to their citizens. In effect, MAVC argues that governments in the Global South do not know how to help those in need or just do not want to. MAVC is supported by a consortium of donors, including the UK Department for International Development, the USAID, the Swedish International Development Agency, Open Society Foundations,[2] and the Omidyar Network.[3] On its website MAVC offers a rolling grant program to help fund "do-ers" and learn from innovative projects that amplify the voices of citizens and enable effective governmental responses to enduring social problems in the Global South.[4]

What is striking about this modern parable, however, is that it was not given by a member of the clergy trying to instill congregants with a moral compass but, rather, by a parishioner trying to find one. In the fast-paced, idea-rich world of humanitarianism, numerous obstacles need to be overcome and hoops must be jumped through: RFPs have to be written, networks have to be cultivated, innovative ideas, tools, and products have to be tested, websites have to designed, and platforms have to be created. And these undertakings have to be successfully accomplished in an ever more crowded and increasingly competitive humanitarian marketplace, where funding (from the land of don-or) is required to make anything happen. And what started as a genuine attempt to "make a difference" in one environment quickly becomes a self-serving enterprise in another, with the best and the worst of intentions.

Another important observation that can be drawn from this story is that donors consistently appear, at least from practitioners' perspectives, to underfund their humanitarian projects, asking too much and giving too little. To this speaker, donors are not simply out of touch with the projects they support and the people they try to help but are from another land [don-or], unable to understand the complex system of meaning and behavior that defines local dispossession and inequality "abroad." This lack of support, many practitioners argue, simply sets them up to fail.

Failure, according Teresa Smyth, the CEO of an international nonprofit organization and an invited speaker at Fail Festival, is squarely due to the allure of the silver bullet metaphor—that "we're just gonna solve it once and for all"—advanced by many large donors. This metaphor has gained much traction among major donors, who are willing to advance large sums of money for silver-bullet campaigns with measurable and definitive outcomes. For example, before the 2015 World Education Forum in South Korea, the World Bank Group announced that it would double its results-based education funding to $5 billion over the next five years. This support, the Bank explained, is part of an initiative to end extreme poverty by 2030. "The goal for 2030," World Bank President Jim Yong Kim explained, "is not just to get all the remaining children in school but also to make sure that they're learning the literacy, math and noncognitive skills they need to escape extreme poverty, share in the benefits of economic growth, and drive innovation and job creation." By linking financing with "pre-agreed results," Kim and other Bank leaders hope to ensure accountability and to better align education systems with managerial incentives. "With nearly a billion people remaining trapped in extreme poverty today," Kim explained, "sustained efforts to improve learning for children will unlock huge amounts of human potential for years to come. Better results in classrooms will help end extreme poverty." This recent financing is part of the Bank's commitment to the SDGs—the new silver bullet for sustainable development—adopted by the United Nations in September 2015. The SDGs will replace the MDGs—the old silver bullet—which ended in 2015, in which the World Bank invested US$40 billion.

However, for Smyth and other practitioners, the notion that a silver bullet even exists is akin to a type of humanitarian entrapment, in which nonprofit organizations are lured into acting in haste and then swiftly "prosecuted" by donors for not succeeding. "Somebody shared with me a paper about what it took in Britain to bring water and sanitation to the poorest people. It took bazillions of British pounds, a lot of money, and a lot of subsidy over 100 years." This is something the World Bank and others are not willing to provide, according to Smyth and other practitioners. "So if you're a donor," Smyth demands, "stop asking for silver bullets, and if you're an implementing partner, stop promising it!" To which the crowd cheered loudly.

A senior advisor at Internews, an INGO that fosters independent media and access to information worldwide, took a more direct tone with donors: "Sometimes you really should look in the face of your donor and USAID people, [and say:] we love you, we really do, but sometimes you really should give them the middle finger." In his remarks, this practitioner blamed their most recent project failure on the ever-increasing demands by donors, governments, and implementing partners. "We decided to help," explains the speaker, "using the most innovative, cutting-edge technology . . . SMS, because we're cool that way, to help community healthcare in Kenya." At the beginning of the project, the speaker explained, "we decided to keep [the objectives] simple. We started . . . talking with donors and also looking at our partners, and we had our first partner looking at the mapping, because you know if you don't have a map in Africa, you're really lame. However, for some donors, the speaker explained, SMS was simply not innovative enough to earn their support." The advice they received from another donor to their SMS proposal was: "You really should do something more innovative." So they decided to include data visualization as part of their revised proposal objectives. "Because who are you if you don't do data visualization!" So, then they took the revised proposal to another donor, who said: "Well, actually, you do data visualization, you collect the data, you should really sum [it] up, you need to do policy [implementation] as well." However, after talking with another donor, they were advised to "work with the government [more directly], because really they are the ones that implement the policies." This interminable review process went on for months, slowly transforming a small pilot project into a silver bullet that could (once again) potentially "solve it once and for all." In the end, its overambitious design also became its Achilles' heel, and "the project . . . never happened."

On the surface, it appears as if this project failed because it tried to do too much with too little—what the World Bank has identified as "overambitious design." An alternative explanation is that the project *was made to fail* because this nonprofit organization was unable to gain specific donor support. Moreover, as it continued to solicit support, the project began to shift from its interests and expertise to those of donor priorities and, as a result, became less focused because of greater donor involvement. For all the hype about entrepreneurialism and innovation, projects continued to be designed by donors and negotiated by practitioners, a relationship that is clearly not one among equals. Eventually, what caused this project to fail was not the failed application of specific technology or poor objective settings, or even overambitious designs, but, rather, the competing goals, interests, and priorities of donors, which made the project unacceptable to all. Moreover, this story also suggests that donors do not have complete confidence in the nonprofit organizations that they support, unless they can "make sure . . . that the grants that we're providing are really having an impact," admitted World Bank President Kim during the 2014 Global Partnership for Social Accountability's Global Partners Forum.

For some, however, failure is not simply about projects but about a state of mind. The perspective that nonprofit organizations lack the imagination to bring about real humanitarian change was clearly illustrated in an op-ed in the *New York Times* (2013) by Peter Buffett, chairman of the NoVo Foundation and the son of the investment magnate and philanthropist Warren Buffett. Buffett likened the contemporary humanitarian assemblage to philanthropic colonialism, a form of interventionism that has not only failed to deliver on its humanitarian promises but also generated damaging unintended consequences for the poor and dispossessed. "It's a massive business," Buffett (2013, 1) wrote, "and has become the 'it' vehicle to level the playing field, generating a growing number of gatherings, workshops, and affinity groups." But this complex "just keeps the existing structure of inequality in place." And as more business-minded folks get into the act, Buffett believes, business principles, and not humanitarian, will drive the philanthropic sector. To respond to this systemic failure, Buffett (2013, 2) calls on nonprofit organizations to get creative, to overcome their "crisis of imagination," and to try "out concepts that shatter current structures and systems that have turned much of the world into one vast market."

This charge did not fall on deaf ears. Writing in response to Buffett's claim that nonprofit organizations lack humanitarian imagination, Wayan Vota (2013), the communications manager at a nonprofit ICT4D organization, admits he, too, is tired of the status quo. Vota writes,

> We find much of the current efforts in philanthropy, aid, foreign assistance, public-private partnerships and all the other categories as hollow and self-serving (except, of course, the projects we're working on!). We know firsthand the hypocrisy of capitalist titans donating pittances and claiming a clean conscience, believing that they know what is best for the poor in other places. And on a daily basis we see what the 1% wrought on those less fortunate—in this country and around the world. . . . What about big bets on emergent leaders who can change business to build, rather than destroy this planet and its people, who can change government to be a strong, positive force for equity between all people, who can lead philanthropy into a new way of interacting with business, government, and those it aims to benefit? . . . We all agree that "safe" decisions beget the status quo. . . . We are tired of the status quo. We're even more tired of those who have the means to change it, not doing so. So with all due respect, please stand up and risk your money. Show us you're willing to fail with 10 big bets to find the 1 approach that changes the world.

Vota offers a real condemnation of those so-called donor agencies trying to structure and control—in effect, manage—the global humanitarian assemblage. In his response, Vota gives as good as he gets. Moreover, while Buffet and Vota are unable to agree upon what makes a humane society possible—in effect, blaming each other—they clearly recognize that this contemporary humanitarian assemblage rarely works counter to existing patterns of global power and inequality; in fact, they agree that it reinforces structural inequality.

The emergence of new humanitarianism and its twin conjuncture of failure and success is symptomatic of the emerging global market of civic virtue in which they are embedded. These new humanitarians concurrently celebrate their failures and achievements while denouncing the conditions of their organization, claiming to be good and successful in the face of grave discontent. Simultaneously, they bet against the system in which they operate and try to leverage their particular advantage. The material reality of this gambling humanitarian culture, however, does not take place at a casino, nor is realized in a lottery ticket or otherwise benevolent sweepstakes but, rather, in the winner-take-all approach that "put[s] the adventure into venture capital," in which gambling is normalized and "tightly woven" into incommensurable networks and conflicted subjectivities of new humanitarianism (Comaroff and Comaroff 2000, 296). The value, however, comes not from simply recognizing humanitarianism's messy, contingent, and unplanned character but, rather, from celebrating its chaotic postcolonial sensibility—namely, to fail, in an effort to recover the ideology of a civilizing mission as a legitimate topic and strategy of Northern Samaritans.

Failing to Succeed and Succeeding in Failure

The history of trying to help those in desperate circumstances is saturated with failure. One only has to look at the great divide between rich and poor, haves and have-nots, in the face of vast investments and hugely creative technologies, to find a glaring example of this contemporary global moment. "Right now," Donna Haraway (2015, 160) reminds us, "the earth is full of refugees, human and not, without refuge," and without help. More than 4 million refugees have fled Syria alone since the civil war there began in 2011. This does not include the humanitarian crises in Sudan, Chad, Libya, Iraq, Nepal, Haiti, and elsewhere around the globe. The real weight of this humanitarian failure came crushing down on many of us after images of a Syrian toddler who washed up on a Turkish beach circulated worldwide in September 2015. "This is a horrific image," said Peter Bouckaert, the emergency director for Human Rights Watch, who shared the picture of the Syrian toddler on social media, "but it is an image that we all need to see because we need to understand that our collective failure to stop the slaughter in Syria for the last four years and not welcome the people who flee its horrors are causing people to die and suffer tremendously."

Governments, donors, nonprofit organizations, and corporations—the global humanitarian complex—together have an equally egregious record when it comes to protecting human rights in the face of imminent peril. This era of humanitarian failure has been called "the age of genocide" by Samantha Power, the US ambassador to the United Nations and the author of the Pulitzer Prize–winning book, *A Problem from Hell: America and the Age of Genocide* (2013). In her survey of major genocides in the twentieth century, including the Bosnian Serbs' eradication of non-Serbs, the Ottoman slaughter of Armenians, the Nazi Holocaust, Pol Pot's terror in Cambodia, Saddam Hussein's destruction of Kurds in northern Iraq, and the Rwandan Hutus' systematic extermination of the Tutsi minority, Power (2013, xv) writes that the United States "had never in its history intervened to stop genocide and had in fact rarely even made a point of condemning it as it occurred." In fact, the responses by the administrations of George H.W. Bush and Bill Clinton to the Bosnian genocide, Power (2013) claims, were jarringly similar to prior ones:

> Early warnings of massive bloodshed proliferated. The spewing of inflamma-tory propaganda escalated. The massacres and deportations started. U.S. policy-makers struggled to wrap their minds around the horrors. Refugee stories and press reports of atrocities became too numerous to deny. Few Americans at home pressed for intervention. A hopeful but passive and ultimately deadly American waiting game commenced. And genocide proceeded unimpeded by U.S. action and often emboldened by U.S. inaction.

Moreover, Power observes, in spite of their lack of activity to curb genocidal events on their watch, American leaders have repeatedly committed themselves to pre-venting the recurrence of genocide. Before becoming president, Power (2013, xxi) writes, "candidate Clinton chided Bush over Bosnia. 'If the horrors of the Holo-caust taught us anything,' Clinton said, 'it is the high cost of remaining silent and paralyzed in the face of genocide.'" After he took office, however, Clinton not only failed but actually assisted—by removing peacekeepers and obstructing the deliv-ery of supplies—in what remains the most rapid and most efficient mass killing in history, which took the lives of 800,000 to 1 million ethnic Tutsis and many moder-ate Hutus in 100 days in the summer of 1994. These men who prided themselves on learning from the past were unable to confront the reality of the dispossessed.

Today, those in the Global North live with the knowledge that the post-Ottoman states of Syria, Iraq, and even Lebanon remain intolerable. On the watch of the 2009 Nobel Peace Prize recipient and US President Barack Obama, an estimated 9 million Syrians have fled their homes since the outbreak of civil war in March 2011, taking refuge in neighboring countries or within Syria itself. Ac-cording to the United Nations High Commissioner for Refugees (UNHCR), over 3 million have fled to Syria's immediate neighbors Turkey, Lebanon, Jordan, and Iraq, and 6.5 million are internally displaced within Syria. Meanwhile, less than 150,000 Syrians have requested asylum in the European Union, and member states have pledged to resettle a further 33,000 Syrians. Today images of refugees and their camplike habitats have become a commonplace and shockingly accepted fact of postmodern life. Moreover, in a post Brexit Europe and a Donald Trump America, these now stateless people have become the raison d'être for a new brand of national populism and institutional racism that once again specifically targets the refugee.

Samantha Power (2013) concludes that the consistent policy of non-intervention by the United States in this age of genocide is a sad testimony, not to an American political system that has failed humanity but to one that is ruthlessly effective in preserving its own interests and those of others. Earlier, the German-born political theorist Hannah Arendt (1951) made a similar observation in her analysis of the Holocaust, the refugee crisis, and mass statelessness that characterized World War II and its aftermath. The concepts of natural or inalienable rights, Arendt writes, failed humanity at the very time that they were needed most, despite having been articulated for over a century and a half (1951, 2). Today, "failure" is "the f-word" not only of international development but also of new humanitarian government and governmentality as well. In a statement commemorating UN World Refugee Day on June 20, 2015, UN High Commissioner for Refugees Antonio Guterres warned that "more people fled last year than at any other time in our records. Around the world, almost 60 million have been displaced by conflict and persecution. Nearly 20 million of them are refugees, and more than half are children." This consequence, Guterres declared, of "a spreading global violence has come to threaten the very foundations of our international system."

It has often been suggested, by advocates and critics alike, that the growing discourse of failure is a consequence of wanting to understand, reflect, and learn from their mistakes, signaling a concerted effort to turn failure into success. However, the real epiphany that comes to light from the many seasonal failure festivals is that the increasing managerial orientation and subjectivity of both nonprofit organizations and their practitioners has led to greater conflict and mistrust with donors and other funding supporters. In effect, the discourse of failure has led to finger pointing, not understanding. For many practitioners, this recent metrics mania by major donors is simply stranger than fiction—from another land. Moreover, in spite of commitments to greater accountability, this most recent managerial turn adopted by those people and institutions *for good* is far from contributing to transparency or reform in humanitarian policy or practice.

What this managerial turn has contributed to, however, is the growth of an army of humanitarian bureaucrats required to keep the emerging global market of civic virtue working. Returning to another Fail Festival stage, a presenter, said the following about managing a recent proposal:

> So here I was in Africa doing my research and writing my project proposal, and I was communicating to my boss, who was in Washington, DC. And he was communicating with the country director who was in Kenya with me, who was communicating with the head of the health program, and all of us were communicating with our partner who was on the West Coast. And my boss was also communicating with that partner, and we also were working with another partner in Boston. And we were also communicating with the person writing the grant proposal, and all of us were also communicating with the person in charge of fundraising. Now after this very simple communication scheme [was put in place], we, of course, got to the point where we needed money because that's what we need at the end of the day—the money to do the project.

The reality of this new humanitarianism is that it has contributed to the rapid growth of what David Graeber (2015, 42) has described as "apparently meaningless, make work, 'bullshit jobs'"—chief program officer, monitoring and evaluation manager, private sector alliances advisor, community development specialist; the list goes on. In fact, one only has to glance at the *International Development Jobs Newsletter*, a "twice weekly publication that connects international development job seekers and recruiters," to see the 2,106 or more jobs needed to sustain this rapidly growing battalion of do-gooders.

For all the attention paid to failure, another simple fact remains obscure: the recognition of failure is driven not by some moral pursuit to change the contemporary conditions of poverty and dispossession but, rather, by an uncharitable imperative to profit from them. The use of interest-rate swaps by Goldman Sachs, which allowed the bank to make millions on Detroit's water crisis—the Detroit Water Department had to pay Goldman and other banks penalties totaling $547 million to terminate costly interest-rate swaps—is just one poignant example of how companies are making a killing on humanitarian crises worldwide (Reich 2015). Of course, this is not the first time that companies have profited from humanitarian crises. Copious examples come to mind during the Holocaust, when major corporations, including IBM, Ford, Coca-Cola (specifically Fanta), Standard Oil, and Chase Bank, aided and profited from this genocidal event. What is different is that in the past it was possible to identify who was profiting and how, even if the evidence comes to light long after the fact. Moreover, this insight was often made by civil society organizations, academics, the media, and governments critical of a capitalism that was causing inexcusable harm. Today, however, it is increasing difficult to determine who is making a killing from poverty and injustice, as all parties involved are now melded together into a single, self-sustaining humanitarian assemblage, whose logics and practices are so deeply entwined that they have become effectively indistinguishable. Now, everyone is in the game—doing well at doing good.

The third and last assumption rooted in the discourse of failure is that it will help to cultivate some sort of reflection, and then change in behavior, about how to deal with contemporary humanitarian crises. In effect, we believe that we will learn from our mistakes, turning our failure into success by providing genuine help to those in need. However, again we see that the way in which failure has been constructed has brought about the opposite behavior—not patience, vigilance, and perhaps, even reflection, but more of the same—gambling, risk taking, and behavior that is in line with making profits and seeking wealth. In effect, the risk taking and venture-type mentality that brought many donors their massive wealth have also come to dominate their humanitarian projects. Donors do not simply want to fund the humanitarian sector; they want to transform it. The theatrics of Fail Festivals reveal that many practitioners not only recognize this fact but are also trying to benefit from it, aligning their ideas and projects with the agendas of powerful donors. Practitioners, too, are ready to risk it all to be able to compete in the transnational market of moral intervention and civic virtue. Fail

Festivals may supply a humanitarian confession booth for those seeking forgiveness for their failure to help those less fortunate, but they do little to change behaviors or the conditions of poverty and injustice worldwide, as these "moments," now deeply neoliberal, remain "the element of profit" (Marx 1976 [1867], 352).

Notes

1. This is also the fourth rule to avoid project failure of the World Bank's Fail-Safe Management Report.

2. The Open Society Foundations were established by the billionaire investor and philanthropist George Soros to provide support to former East-bloc countries as they tried to build vibrant and tolerant democracies whose governments are accountable and open to the participation of all people.

3. The Omidyar Network was established by the eBay entrepreneur and philanthropist Pierre Omidyar.

4. Making All Voices Count runs humanitarian programs in Bangladesh, Ghana, Indonesia, Kenya, Liberia, Mozambique, Nigeria, Pakistan, the Philippines, South Africa, Tanzania, and Uganda.

Conclusion

A Crime against Humanity

O<small>N THE EVE</small> of the blood moon lunar eclipse, Central Park in Manhattan was crammed with tens of thousands of enthusiastic millennials eager to express their solidarity with the world's poor. At one particular moment in the early evening, Pearl Jam frontman Eddie Vedder and recent phenom Beyoncé took center stage together. His acoustic guitar in his lap, Vedder began to strum the familiar introduction to musician and activist Bob Marley's "Redemption Song." Vedder passionately sang the introductory verse, and then Beyoncé, with the roaring crowds' approval, led the next stanza of this iconic melody. As Vedder strummed his guitar and Beyoncé hummed along, the projector behind both of them cast an image of Nelson Mandela delivering a speech in London's Trafalgar Square in 2005 before the Group of Seven finance ministers meeting there. "Like slavery and apartheid," Mandela (British Broadcasting Corporation 2005, 1) announced, "poverty is not natural":

> It is man made. And it can be overcome and eradiated by the actions of human beings. And overcoming poverty is not a gesture of charity. It is the protection of a fundamental human right; the right to dignity and a decent life. While poverty persists, there is no true freedom. Sometimes it falls upon a generation to be great. You can be that great generation. Of course, the task will not be easy. But not to do this would be *a crime against humanity*, against which I ask all humanity now to rise up [emphasis added].

As the projection of Mandela's speech ended, the crowd cheered, Vedder strummed his guitar more emphatically, and the camera panned to a group in the audience holding their palms up to the camera to reveal tattoos of Mandela's face. The duo continued with another verse and chorus as the camera panned the audience, highlighting young couples with their arms together, then returned to the group with Mandela-tattooed palms. The duo closed their performance with an embrace, to which the crowd erupted in cheers.

Vedder and Beyoncé were among a star-studded lineup to mark the fourth Global Citizen Festival. This multihour event held on the Great Lawn in Central Park was hosted by Stephen Colbert, Kerry Washington, Salma Hayek Pinault, Olivia Wilde, and other celebrities. Featured guests included US Vice President Joe Biden, US First Lady Michelle Obama, humanitarian activist and Nobel Prize laureate Malala Yousafzai, Facebook CEO Mark Zuckerberg, Bill and Melinda Gates, and UN Secretary-General Ban Ki-moon. Celebrity activists on stage included Katie Holmes, Hugh Jackman, Bono, and Leonardo DiCaprio. Musical performances were given by Jay Z, Sting, and Coldplay, and, of course, Beyoncé and Pearl Jam.

The star-studded festival was also timed to coincide with the UN General Assembly (UNGA) meeting in New York, appropriately named the United Nations Sustainable Development Summit, where member states adopted seventeen sustainable development goals (SDGs) and indicators intended to frame their agendas and political policies for the betterment of humankind over the next fifteen years. The SDGs follow and expand on the Millennium Development Goals (MDGs), which were agreed to by governments in 2001 and were due to expire at the end of 2015.

In many ways, the United Nations Sustainable Development Summit marks the climax of a recent round of summits, workshops, and meetings by governments, civil society groups, business, and international agencies in a concerted effort to do massive social good. Earlier in the UNGA Week, the annual Social Good Summit convened world leaders, new media and technology experts, and grassroots activists to examine the impact and "unlock the potential" of technology and new media on social good initiatives around the world (Mashable.com 2015). The Clinton Global Initiative (CGI) also coincided with the UNGA meeting. The CGI attendee list included World Bank President Jim Yong Kim, Bill Gates, world leaders, social entrepreneurs, corporate executives, and civil society groups.

Earlier in July, the United Nations organized the third International Conference on Financing for Development in Addis Ababa, Ethiopia. The primary goal of this meeting was to produce a document that outlined the sources of development finance that could be drawn on to implement the SDGs. The third annual Global Humanitarian Policy Forum (GHPF), which took place in New York City in December 2014, brought together over 100 humanitarian practitioners, academics, private sector partners, and representatives of international organizations and nongovernmental organizations. Convened by the United Nations Office for the Coordination of Humanitarian Affairs (OCHA), the GHPF aimed to "build a more inclusive policy community, identify latest trends, showcase research, and foster a coordinated policy and research agenda" that would draw attention to the growing and unprecedented humanitarian need across the world, and contribute to the World Humanitarian Summit (WHS) in May 2016 (Office for the Coordination of Humanitarian Affairs 2014, 2).

Moreover, these high-level meetings cast a shadow on the more pragmatic and frequent gatherings necessary to facilitate the operationalization of contemporary humanitarian government and governmentality. For example, in May, Catholic Relief Services hosted the 2015 ICT4D Conference in Chicago. This conference brought together "thought leaders and experienced professionals from around the world to share and explore methods for systematically integrating information and communications technology innovations into relief and development programs" (Catholic Relief Services 2015, 1). Later in June, a one-day ICTforAg Conference in Washington, DC, brought together more than 150 "thought leaders and decision makers in agriculture and technology from the international development community and the private sector to examine how new innovations can empower smallholder farmers, and the entire value chains that support them, through the use of information and communication technologies" (ICTforAg.org 2015, 1). Then in July, the Institute of Electrical and Electronics Engineers (called the World's Largest Professional Association for the Advancement of Technology) conference on Technological Innovation in Information and Communications Technology (ICT) for Agriculture and Rural Development was held in Chennai, India. Over 600 international participants came together to discuss "innovative ideas on how to do income transfer to poor households during critical times through the use of ICT for agriculture and rural development" (Institute of Electrical and Electronics Engineers 2015, 1).

These now ritual global, multistakeholder, and multifaceted events of new humanitarianism seem to suggest that failure to end poverty and dispossession is not a matter of whether we care, as time and time again, ample gestures of social solidarity appear in the form of institutional efforts and societal reaction to support others in the face of serious and enduring injustices. The paradox, however, rooted in this form of social solidarity is not whether but, rather, *how* we care. Scaffolding "good intentions" to millennial capitalism, no matter how creative, is bound to make matters worse for those less fortunate. The use of interest-rate swaps by Goldman Sachs, discussed in chapter 4, which allowed the bank to make millions from Detroit's water crisis and then turn around to help social entrepreneurs set up water infrastructure facilities via venture capital initiatives in the so-called developing world, is one poignant example of the creative and destructive tendencies inherent in this style of new humanitarian government.

Out front on stage, spectacles like the Global Citizen Festival do important work in raising popular awareness and cultivating social solidarity in response to moments of crises and desperation. However, backstage, much is hidden. Celebrity capitalists, Jim Yong Kim, and the IMF's managing director, Christine Lagarde, may take center stage at glamorous Global Citizen events, but hidden from view of the amassed millennials are the disastrous policies both the IMF and the World Bank have imposed on developing countries, which combined trade liberalization with privatization and deregulation schemes, and later fiscal austerity measures to pry open their markets to foreign investment and multinational interests, concomitantly destroying public services and local industry. Equally hidden from participants' view are Global Citizen sponsors and partnerships, such as the United Nations, Google, Unilever, Citibank, and KPMG, and their equally shady practices of late.

Citigroup, for example, agreed to a $7 billion settlement with the US Department of Justice for its role in defrauding investors with toxic mortgage-backed securities leading up to the financial crisis in 2008. Unilever, too, has admitted to illegally dumping toxicity of another kind—more than 5 tons of mercury from its factory in Kodaikanal, India. According to an Indian government report submitted to the Madras High Court in Chennai, 30 people died, and 550 ex-workers are suffering from health ailments due to mercury exposure (Todhunter 2015). More recently, John William Ashe (who died in 2016), along with others, was accused of bribery during his term as president of the UNGA from 2013 to 2014. KMPG has also been in the scandal spotlight, admitting to criminal wrongdoing and being forced to pay $456 million in fines, restitution, and penalties for designing, marketing, and implementing illegal tax shelters that generated at least $11 billion in phony tax losses for their wealthy clients. And Google, Joseph Stiglitz (2015, 1) writes, "have demonstrated a genius for avoiding taxes that exceeds what they employed in creating innovative products." I, too, eager to show my solidarity with others, considered purchasing a Global Citizen's T-shirt to commemorate the event from its online store, only to be burdened with the fact that its clothing manufacturer, H&M, had recently been cited in a report by Human Rights Watch for labor rights violations, including appalling working conditions, hiring practices, forced overtime, pregnancy discrimination, sexual harassment, and denial of maternity benefits, in its factories in Cambodia (Human Rights Watch 2015).

We might be forgiven for focusing on Beyoncé and Eddie Vedder, as opposed to the numerous other happenings swirling around in the shadows of this spectacle. Yet equally telling is the lack of interest by many millennials in the recent Trans-Pacific Partnership, which, like other free trade agreements, continues to favor corporations' rights over the rights of workers, the environment, and local governments. The very fact that the new SDGs are framed as a business opportunity and that their operationalization should be left to multinational lobbyists does not seem to faze those who went to the park to participate in this exhibition of social solidarity. Why ask such inconvenient questions when there are redemption songs to be sung? Yet without such reflection, Global Citizen and other events of social solidarity run the risk of giving cover to elites, politicians, and companies, rather than holding them accountable to young people who care about poverty alleviation and social and environmental justice.

In particular, millennials and others should recognize that corporations and private investors have steadily muscled their way into formulating the SDGs and an increasing amount of attention is being spent on the role of business in their implementation and management. One not well advertised forum that took place during the music and other theatrics of the UN Summit was the United Nations Private Sector Forum. Hosted by Secretary-General Ban Ki-moon, the forum featured high-level roundtable discussions with 150 private sector participations, government, civil society, and UN leaders, with a view to ushering in a new era of enhanced collaboration between the UN and the private sector. Invited guests included representatives from Citigroup, Unilever, KPMG, Google, other chief executives and UN Global Compact signatories. The session was co-organized by the UN Global Compact, the World Business Council for Sustainable Development, and the Global Reporting Initiative (GRI) (United Nations Global Compact 2015). One only has to listen to a business consultant talk about the SDGs to recognize their importance to the private sector.

> I think getting business to understand that this is about new markets and new business opportunities, and new business models to reach those opportunities, instead of thinking about it as charity and something that is the mandate of the development agencies and the government and the NGOs is a fundamental shift that I think can be very empowering [for business].

"This is a new revenue model for business," concludes Mark Kramer, co-founder and managing director of the consulting firm FSG, in a recent interview (Saldinger 2015).

In addition to showcasing how companies are aligning core business strategies and practices with the SDGs, roundtable discussions focused on three themes: combatting corruption, peace and stability, and rule of law. The implication, of course, is that doing business in the Global South is plagued with corruption, instability, and lawlessness. And these three horsemen have to be tamed in accordance with private sector interests before their commitment to humanitarianism writ large can be ensured. A recent report by the United Nations Economic Commission of Africa on illicit financial flows from Africa estimated that the continent was losing roughly $50 billion each year. This figure exceeds the average annual official development assistance that Africa received from 2008 to 2012. The report also revealed that "commercial illicit financial flows (including tax evasion, trade and services mispricing and transfer pricing abuses by multinational corporations) account for the largest proportion of illicit financial flows, followed by proceeds from criminal activities and corruption" (High-Level Panel on Illicit Financial Flows from Africa 2015, 3). The main receivers of such flows are primarily developed countries (in particular, the United States, Canada, Japan, the Republic of Korea, and European countries) and emerging economies (China and India). These countries and their corporations are also Africa's major trade partners (High-Level Panel on Illicit Financial Flows from Africa 2015). The report concluded that Africa needs mechanisms and strategies to tackle illicit financial flows. "Indeed, curtailing illicit financial flows could become a key delivery mechanism for sustainable development" (High-Level Panel on Illicit Financial Flows from Africa 2015, 12).

Months after the report was released, the UN held the Third International Conference on Financing for Development in Addis Ababa, Ethiopia, to determine how to finance the SDGs, which have been estimated to cost between $2 trillion and $3 trillion a year for fifteen years. During this meeting the developing countries, organized around the Group of Seventy-Seven and China, called for an intergovernmental body with the mandate and resources to create a coherent global framework for international tax cooperation. Until now, the Organization for Economic Cooperation and Development (OECD), whose members are essentially the world's thirty-four richest countries, had continued to set international standards on taxation. Opening up this decision-making body to ensure that developing countries—the world's majority—had an equal say in matters of international taxation would all but guarantee that money earned in their countries by multinational corporations would stay there and contribute to their development and prosperity, without being subjected to illicit flows. But the United States and the European Union blocked the Group of Seventy-Seven's proposal, insisting that the governance of tax cooperation take place exclusively under the OECD, under their control. These same "controls" were recently exposed as part of the "Luxemburg Leaks."[1] for what they really are: elaborate tax scams using complicated accounting and legal structures that move profits to a low-tax country, in this case Luxembourg, from higher-tax countries where they are headquartered. "In some instances, the leaked records indicate, companies have enjoyed effective tax rates of less than 1 percent on the profits they've shuffled into Luxembourg" (International Consortium of Investigative Journalists 2014, 1).

What becomes immediately apparent is that, for all its glamour and effort, the SDG program for development and poverty reduction will not usher in a new set of guiding principles that attend to questions of power and politics but, rather, an old model of industrial growth, which continues to ignore the relationship between the accumulation of wealth and the accumulation of poverty and dispossession. Absent are the urgent changes in tax and trade regulation that developing countries insist are essential to fight poverty and reform international financial institutions that continue to exploit developing countries. The strong role granted to corporations in the SDG process effectively precluded any direct challenge to business interests and all but guarantee access to emerging markets in terms and conditions that were favorable to their and their interests alone. In hindsight, the Global Festival and the UN Summit might be better seen as a sideshow to the actual event—the United Nations Private Sector Forum 2015—that ushered in a new era of enhanced collaboration between the UN and the private sector in the name of poverty reduction and doing good, with minimal fanfare and participation. In truth, the only reason emerging markets are of any interest to the private sector is that they offer historically unparalleled growth potential for business. Emergent markets are the markets of the future.

Part of what makes this current humanitarian conjuncture so extraordinary is the way in which finance capital, corporate philanthropy, social entrepreneurialism, and business management principles have converged and been reconfigured to solve the most pressing problem of modern society: poverty. Moreover, our collective fascination with Silicon Valley–type humanitarianism—entrepreneurial, venture capital, seed funded, strictly technological—has also blinded us to how new humanitarianism is now being done—with methods that are largely bureaucratic, managerial, technologically outmoded, and corporate. Do we really believe that arming the poor with a fleet of cell phones or populating another digital platform will liberate them from structurally created poverty and dispossession? Are we really that naive?

Likewise, this form of new humanitarianism has also blinded us to the spectacular changes in state, market, and civil society institutions as they each endeavor to make the world a better place. Moreover, it should not be lost on us that the current president of the United States is a billionaire businessman—business is now government. The overlapping and active participation of state, market, and civil society in the implementation of new humanitarianism under neoliberal logics has all but made these traditional institutions of modernity indistinguishable from one another. For example, for all their emphasis on entrepreneurialism and innovation, donors and foundations have become remarkably preoccupied with instituting government-like bureaucracies and managerial systems with which to manage new humanitarianism. Similarly, as governments struggle with growing legitimacy questions regarding the dissimilar conditions of their majority poor and exclusive elite citizens, they have increasingly turned to the private sector to help them govern. This new era of enhanced collaboration became most obvious during the US federal government shutdown of 2013, when wealthy philanthropists gave personal gifts to keep public sector services, such as Head Start, going during the shutdown. Basic science research too, once the exclusive domain of governments, is increasingly becoming a private and philanthropic enterprise. Civil society groups, as well, are now providing government services—water and sanitation, agriculture, education, energy, and so on—and using business development models and investment logics to do so, effectively becoming an extension of the financial system, the very system that causes poverty in the first place. Gone are the days when civil society organizations called out coercive governments and shady corporations and held them to account for less than sanguine practices. Today, no one is outside as the core of capitalism and the spirit of humanity are now one and the same. In effect, the discourse of doing good has proved to be a powerful vehicle for reformulating the role not only of civil society groups but of governments and the private sector as well.

A Necessary Condition

But the question really is not whether billionaire philanthropists can replace governments, or capitalism can replace democracy, as wealthy individuals have always used their status to promote a vision for humanity's future that is consistent with their vision. The real question is how we can come to understand this grow-ing ideology at a time when the opposite is so convincing, at a time when the failures of neoliberalism should be exceedingly evident. Humanitarian ideology, to borrow from the anthropologist Clifford Geertz (1964), provides the global citizen with a symbolic outlet and sense of eternal hope in the face of gross inequalities. The Global Citizen's celebrity-packed festival in New York is a poi-gnant example of this symbolism. On the one hand, thousands of millennials came together to sing and express their solidarity against global poverty. However, on the other hand, very few of them bothered to ask how those in extreme poverty got to be so poor, and what continues to impoverish them? In effect, the idea, or ideology, of global citizens is not only a humane one but also a *necessary condition* for an economic and political system that helps the few at the expense of the many. This notion of a humanitarian social solidarity is, in part, the ideology that permits accumulation by dispossession to continue. Without it, we would have to realize that society is inherently inhumane and that we in the Global North have nowhere else to look but ourselves for this inhumanity and its ethnocidal and genocidal tendencies. New humanitarianism, then, masks the exploitative and power rela-tions in *doing good* by reducing questions of inequality and dispossession to economic growth and poverty reduction, instead of political and economic reform. In effect, new humanitarianism both constructs and manages the realm of poverty and dispossession to be *regulated* and not eradicated, and as a result, (these) good intentions are simply not enough.

I want to close by asking, as others have, a simple question: what do we want in the absence of the welfare state beyond denouncing neoliberalism and providing silver bullets? Of course, the answer to this question depends on whom you ask. But if we accept the premise laid out in this book that what amounts to sovereign decisions over life and death are limited not only to decisions of governments but also to the discretion of civil society, and the goodwill of corporations, then what are the implications for doing good? What does it mean to be political-postcolonial? And in what ways are we contributing to infrastructures of exploitation and violence in the Global South with our good intentions? What might such a perspec-tive also signal for neoliberalism in the face of massive failure?

We can look at the recent attempt by developing countries, organized by the Group of Seventy-Seven and China, at the Third International Financing for Development conference in Addis Ababa, Ethiopia, for an intergovernmental committee on tax cooperation as one political alternative. Despite the disap-pointment of the failure in Addis Ababa to create a representative tax body that would ensure that profits made in their mines, their fields, and their factories would remain inside their borders, the increasingly audible call for reform of the international tax system by developing countries is not likely to be silenced any time soon.

We can also look at the increasing role of government regulation, particularly by countries in the Global South, concerning nonprofit organizations and their funding mechanisms as another possible marker of change. India's Prime Minister Narendra Modi's government recently froze $4 million in funding of the US-based Ford Foundation for failing to register its Indian arm under the Foreign Exchange Management Act, a mandatory requirement for all foreign agencies operating in the country. Although previous governments never insisted on compliance with the law, the Modi government toughened rules governing INGOs, and this year the government cancelled the registration of nearly 9,000 groups for failing to declare details of overseas donations (Jain 2015). China, too, has proposed new legislation—the Overseas NGO Management Law—to standardize and guide all activities carried out by overseas NGOs within its borders. The proposed law requires overseas NGOs to register with a legally designated representative office. Under the proposed law, overseas NGOs must operate "according to Chinese laws; not threaten China's security or national and ethnic unity; must not harm China's national interests, societal public interests, or the legal rights of other groups and citizens; and must not disrupt public order and morality" (China Development Brief 2015, 2). China is the most recent notable government to join a growing group of countries, including South Sudan, Cambodia, Ethiopia, Uganda, Kenya, and Eretria, to introduce specific legislation to govern INGOs operating within their borders. Most of the new legislation, government officials argue, is designed to require better reporting mechanisms by Western-based NGOs to force them to be transparent and accountable, including declaring their sources of income and obtaining permits from local government authorities to operate.

This tougher scrutiny of INGOs by developing countries has many in the Global North concerned. And given the oppressive regimes and ongoing crises in some of these areas, these concerns may certainly be warranted. Nevertheless, these countries argue that the latest round of demands for reforms in international tax cooperation and nonprofit regulation are essential for fighting poverty and illicit financial flows that continue to undermine their economic, sociopolitical, and environmental sustainability. In 2015, Kenya shut down 500 NGOs for noncompliance with its new law, accusing some of using their charitable status as a front for raising cash for terrorism (Mwesigwa 2015). Many humanitarians in the Global North vehemently oppose these new reforms, arguing that government control over civil society organizations risks negating the very essence of freedom of association. Most Western governments, NGOs, and even businesses have demanded that China, India, and other countries throw out their new or proposal legislation or change it entirely. Yet these same devotees of the poor and oppressed remain strangely silent about the billions in illicit flows that leave developing countries each year en route to the Northern multinational headquarters, via one or two tax havens, to ensure that these mavericks of capital pay little or no tax on the profits and wages they earn abroad. The ability to evade taxes, Donald Trump proudly declared, made him smart not criminal. According to the Economic Commission for Africa (ECA), total annual illicit financial flows are estimated at some $50 billion. Corporate crime in the United States alone is estimated to total $200 billion a year. These practices disproportionately affect the poor and powerless, as CEO after CEO walks away from a company's transgressions, while taxpayers are left to pick up the tab. If people looked carefully at what developing countries are trying to do—albeit using very different methods and in some cases for very different reasons—they might begin to see the foundations of welfare state–type strategies of rule in situ, to the extent possible.

If this tougher scrutiny of INGOs is, in fact, about protecting the social fabric of developing countries, then it seems to suggest that the Global North has very little to teach the Global South as the latter slowly and strategically maneuvers to take social justice matters within its borders into its own hands. Only in government's willingness to tax income and wealth, and regulate well-being can both be realized for the many instead of the few. This is as true today as it was in the past: state-led planning and, in some cases, state ownership went hand in hand with relatively high rates of growth and a relatively fair share of the economic pie. In the United States, for example, the share of national income taken by the top 1 percent of income earners remained close to 8 percent during the post–World War II decades (Harvey 2005). In 2012, however, after more than thirty years of neoliberalism, the top 10 percent of earners took more than half the country's total income, the highest level recorded since the government began collecting relevant data a century ago. There is nothing inherent about this level of global inequality.

The South may be growing impatient with the same old talk of blueprints for sustainability filled with many of the same guidelines and plans that made these once-rich countries dependent on Northern generosity and charity. Listening to General Electric's Sustainable Healthcare Solutions chief executive Terri Bresenham talk about the firm's blueprint for improving health outcomes—SDG's third goal—one cannot help but conclude that the SDGs, like the MDGs before them, mean business as usual. GE's blueprint for innovating in technology, business models, and partnerships, Bresenham concludes will give "business enough room to flourish and decide, and be empowered to make the right choices" in emerging markets. We should remember that of the eight MDGs adopted by world leaders fifteen years ago, only one has been achieved: halving the number of people living in extreme poverty. And this was achieved largely by economic growth in China and by defining extreme poverty as the daily consumption of $1.25 or less. One could go back further to the World Commission on Environment and Development in 1987 (the Brundtland Commission) when the concept of sustainable development was firmly established. This blueprint was also the result of a UNGA resolution. The message of the Brundtland Report was that humanity has the ability to make development sustainable—to ensure it meets the needs of the present genera-tion without compromising the ability of future generations to make their own needs—socially, economically, and ecologically. This blueprint, too, was business as usual.

Yet in spite of these and numerous other failures, most Western humanitar-ians either live in a state of denial, refusing even to hear that there might be an alternative to kind-hearted capitalism or, if they do hear it, passively justify it as the normal cost of doing fundamental honest and good work in an otherwise coercive and corrupt world. Against evidence to the contrary, they continue to believe they are acting in the general interest of all of humanity. In effect new humanitarianism has become a central fabric of our society. It has become this because to question the current state of human affairs for most of the world's popu-lation leads to some serious soul searching on the part of the self-proclaimed good Samaritans from the West. How has it come to be that in a time of unprecedented humanitarianism we continue to observe unparalleled physical and economic dis-possession? Witness the thousands who have recently perished in their futile at-tempt to leave the atrocious conditions in Syria for a better life in Europe. Many who hope for a better life leave to encounter conditions of imprisonment and abuse, often ending in their death. Nearly 60 million people—half of them children—around the world have been displaced by war and persecution, more than at any time since World War II, a *New York Times Magazine* article reports (Silverstein 2015). Or con-sider the recent investigation into the Red Cross—the charity of choice for ordi-nary Americans and corporations alike—and its struggles in Haiti after its most recent earthquake, which killed more than 160,000 and displaced close to 1.5 mil-lion Haitians. The Red Cross received an outpouring of donations after the 2010 quake, nearly half a billion dollars. However, five years later, many residents live in shacks made of rusty sheet metal, without access to drinkable water, electricity, or basic sanitation (Elliott and Sullivan 2015). We don't have to guess about the dire consequences of President Trump's Muslim ban as increased racism at the hands of white supremacists is already on the rise.

A recent World Bank report about increasing dispossession and displace-ment in the face of climate change could lead an additional 100 million people to live in extreme poverty by 2030. Yet the key question of the report was how much climate change will influence the flows in and out of poverty and affect poverty over time, with no mention of the Global North's role or responsibility, as if cli-mate change just happened! However, despite mostly hollow pledges to rein in emissions of carbon dioxide and other gases that contribute to global warming, countries in the Global North have been slow to introduce policies that might ac-tually delay the uneven consequences of climate change for poor people and poor countries. And given this perspective, the North, once again, can take on the role of good Samaritan, helping those less fortunate, this time via finance and insurance directed at what the Bank has called "climate-informed development." Yet this seemingly helpful suggestion advanced by the Bank that the poor should first save or then borrow from financial institutions and insurance companies to help them adapt to the effects of climate change–induced poverty and dispossession suggests that we in the North are much more a part of the problem of humanitarianism than the solution. What will it take for us in the North to face the undeniable truth of climate change—a direct response of millennial capitalism—and its disproportionate impact on the world's already poor and dispossessed? Clearly, appointing a self-proclaimed climate change denialist to head the US Environmental Protection Agency was not the answer many of us were looking for.

The important question of how poverty can be eliminated has no easy answers. Even if one recognizes that my way of life and my culture are part of the problem, what can I do as an individual with this information? One of the greatest challenges in understanding poverty and dispossession is the continued emphasis on poverty and dispossession as object, and not relationality. This *new humanitarian* governmentality continues to construct and manage poverty and dispossession as a thing that exists in the slums of Kolkata or the fields of Rwanda, a thing that can be quantified in some meaningful way, captured, and then managed. A relational perspective, in contrast, would attend to questions of power, politics, identity, and culture—raising awareness and building skills to move the entrepreneur, the investor, the volunteer, the intellect, the politician, and the public beyond notions of the Global South based on compassion and charity to an understanding of political, economic, and environmental interdependence. Moreover, in order to promote ways of thinking (ideology), being (professions, volunteering), and understanding that encourage and enable people to think critically about eradicating poverty, and not just regulating it (a social movement), we also need to acknowledge the uneven levels of power (white, male, and Western) inherent in the everyday practices of trying to do good. Another challenge is in recognizing the extent to which civil society has become truly governmental. This admission is an important first step in understanding the degree to which participating in civil society is now also politics by other means; civil society is now constitutive of a political superstructure that is ill-equipped to embrace either the idea (ideology) or the material reality of freedom and equality for all.

What I have outlined in this book is as much about a crisis of imagination and a crisis of humanity. The Global South is becoming increasingly impatient with the Global North's humanitarian life preserver of free markets, corporate rights, and global finance. It is time for us in the Global North to come to terms with our privileged lives and perspectives and to start singing a different tune—not one of redemption but one of pedagogy: a pedagogy of the oppressed, which the Brazilian educator Paulo Freire (2011) remarkably identified over a decade ago. A pedagogy forged *with*, and not *for*, the oppressed in their and our incessant struggle to regain their humanity. Freire (2011) cautions us do-gooders that when people are already dehumanized, the process of their liberation must not employ the same methods of dehumanization. The correct method lies in genuine dialogue, communication that does not begin with the egoistic interests of the Global North but, rather, is rooted in the experiences and knowledge of those who really understand poverty and dispossession. Such a turn or change would also signal the end of transcendental claims of doing good and the end of grand narratives of development and sustainability. In such a place of thought and action, the ideology, professionalism, and social movements associated with doing good would become a social justice question, rather than a device of development. This type of inquiring would also include questions of accountability and responsibility that so many good neoliberals demand, but these questions would need to be directed at our privileged perspectives much more than the dispossessed. The real question is: are we finally ready to listen?

Notes

1. Luxemburg Leaks is the name given to the financial scandal where multinational corporations were benefitting from tax rulings and tax avoidance schemes in Luxembourg. The scandal was revealed in November 2014 by International Consortium of Investigative Journalists (ICIJ).

Bibliography

Agamben, Giorgio. 2005. *State of Exception.* Chicago: University of Chicago Press.

Alfred Santos, Lean. 2014. "ADB Directly Funding NGOs, CSOs—Why Not?" *Development Newswire*, Devex. May 7. https://www.devex.com/news/adb-directly-funding -ngos-csos-why-not-83440?mkt_tok=3RkMMJWWfF9wsRoku6jLe%2B%2FhmjTE U5z17eQkWqe1iokz2EFye%2BLIHETpodcMTcBnNLrYDBceEJhqyQJxPr3DJNUN oddxRhbkDQ%3D%3D.

Alwaleed Philanthropies. 2015. "Prince Alwaleed Pledges His Wealth to Philanthropy— $32B, a Groundbreaking Gift Dedicated to Philanthropy." Press release. http:// www.alwaleedphilanthropies.org/prince-alwaleed-pledges-his-wealth -philanthropy-32b-groundbreaking-gift-dedicated-philanthropy.

Anderson, Chris. 2008. "The End of Theory." *Wired* 16:108–109.

Andreotti, Vanessa. 2006. "The Contributions of Postcolonial Theory to Development Education." *DEA Thinkpieces.* http://www.dea.org.uk/thinkpieces/.

Andrews, Edmund, and Peter Baker. 2009. "A.I.G. Planning Huge Bonuses after $170 Billion Bailout." *New York Times.* March 14.

Appadurai, Arjun. 1990. "Disjuncture and Difference in the Global Cultural Economy." In *Global Culture: Nationalism, Globalization and Modernity,* ed. Michael Featherstone, 295–310. London: Sage.

Arendt, Hannah. 1951. *The Origins of Totalitarianism.* New York: Harcourt, Brace.

Arnove, Robert. 1980. *Philanthropy and Cultural Imperialism.* Boston: G.K. Hall.

Arrighi, Giovanni. 2007. *Adam Smith in Beijing. Lineages of the Twenty-First Century.* New York: Verso.

Arum, Richard, and Josipa Rosksa. 2011. *Academically Adrift: Limited Learning on College Campuses.* Chicago: University of Chicago Press.

Asian NGO Coalition for Agrarian Reform and Rural Development. 1994. "A Country Paper of Bangladesh on Promoting Dialogue and Collaboration in Sustainable Agriculture & Rural Development (SARD) Between NGOs/RPOs and Government." United Nations Food and Agriculture Organization, Quezon City, Metro Manila, Philippines.

Association of Universities and Colleges of Canada. 2014. "Canada's Universities in the World." Association of Universities and Colleges of Canada, Ottawa, Ontario.

Atkinson, Paul. 1990. *The Ethnographic Imagination: Textual Constructions of Reality.* New York: Routledge.

Baer, Justin, and Joe Light. 2014. "Goldman Sachs Settles FHFA Lawsuit for About $1.2 Billion." *Wall Street Journal*, August 22. http://www.wsj.com/articles/goldman -sachs-close-to-settling-fhfa-lawsuit-for-more-than-1-billion-1408737438.

Barnett, Michael. 2011. *Empire of Humanity: A History of Humanitarianism.* Ithaca: Cornell University Press.

Batavia, Hima, Justin Chakma, Hassan Masum, and Peter Singer. 2011. "Market-Minded Development." *Stanford Social Innovation Review* 5:1–3.

Bebbington, Anthony. 1997. "New States, New NGOs? Crises and Transitions among Rural Development NGOs in the Andean Region." *World Development* 25:1155–1765.

Beloe, Seb, John Elkington, Katie Fry Hester, and Sue Newell. 2003. "The 21st Century NGO in the Market for Change." Sustainability, London, UK. http://www .sustainability.com/library/the-21st-century-ngo/.

Benham Rennick, Joanne, and Michael Desjardins. 2013. *The World Is My Classroom: International Learning and Canadian Higher Learning.* Toronto: University of Toronto Press.

Benjamin, Walter. 1942. "On the Concept of History." In *Walter Benjamin: Selected Writings.* Vol. 4, *1938–1940*, ed. Howard Eiland and Michael W. Jennings. Cambridge, MA: Harvard University Press, 2003.

Bhabha, Homi. 1990. "The Other Question: Difference, Discrimination, and the Discourse of Colonialism." In *Out There: Marginalization and Contemporary Culture*, ed. Russell Ferguson, Martha Gever, Trinh T. Minh-ha, and Cornell West, 71–89. Cambridge, MA: MIT Press.

Bill & Melinda Gates Foundation. 2014. "Water for People Receives Funding for Sanitation as a Business Program." Press Release. Bill & Melinda Gates Foundation, Seattle.

———. 2015. "Africa Health Foundation." http://www.gatesfoundation.org/How-We -Work/Quick-Links/Program-Related-Investments/Africa-Health-Fund.

Blackwood, Amy S., Katie L. Roeger, and Sarah L. Pettijohn. 2010. "The Non-Profit Sector in Brief: Public Charities, Giving, and Volunteering, 2012." The Urban Institute, Washington, DC.

Bolton, John. 2009. "Future of the Humanitarian System: Impacts of Internal Changes." Feinstein International Center, Medford, MA.

Bourgois, Philippe. 2000. "Violating Apartheid in the United States." In *Racing Research, Researching Race*, ed. France W. Twine and Jonathan Warren, 204–214. New York: New York University Press.

Brandon, Katrina. 1996. "Ecotourism and Conservation: A Review of Key Issues." World Bank, Washington, DC.

British Broadcasting Corporation. 2005. "In Full: Mandela's Poverty Speech." *BBC News.* http://news.bbc.co.uk/2/hi/uk_news/politics/4232603.stm.

———. 2016. "Uganda Court Orders Closure of Low-Cost Bridge International Schools." November 4. http://www.bbc.com/news/world-africa-37871130.

Browne, Andrew. 2004. "Tsunami's Aftermath: On Asia's Coasts, Progress Destroys Natural Defenses." *Wall Street Journal,* December 31. http://online.wsj.com/news /articles/SB110443750029213098.

Bryant, Raymond, and Michael Goodman. 2004. "Consuming Narratives: The Political Ecology of 'Alternative' Consumption." *Transactions of the Institute of British Geographers* 29:344–366.

Buffett, Peter. 2013. "The Charitable-Industrial Complex." *New York Times*, July 26. http://www.nytimes.com/2013/07/27/opinion/the-charitable-industrial-complex .html?_r=1.

Burawoy, Michael. 1998. "The Extended Case Method." *Sociological Theory* 16:4–33.

———. 2001. "Manufacturing the Global." *Ethnography* 2:147–159.

Burawoy, Michael, Joseph A. Blum, Sheba George, Zsuzsa Gille, Teresa Gowan, Lynne Haney, Maren Klawiter, Steve H. Lopez, Sean O' Riain, and Millie Thayer. 2000. *Global Ethnography: Forces, Connections, and Imaginations in a Postmodern World*. Berkeley: University of California Press.

Burawoy, Michael, Alice Burton, Ann Arnett Ferguson, Kathryn Fox, J., Joshua Gamson, Nadine Gartrell, Leslie Hurst, Charles Kurzman, Leslie Salzinger, Josepha Schiffman, and Shiori Ui. 1991. *Ethnography Unbound. Power and resistance in the Modern Metropolis*. Berkeley: University of California Press.

Calder, Ian. 1999. *The Blue Revolution: Land Use & Integrated Water Resources Management*. London: Earthscan.

Canadian Broadcasting Corporation. 2006. "How Charities Spend." *CBC News*. http://www.cbc.ca/news/background/asia_earthquake/how-charities-spend.html.

———. 2011. "Thousands of Charity Workers Earn Big Salaries: Report." *CBC News*, July 10. http://www.cbc.ca/news/canada/thousands-of-charity-workers-earn-big-salaries-report-1.1022805.

Caprara, David, Kevin F. F. Quigley, and Lex Rieffel. 2009. "International Volunteer Service: A Smart Way to Build Bridges. Recommendations on How to Enhance U.S. Volunteer Efforts." Brookings Institution, Washington, DC.

Catholic Relief Services. 2015. "Proceedings from ICT4D 2015. Increasing Impact Through Innovation." http://www.ict4dconference.crs.org/.

Center on Philanthropy. 2013. "Giving USA 2013. The Annual Report on Philanthropy for the Year 2013. 58th Annual Issue." Center on Philanthropy at Indiana University, Bloomington, IN.

Chatterjee, Partha. 2004. *The Politics of the Governed. Reflections on Popular Politics in Most of the World*. New York: Columbia University Press.

Cherryholmes, Cleo. 1988. "Construct Validity and the Discourse of Research." *American Journal of Education* 96:421–457.

China Development Brief. 2015. "CDB English Translation of the Overseas NGO Management Law (Second Draft)." http://chinadevelopmentbrief.cn/articles/cdb-english-translation-of-the-overseas-ngo-management-law-second-draft/.

Choge, Cheryl, Courtney Harrison, Peter McCornick, and Ryan Bartlett. 2011. "A Review of U.S. Efforts in Water and Sanitation." Nicholas Institute for Environmental Policy Solutions, Durham, NC.

Chomsky, Noam. 1992. *Deterring Democracy*. New York: Hill & Wang.

The Chronicle of Philanthropy. 2013. "How America's Biggest Companies Gave in 2012." http://philanthropy.com/article/How-America-s-Biggest/140269/#id=101092.

Clifford, James. 1986. "Introduction: Partial Truths." In *Writing Culture: The Poetics and Politics of Ethnography*, ed. James Clifford and George Marcus, 1–26. Berkeley: University of California Press.

———. 1988. *The Predicament of Culture: Twentieth-Century Ethnography, Literature, and Art*. Cambridge, MA: Harvard University Press.

Comaroff, Jean, and John L. Comaroff. 2000. "Millennial Capitalism: First Thoughts on A Second Coming." *Public Culture* 12:291–343.

Craig, David, and Doug Porter. 2006. *Development Beyond Neoliberalism? Governance, Poverty Reduction and Political Economy*. New York: Routledge.

Crapanzano, Vincent. 1986. "Hermes' Dilemma: The Making of Subversion in Ethno-graphic Description." In *Writing Culture: The Poetics and Politics of Ethnography*, ed. James Clifford and George Marcus, 51–76. Berkeley: University of California Press.

"Cross-Cultural Solutions." 2015. http://www.crossculturalsolutions.org/.

Dallaire, Roméo. 2003. *Shake Hands with the Devil: The Failure of Humanity in Rwanda.* Cambridge, MA: Da Capo Press.

Davis, Mike. 2004. "Planet of Slums: Urban Involution and the Informal Proletariat." *New Left Review* 26:5–34.

Denzin, Norman, and Yvonna Lincoln. 1994. *Handbook of Qualitative Research.* Thousand Oaks, CA: Sage.

Dezalay, Yves, and Bryant Garth. 1998. "Droits de l'homme et philanthropie. hegemo-nique." *Actes de la Recherche en Sciences Sociales* 121 (1): 23–41.

Dijkzeul, Dennis, Dorothea Hilhorst, and Peter Walker. 2013. "Introduction: Evidence-Based Action in Humanitarian Crises." *Disasters* 37:S1–S19.

Du Bois, W. E. B. 2014 [1903]. *The Souls of Black Folk.* New York: Millennium Publications.

Duffield, Mark. 2007. *Development, Security and Unending War. Governing the World of Peoples.* Cambridge, UK: Polity Press.

Edwards, Michael, and David Hulme. 1996. "Too Close for Comfort? The Impact of Official Aid on Nongovernmental Organizations." *World Development* 24:961–973.

Eisner, Elliot. 1994. *The Educational Imagination. On the Design and Evaluation of School Programs.* New York: Macmillan College.

Elliott, Justin, and Laura Sullivan. 2015. "How the Red Cross Raised Half a Billion Dollars for Haiti—and Built Six Homes." ProPublica, New York.

Escobar, Arturo. 1995. *Encountering Development. The Making and the Unmaking of the Third World.* Princeton: Princeton University Press.

Fine, Gary Allan. 1993. "Ten Lies of Ethnography: Moral Dilemmas of Field Research." *Journal of Contemporary Ethnography* 22:267–294.

Fisher, William. 1997. "DOING GOOD? The Politics and Antipolitics of NGO Practices." *Annual Review of Anthropology* 26:439–464.

Food and Agriculture Organization (FAO). 2008. "Report of the Expert Consultation on Improving Planning and Policy Development in Aquaculture." FAO Fisheries Report No. 858. FAO, Rome, February 26–29.

Foucault, Michel. 1997. *Michel Foucault: "Society Must Be Defended." Lectures at the College de France, 1975–1976*, ed. M. Bertani and A. Fontana; gen. ed. Francois Ewald and Alessandro Fontana; trans. David Macey. New York: Picador.

———. 2008. *The Birth of Biopolitics: Lectures at the College de France, 1978–1979.* New York: Palgrave Macmillan.

Fox, Fiona. 2001. "New Humanitarianism: Does It Provide a Moral Banner for the 21st Century?" *Disasters* 25:275–289.

Freeland, Chrystia. 2012. *Plutocrats: The Rise of the New Global Super-Rich and the Fall of Everyone Else.* New York: Penguin Books.

Freire, Paulo. 2011. *Pedagogy of the Oppressed: 30th Anniversary Edition.* New York: Bloomsbury Academic.

Geertz, Clifford. 1964. "Ideology as a Cultural System." In *Ideology and Discontent*, ed. David Apter, 47–76. New York: Free Press of Glencoe.

———. 1973. *The Interpretation of Cultures: Selected Essays*. New York: Basic Books.

———. 1988. *Works and Lives: The Anthropologist as Author*. Stanford: Stanford University Press.

Global Crossroads. 2015. "Global Crossroad—Meaningful Volunteering Abroad." http://www.globalcrossroad.com/.

Global Glimpse. 2015. "Global Glimpse. Opening the Eyes of Tomorrow's Leaders." https://www.globalglimpse.org/who-we-are/.

Global Innovation Fund. 2015. "Transforming Ideas into Impact." http://www .globalinnovation.fund/.

Global Urban Observatory. 2003. *Slums of the World: The Face of Urban Poverty in the New Millennium?* New York: United Nations Human Settlements Programme.

Goldman, Michael. 2005. *Imperial Nature: The World Bank and Struggles for Social Justice in the Age of Globalization*. New Haven: Yale University Press.

Goodman, Allan, and Stacie Nevadomski Berdan. 2014. "Every Student Should Study Abroad." *New York Times*, May 12. http://www.nytimes.com/roomfordebate/2013 /10/17/should-more-americans-study-abroad/every-student-should-study-abroad.

Graeber, David. 2015. *The Utopia of Rules. On Technology, Stupidity, and the Secret Joys of Bureaucracy*. Brooklyn, NY: Melville House.

Gramsci, Antonio. 2000 [1935]. *The Gramsci Reader: Selected Writings, 1916–1935*, ed. David Forgacs. New York: New York University Press.

Gregory, Ann Goggins, and Don Howard. 2009. "The Nonprofit Starvation Cycle." *Stanford Social Innovation Review* (Fall): 49–53.

Hammersley, Martyn, and Paul Atkinson. 1995. *Ethnography: Principles in Practice*. 2nd ed. New York: Routledge.

Haraway, Donna. 2015. "Anthropocene, Capitalocene, Plantationocene, Chthulucene: Making Kin." *Environmental Humanities* 6:159–165.

Harding, Sandra. 2012. "Moving South and East: Epistemic Modernization for Global Northern Philosophies of Science." Paper presented at *Relocating Science and Technology Max Planck Institute for Social Anthropology*, Halle, Germany, July 18–20, 2012.

Hardt, Michael, and Antonio Negri. 2001. *Empire*. Cambridge, MA: Harvard University Press.

———. 2004. *Multitude: War and Democracy in the Age of Empire*. New York: Penguin Press.

Hart, Gillian. 2001. "Development Critiques in the 1990s: Culs de Sac and Promising Paths." *Progress in Human Geography* 25:649–658.

———. 2002. *Disabling Globalization. Places of Power in Post-Apartheid South Africa*. Berkeley: University of California Press.

———. 2004. "Geography and Development: Critical Ethnographies of D/development in the Era of Globalization." *Progress in Human Geography* 28:91–100.

———. 2009. "D/developments after the Meltdown." *Antipode* 41:117–141.

———. 2013. "Beyond Dichotomies: Challenges in Reframing 'The Global.'" Paper presented at "Framing the Global" Conference. September 26–28. Indiana University, Bloomington, IN.

Harvey, David. 2003. *The New Imperialism*. Oxford: Oxford University Press.

———. 2005. *A Brief History of Neoliberalism*. Oxford: Oxford University Press.

———. 2006. *Spaces of Global Capitalism. Towards a Theory of Uneven Geographical Development*. London: Verso.

———. 2010. *The Enigma of Capital and the Crises of Capitalism*. New York: Profile Books.

———. 2011. *The Enigma of Capital and the Crises of Capitalism*. London, UK: Profile Books.

Hegel, Georg. 2005 [1821]. *Philosophy of Right*. Trans. S. W. Dyde. Mineola, NY: Dover.

Heilprin, J. 2013. "Almost $13B in aid needed for world's biggest crises in 2014: UN." Associated Press. December 16. http://www.ctvnews.ca/world/almost-13b-in-aid -needed-for-world-s-biggest-crises-in-2014-un-1.1595087.

Hermes, Mary. 1998. "Research Methods as a Situated Response: Towards a First Nations' Methodology." *Qualitative Studies in Education* 11:155–168.

Hey, Tony, Stewart Tansley, and Kristin Tolle. 2009. "The Fourth Paradigm. Data-Intensive Scientific Discovery." Microsoft Research, Seattle, WA.

High-Level Panel on Illicit Financial Flows from Africa. 2015. "Illicit Financial Flows: Why Africa Needs to "'Track It, Stop It and Get It.'" United Nations Economic Commission for Africa, Addis Ababa, Ethiopia.

High-Level Panel on Threats, Challenges and Change. 2004. "A More Secure World: Our Shared Responsibility." United Nations, New York.

Hilhorst, Dorothea. 2003. *The Real World of NGOs. Discourses, Diversity, and Development*. New York: Zed Books.

Human Rights Watch. 2015. "'Work Faster or Get Out.' Labor Rights Abuses in Cambodia's Garment Industry." Human Rights Watch, Washington, DC.

ICTforAg.org. 2015. "ICTforAg Conference." http://ictforag.org/.

Idealist.org. 2015. "Volunteering with a Program or Volunteer-Sending Organization." Action Without Borders, New York.

Independent Evaluation Group. 2011. "IEG Annual Report 2011: Results and Performance of the World Bank Group. Volume I: Main Report." World Bank Group, Washington, DC.

Indiana University. 2014. *School of Global and International Studies*. Bloomington, IN: College of Arts and Sciences, Indiana University.

Institute of Electrical and Electronics Engineers. 2015. "2015 IEEE Technological Innovation in ICT for Agriculture and Rural Development (TIAR)." https://www .ieee.org/conferences_events/conferences/conferencedetails/index.html?Conf_ID =33747.

Institute of International Education, Inc. 2014. "Opendoors 2014 'Fast Facts.'" http:// www.iie.org/Research-and-Publications/Open-Doors/Data/Fast-Facts.

———. 2015. "Generation Study Abroad." http://www.iie.org/Programs/Generation -Study-Abroad/About.

International Consortium of Investigative Journalists. 2014. "Leaked Documents Expose Global Companies' Secret Tax Deals in Luxembourg." Center for Public Integrity, Washington, DC.

Ip, Greg. 2008. "Soros, the Man Who Cries Wolf, Now Is Warning of a 'Superbubble.'" *Wall Street Journal*. June 21. http://www.wsj.com/articles/SB121400427331093457.

Jain, Bharti. 2015. "Ford Foundation-Govt Stand-Off Ends as NGO Agrees to Come Under FEMA." *Times of India*, July 16. http://timesofindia.indiatimes.com/india

/Ford-Foundation-govt-stand-off-ends-as-NGO-agrees-to-come-under-Fema
/articleshow/48092013.cms.

Kaufman, Frederick. 2012. "Wall Street's Thirst for Water." *Nature* 490:469–471.

Khagram, Sanjeev. 2004. *Dams and Development: Transnational Struggles for Water and Power.* Ithaca: Cornell University Press.

Klein, Naomi. 2007. *The Shock Doctrine: The Rise of Disaster Capitalism.* New York: Metropolitan Books.

Labaree, David. 1997. "Public Goods, Private Goods: The American Struggle Over Educational Goals." *American Educational Research Journal* 34:39–81.

———. 2012. "School Syndrome: Understanding the USA's Magical Belief That Schooling Can Somehow Improve Society, Promote Access, and Preserve Advantage." *Journal of Curriculum Studies* 44:143–163.

Labbe, Jeremie. 2012. "Rethinking Humanitarianism: Adapting to 21st Century Challenges." International Peace Institute, New York.

Ladika, Susan. 2012. "Transforming Lives." *International Educator* 21:15–24.

Lakner, Christoph, and Branko Milanovic. 2013. "Global Income Distribution. From the Fall of the Berlin Wall to the Great Recession." World Bank Development Research Group Poverty and Inequality Team, New York.

Lareau, Annette. 2000. *Home Advantage: Social Class and Parental Intervention in Elementary Education.* New York: Rowman & Littlefield.

Lather, Patti. 2002. "Validity as an Incitement to Discourse. Qualitiative Research and the Crisis of Legitimation." In *Handbook of Research on Teaching*, ed. Virginia Richardson, 241–258. Washington, DC: American Educational Research Association.

Latour, Bruno. 1996. *Aramis or the Love of Technology.* Cambridge, MA: Harvard University Press.

———. 2005. *Reassembling the Social. An Introduction to Actor-Network-Theory.* New York: Oxford University Press.

Lee, Jo-Anne, and John Lutz. 2005. *Situating "Race" and Racisms in Time, Space, and Theory.* Montreal: McGill-Queen's University Press.

Lough, Benjamin J. 2012. "International Volunteerism from the United States, 2004–2010." Center for Social Development, Washington University, St. Louis, MO.

Lyotard, Jean-François. 1979. *The Postmodern Condition: A Report on Knowledge.* Trans. Geoff Bennington and Brian Massumi. Minneapolis: University of Minnesota Press.

Macrae, Joanna. 2002. "The New Humanitarianisms: A Review of Trends in Global Humanitarian Action." Overseas Development Institute, London, UK.

Maliniak, Daniel, Susan Peterson, Ryan Powers, and Michael J. Tierney. 2014. "The Best International Relations Schools in the World." *Foreign Policy.* http://foreignpolicy.com/2015/02/03/top-twenty-five-schools-international-relations/.

Marx, Karl. 1976 [1867]. *Capital: A Critique of Political Economy.* Vol. 1. London: Penguin Books.

———. 1978 [1852]. "The Eighteenth Brumaire of Louis Bonaparte." In *The Marx-Engels Reader*, ed. Robert Tucker, 594–617. New York: W.W. Norton.

———. 1991. *Capital: A Critique of Political Economy.* Vol. 3. London: Penguin Books.

Mashable.com. 2015. "Social Good Summit 2015." http://mashable.com/sgs/.

Mayer-Schönberger, Viktor, and Kenneth Cukier. 2013. *Big Data: A Revolution That Will Transform How We Live, Work, and Think*. New York: Eamon Dolan/Houghton Mifflin Harcourt.

McGhee, Tom. 2006. "CH2M Hill Finds Opportunity in Disasters, War." *Denver Post*, January 29. http://www.denverpost.com/search/ci_3446246.

McGray, Douglas. 2004. "The Rise in Voluntourism." *Travel and Leisure*, February. http://www.travelandleisure.com/articles/going-the-distance-february-2004.

Miraftab, Faranak. 1997. "Flirting with the Enemy." *Habitat International* 21:361–375.

Mohanty, Chandra. 1988. "Under Western Eyes: Feminist Scholarship and Colonial Discourses." *Feminist Review* 30:61–88.

———. 1991a. "Cartographies of Struggle: Third World Women and the Politics of Feminism." In *Third World Women and the Politics of Feminism*, ed. C. Mohanty, A. Russo, and L. Torres, 1–47. Bloomington: Indiana University Press.

———. 1991b. "Under Western Eyes: Feminist Scholarship and Colonial Discourses." In *Third World Women and the Politics of Feminism*, ed. Chandra T. Mohanty, Ann Russo, and Lourdes Torres, 51–80. Bloomington: Indiana University Press.

Mosse, David. 2005. *Cultivating Development: An Ethnography of Aid Policy and Practice*. New York: Pluto Press.

Mostafanezhad, Mary. 2013. "The Geography of Compassion in Volunteer Tourism." *Tourism Geographies: An International Journal of Tourism, Space, Place, and Environment* 15:318–337.

Moyo, Dambisa. 2010. *Dead Aid. Why Aid Is Not Working and How There Is Another Way for Africa*. London: Penguin Books.

Mwesigwa, Alon. 2015. "Uganda: NGO Bill Aims to Muzzle Civil Society, Say Activists." *The Guardian*, June 24. http://www.theguardian.com/global-development/2015 /jun/24/uganda-ngo-bill-aims-muzzle-civil-society-say-activists.

Nader, Laura. 1972. "Up the Anthropologist—Perspectives Gained from Studying Up." In *Reinventing Anthropology*, ed. Dell H. Hymes, 284–311. New York: Random House.

———. 2008. "Keynote Address." Presented at Fifth Annual Public Anthropology Conference, "Supporting Social Movements." October 27. American University, Washington, DC.

Neuman, Michaël. 2012. "The Shared Interests Which Make Humanitarianism Possible." *Humanitarian Aid on the Move Newsletter* no. 9 (March):2–4. http://reliefweb .int/sites/reliefweb.int/files/resources/Full%20Report_653.pdf.

Nordstrom, Carolyn. 2007. *Global Outlaws: Crime, Money, and Power in the Contemporary World*. Berkeley: University of California Press.

O'Connor, James. 1998. *Natural Causes: Essays in Ecological Marxism*. New York: Guilford Press.

Odun Balogun, Fidelis. 1995. *Adjusted Lives: Stories of Structural Adjustment*. Trenton, NJ: Africa World Press.

Office for the Coordination of Humanitarian Affairs. 2014. "Third Annual Global Humanitarian Policy Forum: Analytical Summary: Enhancing Cooperation, Enhancing Effectiveness." Office for the Coordination of Humanitarian Affairs, New York, NY.

Opoku-Mensah, Paul. 2001. "The Rise and Rise of NGOs: Implications for Research." Institutt for Sosiologi og Statsvitenskap. http://www.svt.ntnu.no/iss/issa/0101 /010109.shtml.

————. 2007. "Reconceptualising NGOs and Their Roles in Development: An Outline of the Issues." In *Reconceptualising NGOs and Their Roles in Development: NGOs, Civil Society and the International Aid System*, ed. Paul Opoku-Mensah, David Lewis, and Terje Tvedt, 9–14. Aalborg, Denmark: Aalborg University Press.

Opoku-Mensah, Paul, David Lewis, and Terje Tvedt. 2007. *Reconceptualising NGOs and Their Roles in Development: NGOs, Civil Society and the International Aid System*. Aalborg, Denmark: Aalborg University Press.

Organization for Economic Cooperation and Development. 2012. "ODA Trends from 1960 to 2012." http://www.oecd.org/dac/stats/odatrendsfrom1960to2012.htm.

O'Toole, James, and Evan Perez. 2013. "JPMorgan Agrees to $13 Billion Mortgage Settlement." *CNNMoney*, November 19. http://money.cnn.com/2013/11/19/investing/jpmorgan-mortgage-settlement/.

Oxfam GB. 2006. "Education for Global Citizenship. A Guide for Schools." Oxfam GB, London, UK.

Oxfam International. 2014. "Working for the Few. Political Capture and Economic Inequality." Oxfam GB, London, UK.

Peace Corps. 2015. "The Peace Corps Announces Record-Breaking Application Numbers in 2014." http://www.peacecorps.gov/media/forpress/press/2447/.

Pearce, Jenny. 2000. "Development, NGOs, and Civil Society: The Debate and Its Future." In *Development, NGOs, and Civil Society: Selected Essays from Development in Practice*, ed. Deborah Eade, 15–43. Oxford: Oxfam GB.

Petras, James. 1999. "NGOs: In the Service of Imperialism." *Journal of Contemporary Asia* 29:429–440.

Phadke, Roopali. 2005. "People's Science in Action: The Politics of Protest and Knowledge Brokering in India." *Society and Natural Resources* 18:363–375.

Polanyi, Karl. 1944. *The Great Transformation: The Political and Economic Origins of Our Time*. Boston: Beacon Press.

Polman, Linda, and Kathie Klarreich. 2012. "The NGO Republic of Haiti." *The Nation*. October 31. http://www.thenation.com/article/170929/ngo-republic-haiti.

Power, Michael. 1997. *The Audit Society: Rituals of Verification*. Oxford: Oxford University Press.

Power, Samantha. 2013. *A Problem from Hell. America and the Age of Genocide*. New York: Basic Books.

Reich, Robert. 2015. "How Goldman Sachs Profited from the Greek Debt Crisis." *The Nation*. July 16. http://www.thenation.com/article/goldmans-greek-gambit/.

Richardson, Laura. 1994. "Writing: A Method of Inquiry." In *Handbook of Qualitative Research*, ed. Norman K. Denzin and Yvonna S. Lincoln, 516–529. Thousand Oaks, CA: Sage.

Rist, Gilbert. 1997. *The History of Development from Western Origins to Global Faith*. London: Zed Books.

————. 2008. *The History of Development: From Western Origins to Global Faith*. 3rd ed. New York: Zed Books.

Rosenberg, Justin. 2005. "Globalization Theory: A Post Mortem." *International Politics* 42:2–74.

Said, Edward. 1979. *Orientalism*. New York: Vintage Books.

Salamon, Lester M. 1994. "The Rise of the Nonprofit Sector." *Foreign Affairs* 73:109–122.

Salamon, Lester M., S. Wojciech Sokolowski, and Stephanie L. Geller. 2012. "Holding the Fort: Nonprofit Employment During a Decade of Turmoil." Johns Hopkins Center for Civil Society Studies, Baltimore, MD.

Saldinger, Adva. 2015. "SDGs—A Business Opportunity?" *Devex Impact*. July 20. https://www.devex.com/news/sdgs-a-business-opportunity-86564.

Salmon, Felix. 2009. "Recipe for Disaster: The Formula That Killed Wall Street." *Wired Magazine* 17(3). February 23. http://archive.wired.com/techbiz/it/magazine/17-03/wp_quant?currentPage=all.

Schellnhuber, Hans Joachim, Bill Hare, Olivia Serdeczny, Michiel Schaeffer, Sophie Adams, Florent Baarsch, Susanne Schwan, Dim Coumou, Alexander Robinson, Marion Vieweg, Franziska Piontek, Reik Donner, Jakob Runge, Kira Rehfeld, Joeri Rogelj, Mahe Perette, Arathy Menon, Carl-Friedrich Schleussner, Alberte Bondeau, Anastasia Svirejeva-Hopkins, Jacob Schewe, Katja Frieler, Lila Warszawski, and Marcia Rocha. 2013. "Turn Down the Heat: Climate Extremes, Regional Impacts, and the Case for Resilience." World Bank, Washington, DC.

Schemo, Diana Jean. 2007. "In Study Abroad, Gifts and Money for Universities." *New York Times*. August 13.

Scott, James C. 1998. *Seeing Like a State: How Certain Schemes to Improve the Human Condition Have Failed*. New Haven: Yale University Press.

Segall, Avner. 2001. "Critical Ethnography and the Invocation of Voice: From the Field/in the Field—Single Exposure, Double Standard." *Qualitative Studies in Education* 14:579–592.

———. 2013. "Revitalizing Critical Discourses in Social Education: Opportunities for a More Complexified (Un)Knowing." *Theory & Research in Social Education* 41:476–493.

Seth, Suman. 2009. "Putting Knowledge in Its Place: Science, Colonialism, and the Postcolonial." *Postcolonial Studies* 12:373–388.

Shapin, Steven. 1998. "Placing the View from Nowhere: Historical and Sociological Problems in the Location of Science." *Transactions of the Institute of British Geographers* 23:5–12.

Silverstein, Jake. 2015. "The Displaced." *New York Times Magazine*. November 8.

Smith, Neil. 1998. "Nature at the Millennium: Production and Re-enchantment." In *Remaking Reality: Nature at the Millennium*, ed. Bruce Braun and Noel Castree, 271–285. New York: Routledge.

———. 2008. *Uneven Development: Nature, Capital, and the Production of Space*. Athens: University of Georgia Press.

Sorkin, Andrew Ross. 2014. "Everything Is Illuminated." *New York Times Magazine*, September 7, 30–70.

Stiglitz, Joseph. 2015. "America in the Way." *Project Syndicate*. August 6. http://www.project-syndicate.org/commentary/us-international-development-finance-by-joseph-e--stiglitz-2015-08.

Sulaiman, Tosin. 2014. "For-Profit School Chains Educate Africa's Poor." *beyondbrics* (blog). FT.com. December 17.

Sunday Times. 2005. "Better Corporate Profits Seen Leading to Higher Investments." *Sunday Times* (Sri Lanka). http://www.sundaytimes.lk/051009/ft/8.html.

Telegraph. 2009. "Merrill Lynch Paid Billions in Bonuses Before Bailout." *Telegraph*. January 22. http://www.telegraph.co.uk/finance/financialcrisis/4316475/Merrill-Lynch-paid-billions-in-bonuses-before-bailout.html.

Thomas, Caroline. 1999. "Where Is the Third World Now?" *Review of International Studies* 25:225–244.

Tilley, Helen. 2011. *Africa as a Living Laboratory: Empire, Development, and the Problem of Scientific Knowledge 1870–1950.* Chicago: University of Chicago Press.

Todhunter, Colin. 2015. "Toxic Mercury in the Mist: Holding Unilever in India to Account." *Global Research.* April 30. http://www.globalresearch.ca/toxic-mercury -in-the-mist-holding-unilever-in-india-to-account/5446324.

Toope, Stephen. 2012. "Strengthening Education and Research Connectivity between Canada and Asia: Innovative Models for Engagement." Canadian Council of Chief Executives, Ottawa, Ontario.

Truman, Harry. [1949] 1964. *Public Papers of the Presidents of the United States: Harry Truman.* Washington, DC: U.S. Government Printing Office.

UN-Habitat. 2003. "The Challenge of the Slums: Global Report on Human Settlements 2003." United Nations Human Settlements Programme, London.

UNICEF Innovation. 2013. "Invitation: FAILFaire—Fail to Scale." UNICEF, New York.

Union of International Associations. 2008. *Yearbook of International Organizations 2007/2008: Volume 5: Statistics, Visualizations, and Patterns.* Brussels: Brill.

United Nations. 2013. "UN, Partners Seek Record $13 Billion to Bring Life-Saving Aid to Millions in 2014." *UN Daily News.* December 16. http://www.un.org/news/dh/pdf /english/2013/16122013.pdf.

———. 2014. "The Responsibility to Protect." Department of Public Information, United Nations, New York. http://www.un.org/en/preventgenocide/rwanda/pdf /Backgrounder%20R2P%202014.pdf.

United Nations Development Programme. 1991. *Human Development Report 1993.* New York: Oxford University Press.

United Nations Global Compact. 2015. "United Nations Private Sector Forum 2015." United Nations Global Compact, New York.

United States Senate. 2010. "Goldman Sachs and the Financial Crisis." Washington DC: Senate Permanent Subcommittee on Investigations. http://www.hsgac.senate .gov//imo/media/doc/Financial_Crisis/042710Exhibits.pdf?attempt=2.

Van Maanen, John. 1988. *Tales of the Field: On Writing Ethnography.* Chicago: University of Chicago Press.

Vota, Wayan. 2013. "Using ICT to Make a Better World" (Blog post). https://plus.google .com/+WayanVota.

Wall Street Journal News Roundup. 2004. "Tsunami's Aftermath: Donations Pile in From Companies, Individuals." *Wall Street Journal.* December 30. http://online .wsj.com/news/articles/SB110424799797311011.

Wallace, Tina. 2003. "NGO's Dilemmas: Trojan Horses for Global Neoliberalism." *Socialist Register* 40:202–219.

Water for People. 2011. "World Water Corps." http://web.archive.org/web /20110107000347/http://www.waterforpeople.org/programs/how-we-work/world -water-corps/.

———. 2014. "Board Members." http://www.waterforpeople.org/about/people/board -members/.

Weerakoon, Dushni, Sisira Jayasuriya, Nisha Arunatilake, and Paul Steele. 2007. "Economic Challenges of Post-Tsunami Reconstruction in Sri Lanka." Asian Development Bank Institute, Tokyo, Japan.

Weiss, Thomas, and Leon Gordenker. 1996. *NGOs, the UN, and Global Governance.* Boulder: Lynn Rienner.

Will, George F. 1999. "Hooked on Gambling: Other Comment." *Herald Tribune.* June 26–27.

World Bank. 2002. "States and Markets." World Bank, New York.

———. 2012. "World Bank Statement on Padma Bridge." World Bank, Washington, DC.

World Health Organization. 2010. "U.N.-Water Global Annual Assessment of Sanitation and Drinking-Water (GLAAS)." World Health Organization, Geneva.

World Resources Institute. 1996. *World Resources: 1996–97.* Oxford: Oxford University Press.

World Travel & Tourism Council. 2012. "The Comparative Economic Impact of Travel & Tourism." Oxford Economics, London.

Zaidman, Yasmina. 2013. "An Approach to Building Diverse Global Networks and Unlikely New Alliances in an Interconnected World." Paper presented at "Framing the Global" Conference. September 26–28. Indiana University, Bloomington, IN.

Zall Kusek, Jody, Marelize Görgens Prestidge, and Billy C. Hamilton. 2013. "Fail-Safe Management: Five Rules to Avoid Project Failure." World Bank, Washington, DC.

Index

accumulation by dispossession, 103–107, 140

Acumen Fund, 20, 28n12, 90–92, 93, 94, 96–100, *97–98*, 110–111, 112, 112n1

Acumen Fund Fellows program, 99–100

Africa: illicit financial flows in, 137; slums in, 107. *See also individual countries*

African Development Bank (AfDB), 42, 82, 92

Ahearn, John, 10

American International Group (AIG), 108, 111

Amos, Valerie, 8

Anastasie, Tabu, 57

Annan, Kofi, 5

Arendt, Hannah, 130

Arnove, Robert, 103

Ashe, John William, 136

Asian Development Bank, 11, 35, 36–37, 48, 50, 82

Atkinson, Paul, 43, 54

audit culture, humanitarian organizations and, 34, 120–123

bailout of corporations in financial crisis, 108–109

Ban Ki-Moon, 134, 136–137

Barnett, Michael, 14, 31

baseline assessment of water, sanitation and hygiene education programs in Rwanda, 10–11, 39–41, 43–59, 61–62

Benjamin, Walter, 7

Berdan, Stacie Nevadomski, 79

Bhabha, Homi, 18

big data, 32–34, 42–43, 49

Bill & Melinda Gates Foundation, 55, 90, 92, 96, 102

Blavatnik, Len, 102

boards of directors: corporate links of NGO, 10; Water for People, 94–96, 97–98

Bouckaert, Peter, 128

Bourgois, Philippe, 41

Bresenham, Terri, 142

Breslin, Ned, 93–94

Bridge International Academies, 100–101

Buffett, Peter, 126–127

Bush, George H. W., 129

Bush, George W., 108

business, humanitarian, 107–112; accumulation by dispossession, 103–107; Acumen Fund, 90–92, 93, 94, 96–100, 110–111, 112; Global Innovation Fund, 92–93; local conditions and, 93–94; private education, 100–102; social venture capital funds, 90–92; Water for People and, 93–96; wealth inequality, 102–103

Capital (Marx), 64n1, 117

capitalism: accumulation by dispossession and, 103–107; double movement, 22–23, 104; philanthropy combined with, 90–92

Card, Robert, 10

certificates, in international relations, 86–87, 89n7

"The Challenge of the Slums" (UN-Habitat), 106

CH2M Hill, 3, 10, 47, 96

civil society organizations (CSOs), 9, 36, 139

classic humanitarianism, 4–5, 6

Clifford, James, 60

climate change, dispossession and displacement and, 8, 143–144

Clinton, Bill, 129

Clinton, Hillary, 90

Coca-Cola Company, 1, 82, 110–111, 131

Cohen, Naomi, 2

collateralized debt obligations (CDOs), 109, 112, 112n6, 119

Colombel, Andrea Soros, 92

colonialism, state-led development to assist in overcoming effects of, 12–13

Columbia University Mailman School of Public Health, 85–87

Comaroff, Jean and John, 118

Commonwealth Scholarship, 25, 66

construct validity, 58–59, 60

corporate philanthropy: capitalism combined with, 90–92; corruption and, 17; humanitarian organizations and, 1, 24–25, 69, 95; rise in, 4, 14–15; water and sanitation efforts and, 36

MICHAEL MASCARENHAS is Associate Professor in the Science and Technology Department at Rensselaer Polytechnic Institute. A sociologist with scholarly interests in the fields of postcolonial and development studies, environmental justice and racism, and science and technology studies, he is author of *Where the Waters Divide: Neoliberalism, White Privilege, and Environmental Racism in Canada* (2012).

CPSIA information can be obtained
at www.ICGtesting.com
Printed in the USA
BVHW041305141218
535641BV00013B/157/P